The Spirituality
of the Diocesan Priest

Donald B. Cozzens
Denis Edwards
William D. Hammer
Frank McNulty
Robert F. Morneau
Edward G. Pfnausch
James H. Provost
Sylvester D. Ryan
Robert M. Schwartz
William H. Shannon
Richard J. Sklba
Kenneth Untener

Donald B. Cozzens, Editor

A Liturgical Press Book

 THE LITURGICAL PRESS
Collegeville, Minnesota

1   2   3   4   5   6   7   8   9

Library of Congress Cataloging-in-Publication Data

The spirituality of the diocesan priest / Donald B. Cozzens . . . [et al.].
     p.   cm.
    Includes bibliographical references.
    ISBN 0-8146-2421-9
    1. Priests—Religious life. 2. Spirituality—Catholic Church.
  3. Catholic Church—Clergy—Religious life. I. Cozzens, Donald B.
  BX1912.5.S66 1997
  248.8'92—dc21   96-51709
                                            CIP

For the presbyters
of North America and Australia

Contents

Introduction   vii
   Donald B. Cozzens

1 Servant of the Servants of God: A Pastor's Spirituality   1
   Robert M. Schwartz

2 Using the Wrong Measure?   20
   Kenneth E. Untener

3 Ruminations of a Canonist   27
   James H. Provost

4 Tenders of the Word   42
   Donald B. Cozzens

5 Paul of Tarsus: A Model for Diocesan Priesthood   59
   Richard J. Sklba

6 Personal Symbol of Communion   73
   Denis Edwards

7 Priestly Spirituality: "Speaking Out *for the Inside*"   85
   William H. Shannon

8 A Glorious and Transcendent Place   104
   Robert F. Morneau

9 Heralds of the Gospel and Experts in Humanity   121
   Sylvester D. Ryan

10 A Kindled Heart   143
   Frank McNulty

11 The Conciliar Documents and the 1983 Code   156
    Edward G. Pfnausch

12 Confessions of a Pilgrim Pastor   173
    William D. Hammer

Afterword   184

Contributors   191

Introduction

The clarity of role and purpose that long sustained my colleagues in the ministerial priesthood no longer holds. While we welcome the theological investigations probing the deeper reality and identity of the priest, there is no denying that the model is shifting with the mining of richer veins of thought concerning the nature and meaning of the diocesan priesthood. The meantime, *this* time in the history of the Church, challenges our maturity and unsettles our spirituality. To priests living in this meantime, this time between commonly held understandings of the nature and meaning of the ministerial priesthood, we speak a word about *the* Word sustaining us, nourishing us, and directing our earnest seeking after a renewed theology of priesthood. Never has the interior life of today's priest been so important to his spiritual and personal health and to his effectiveness as pastor and shepherd as it is during this time of seeking and waiting.

My own search for the core and charism of diocesan priestly spirituality is the genesis of this collection. I began putting this book together believing I knew something about the priesthood. And I thought I knew priests. I had counseled priests, directed their spiritual journeys, and preached their retreats. As a former vicar for clergy, I knew the wounds of the priesthood, the pain of it, the unspeakable privilege of it. But the past few years seem to have laid bare, more than anything else, the unfathomable mystery of the priesthood. It was not always so. Since the time of Trent, the priesthood was clearly defined, safely moored in Trent's theological harbor. Few winds of change threatened the safe mooring. It was a time when the status of the priest went unquestioned and his authority unchallenged.[1] One could catch a glimpse of awe and reverence in the eyes of some parishioners when they encountered their parish priest—yet even here I suspect it was more the mystique of the priesthood than its transcendent mystery. But as we shall see, change was in the air. The Catholic imagination, awakened by the conciliar renewal's attention to the mystery and depth of the Church, spawned serious reflection on the theology of the priesthood that in turn has led to a reexamination of the priest's identity and spirituality.

Ordained over thirty years ago at the closing of Vatican II, my classmates and I were launched into a priestly orbit as exciting and adventurous as the Apollo 13 flight. The priesthood we entered in the middle sixties looked like the priesthood of our seminary dreams—but only on the surface. We were assigned to parishes that resembled the parishes of today, to seasoned pastors with little idea that the medieval model of benefice and the priestly identity that so comfortably sustained them was about to be transformed. We offered Mass, celebrated the sacraments, visited the sick, and taught in the school. The game plan was simple—if we remained faithful to our prayer and cultivated an interior life the grace of the sacrament of orders would sustain us. Of course it was difficult at times, especially when the loneliness of the rectory and the inner tension associated with sexuality and intimacy needs unsettled our souls. Celibacy on the other side of the seminary wall, we discovered, took on different challenges. The numbing of our sexual impulses brought about by seminary routine and structured spirituality gave way to a sexual reawakening fueled by the revolutions and rebellions of the sixties. The more perplexing and disturbing challenges, however, did not come from the structures of parish or diocese or from the disquietude of celibacy. The real adventure was something we could not yet name since it was just beginning to surface from the collective unconscious of our priesthood. We were shaken to our foundations as we came to understand that the conciliar documents had profound implications for our identity as priests. We had a mountain of soul work to do just as we discovered that many of the traditional supports systems of our seminary years no longer made sense. The quasi-monastic and religious spirituality of our seminary years simply didn't fit. Precisely at this time of spiritual crisis we discovered that at the heart of the theological renewal of the diocesan priesthood were the seeds of a spirituality that was appropriately our own.

Still, lingering questions shook our confidence—who were we as priests in this post-conciliar Church? What was our charism as diocesan priests? Did we possess a spirituality grounded in the ministry and life we lived? All of this interior work absorbed our energies even as we struggled to assimilate the council's new directions. I have come to take a certain consolation in discovering that God is not the only mystery, that creation itself, and this priesthood that has so captured our spirit and imagination is, perhaps above all else, mystery—a mystery grounded in the saving love of God.

If the essays in this collection capture the spirituality of the diocesan priest, then the fog engulfing the priesthood in English-speaking countries over the past decade is lifting. In spite of the unprecedented scandal of sexual misconduct with minors, the sharp decline in candidates for seminary training, the graying of the clergy, and the staggering demands of pastoral care for a growing Catholic population, priests, for the most part, have held their ground. They have stood in the fire of suspicion and criticism and emerged wiser, more mature, and spiritually renewed.

The metal of priests has been tested on other fronts as well. As we have noted, Vatican II's unfolding of a deeper and broader understanding of the nature of the Church stimulated a corollary unfolding of the nature and identity of the ministerial priesthood. For many priests the conciliar insights were exciting and liberating. With all baptized, they were to enter on the paschal path to holiness. They were to preach the word as men who listened to the word proclaimed by voices other than their own, by parishioners and other believers more at home in the marketplaces of city and suburb. Their role as leaders was now understood as service to their sisters and brothers. As presbyters they were to serve in collaboration with religious and lay ministers whose gifts were manifest and whose numbers were growing. They were both elder to the community as representative of the diocesan bishop and truly brother to the people of the parish community. While the essence of the priesthood was consonant with the tradition of the Church, the context, and consciousness of priestly ministry was profoundly affected.

While exciting and liberating for many priests, the post-conciliar horizon was disturbing and threatening to others. With religious imaginations formed and in some cases hardened by four centuries of relative uniformity in theology and ecclesial culture, the new insights stretched their minds and imaginations. And the stretching proved painful. The feeling persisted that something was being lost. Some understood the external respect and reverence sustained by this culture to be a confirming sign of the sacredness, the *special* sacredness of the priesthood. Others came to see they were being held "prisoners of privilege"[2] to a clerical culture taken as a given. So it was difficult for many to understand that not only were they priests to the people of God and for the people of God but they were also members *of* the people of God. A cloud seemed to engulf the priestly identity that for so long served them well, that validated the sacrifices inherent to the life-long commitment of celibate ministry. In some cases priests were more than disturbed and frightened; they were angry and hostile. Their center of security was shaken and for the first time (in centuries?) they didn't quite know their place. Their Vatican II oriented colleagues in the priesthood seemed more at home with the softening of lines between clergy and laity and the underscoring of the dignity of the baptized as the people of God. For these priests the past decades generated altogether too much excitement, too much liberation. What were they to make of the emerging models of priesthood? Avery Dulles, for example, identified three paradigms or foci of the priesthood: theologians such as Karl Rahner and Joseph Ratzinger perceive priesthood as essentially a ministry of the word; a second paradigm, represented by Otto Semmelroth and Roger Vekemans, emphasizes the cultic role of the priest; Thomas O'Meara and Robert Schwartz in the United States and Walter Kasper and Hans Urs von Balthasar in Europe, stressed the community leadership dimension of priesthood.[3] Each of these models influenced the identity and spirituality of the diocesan priest. The restlessness of both the inspired and fearful priests turned their attention inward in search of their unfolding identity, their priestly charism, and above all their authentic spirituality.

They came to see that their spirituality was eclectic, an amalgam of quasi-monastic Jesuit, Dominican, and Franciscan spiritualities often filtered through Sulpician and Irish approaches to the spiritual life. Alongside these traditions, a contemplative strain, mostly Cistercian and Carmelite in character, was observable in the spiritual lives of a growing number of diocesan priests. Thomas O'Meara writes: "The diocesan priest for long has had, at best, spiritualities which were derivative: that of the Benedictine monks, of the Jesuits, of the clerics regular. Church authorities are right to be concerned over the spirituality . . . of the priest and seminarian."[4] While enriched by these various spiritual traditions and indeed indebted to them, diocesan priests conceded that they had grown out of charisms not necessarily their own.

Recognizing the currents buffeting the souls of their brothers, twelve authors agreed to address the issue of the spirituality of the diocesan priest. They are poets and pastors, theologians, canonists and bishops—priests who have walked straight into the darkness of the mystery until the shadows gave way to light. The common threads of their stories weave a surprisingly passionate tapestry. The essays you are about to read come from the experiences, the ordeals, the failures and triumphs of the writers. They come from men who have become, by the grace of God, ministers of mystery and grace. Their passion is the liberating power of the Gospel; their mission is to name the mysterious workings of grace to a world in search of meaning and hope. There is, to be sure, a theology of diocesan priestly spirituality here, but it is clearly grounded in the authors' journey of soul. They bear witness to their love of God, their love of the Church, their struggles to love and hope and believe. They write without illusion, fully aware of the issues that have led to the crisis facing the priesthood today. But most of all, they touch the mystery of the priesthood and unveil personal, often moving, dramas of grace.

> *Donald Bernard Cozzens*
> *Saint Mary Seminary and*
> *Graduate School of Theology*
> *Wickliffe, Ohio*

Notes

[1]Raymond Hedin's *Married to the Church* (Bloomington and Indianapolis, Indiana University Press, 1995, 129) probes the intricacies and complexities of clerical culture, laying bare the dynamics that bind the souls of men who have studied for the priesthood. Hedin provides by far the best analysis of the psyche of the seminarian, the former seminarian, the priest and former priest currently available. See especially chapter 6, "Finding a place in the world."

[2]For a sustained discussion of the spiritual and psychological effects of clericalism, see Michael H. Crosby's *Celibacy: Means of Control or Mandate of the Heart?* (Notre Dame, Ind., Ave Maria Press, 1996).

[3]Avery Dulles, "Models for Ministerial Priesthood," *Origins* 20 (1990) 286–87.

[4]Thomas F. O'Meara, "The Ministry of the Priesthood and Its Relationship to the Wider Ministry in the Church," *Seminaries in Dialogue* 11 (September 1985) 6.

1

Servant of the Servants of God: A Pastor's Spirituality

Robert M. Schwartz

Nothing has surprised me as much as the power that lay people have in my life as a priest. For a long time my theology insisted that this should be true. Vatican II had chosen to place its consideration of ordained ministry within the context of the Church as a whole. I knew well that the focus of post-conciliar theology was on the great sacrament of the Church, not on the priest as such. I understood that baptism, confirmation, and Eucharist were the sacraments of initiation into the life and mission of the Church, not ordination. My theology told me that lay people were crucial in the life of the contemporary parish. I knew all of this in my head, and then I became a pastor on my twenty-fourth anniversary as a priest—and the experience was overwhelming. I was surprised that everything I believed and taught suddenly became power and grace. The people of God were not only crucial in the life of the Church; they were an indispensable source of spiritual vitality for me as well.

Both historically and theologically, the primary identity of the bishop, with the presbyters gathered around him, is that of pastor. While ordained priests exercise their ministry in many contexts, Vatican II has again made it clear that the overarching and fundamental model for priestly ministry is pastoral leader within a community of faith. Some priests, diocesan and religious, better emulate the role of the ancient presbyterate as a council of elders who always made the bishop look wise. All priests, no matter where they minister, share in the pastoral leadership of the Church by the very fact of their ordination.

Having made room for the many faces of ordained priesthood, it is important to focus on the core meaning of ordination. Through sacramental ordination the Church designates and empowers the pivotal pastoral leaders of the community. The relationship between community and community leader lies at the very heart of priestly identity and priestly spirituality.

Vatican II underscored the relationship between the mission of the priest as pastoral leader and the spiritual life of the priest by affirming that pastoral charity is the way to priestly perfection *(Presbyterorum ordinis* 14). Therefore, holiness is not something a priest can attain by himself or apart from the community of faith. The priest becomes holy within the community by ministering to it and leading it. A spirituality that is truly "priestly" comes to be as a priest surrenders himself to his role in the community, ministers to it, and allows himself to be enriched and enlivened by the people he serves.

The image of Archbishop Oscar Romero easily comes to mind in this regard because he was so unlikely a candidate for bishop, especially a pastoral one. Two factors worked together in the archbishop's life. First, he was ordained—designated and empowered by the action of the Church and the Holy Spirit to be a bishop. But the grace given in ordination remained fallow until he surrendered his life to the people of San Salvador. The faith and courage of the laity in expressing their baptismal priesthood activated and called forth the grace of pastoral leadership in Romero. In a real sense, the people made a bishop out of Romero, and he made them the people of God. Priestly spirituality is found in the interaction between priest and people. By the very nature of the Church, the priesthood of the laity and the priesthood of the ordained are interacting components of a larger whole. The priest meets God in the community he serves, and the experience of God is unlocked and deepened in the community through the words and actions of the priest.

There are certainly other ways of experiencing God in the Catholic tradition, and are members of the community have a profound influence on one another. Even though this is true, my point remains—ecclesial relationships are the key to understanding any spirituality which is truly Catholic. This is true in spades of the spirituality of the ordained priest. Far from limiting and controlling our experience of God, the sacraments, rituals, roles, ministries, and interactions of the community are the place where God's presence is revealed, recognized and lived out.

Vatican II insisted that the priesthood of the ordained and the priesthood of the baptized are different in kind and not only in degree. They are different ways of participating in the one priesthood of Christ and the Church. The council also affirmed that these two ways of participating in Christ's priesthood are related to one another by their very nature. Neither the priesthood of the ordained nor the priesthood of the laity stands alone. Hidden within this affirmation is a strong message to the ordained. There is no priesthood apart from the community of the Church. The spirituality of the ordained priest comes to birth in the priest's relationship to the people of God. Pope John Paul affirmed this relational understanding of ordained ministry in his 1990 Holy Thursday letter to priests:

> The priesthood is not an institution that exists alongside the laity, or "above" it. The priesthood of bishops and priests, as well as the ministry of deacons, is "for" the laity, and precisely for this reason it possesses a ministerial character, that is to say one "of service."

What does this mean in practice? To understand the relational nature of priestly spirituality, we must remember that the presbyter is ordained to three interrelated roles in the community: shepherd, prophet, and priest. As I have already said, the glue which holds the three together is pastoral leadership. The presbyter acts, first of all, *in persona Christi*—in the person of Christ who is the head and shepherd leader of the community. In his role as shepherd leader, the presbyter is empowered to be prophet or proclaimer of God's word and priest or leader in divine worship. The uniqueness of the preaching of the presbyter or his priestly ministry in worship rests on his sacramental role as the shepherd of the community. Others also proclaim God's word and lead in worship. The presbyter does this as pastor of the community, or as one joined to the bishop and the presbyterate in the sacrament of pastoral leadership in the Church. The separation of community leadership from the prophetic and priestly functions of the presbyter strikes a blow at the integrity of both the community and the sacramentality of ordained ministry. The presbyter cannot be reduced to a sacramental circuit rider without doing great harm to our understanding of community, liturgy and the significance of sacramental ordination.

Shortly before he was murdered, Archbishop Romero said that if he should be killed, he would rise again in the people of San Salvador. Bishop and people together had become good shepherd for the people of San Salvador. The people had shared their wants and their needs, their courage, and their love with their bishop, and Romero had helped them transform their faith-filled desperation into active care and involvement with the oppressed and the poor. Acting alone there was little the bishop could do to better the situation of the masses. Romero was shepherd by ordination and by the people's trust. He was sacramental presence of the Good Shepherd, but his role as shepherd would be effective only if he could fan into flame the baptismal grace of the community as a whole. Every member of his Christian community had been anointed priest, prophet, and shepherd-king on the day each was baptized. It was not poetic dreaming which prompted him to say that the shepherd would rise in the people—it was profound theological insight into the nature of the Church. The shepherding role of the bishop or presbyter is related by its very nature to the shepherding role of the laity. The bishop or priest who remains alone as shepherd has not yet discovered either the grace of his own ordination or the grace of the baptized. The spirituality of the ordained priest is experienced not only in being shepherd to the community, but in being shepherd to a community of shepherds. As pastor of the community, the presbyter not only makes the Great Shepherd present through his ministry but also challenges, supports, and empowers the total community as it takes on the shepherding image of Christ.

When the disciples of Jesus noticed that the crowd was without food in a deserted place after having listened to him preach all day, they brought their concern to Jesus. His reaction to their observation is both surprising and challenging. Jesus didn't say that he would take care of things; no, he said: "You give them something to eat yourselves" (Luke 9:13). Their immediate reaction was panic at how little they had to feed so many. Jesus did not replace their shepherding role with his own, nor did he abandon them to do something which would be impossible to do alone. Jesus empowered them and worked a miracle with them and through them. Jesus shows the way around the twofold temptation in the life of every pastor. The first is to take over the shepherding role of the laity, replacing their ministry with his own. The second is to abandon the community to do what it has neither the experience, the skill nor the resources to do by itself. Jesus interacted with the disciples in a way which enabled them to feed the hungry. This interaction helped the disciples find their rightful place as shepherds in the Church.

The ordained pastor exists for the empowerment of the community. In acting as shepherd, the presbyter experiences his own transformation in the image of the One he represents. This is how he becomes holy. In calling forth the gifts of the whole community, he also experiences himself being loved, cared for, and supported by the embrace of a shepherding Church. Leadership can be a stress-filled and lonely responsibility. The pastor may well have to take courageous and unpopular stands. The presbyter may have to stand up to the community as well as take his place within it. Yet, the days of the rugged, lonely, and stand-alone pastor are over. The pastor exists to lead and serve a faith community; at the same time he finds both God and support for his own priestly life in the embrace of the Church. The bishop and other presbyters are certainly an important part of that embrace. Most surprising to me as a pastor is the powerful way that the lay community cares for me. They call forth the best from me, as I attempt to do the same for them. The daily experience of the way we are related to one another is the main thrust of my spirituality as a priest.

In a Church in which preaching had often been perfunctory and people felt only a less serious obligation to be present for the proclamation of the Scriptures and the homily, Vatican II affirms that the first responsibility of the priest is to proclaim the word of God to all (*Presbyterorum ordinis* 4). Presbyters are told that people have a right to hear the word of God from the priest. The rites and rituals that came out in the wake of the council tied the proclamation of the word and a homily or exhortation to the celebration of every sacrament. Today's priest is to be a person steeped in the Scriptures, and the contemporary Catholic has come to hunger for insight into God's word in the preaching of the priest.

The priest is ordained to be much more than a student of the Scriptures—the priest is empowered to be a prophetic person sent to insert the living word of God into the daily life of the Church. The student of Scripture studies the text and its context. To be a good preacher, the presbyter must do this too. But because the ordained are also pastors called to preach God's word, the task is a much larger one. The presbyter must understand the people whom he addresses, and he must understand the relationship between the word and this particular community of faith and the individuals within it. The purpose of preaching is twofold: the transformation of the community through the power of the Gospel, and the awakening of the community to its own prophetic task and mission.

By the very nature of the presbyteral mission, the spirituality of the priest is contemplative. The priest must study, contemplate and internalize God's word until it becomes the very fabric of his being. The priest must reek with the word and be a living sign of its meaning and power. The holiness of the priest is the first and most effective proclamation of the word. The priest must take his place at the feet of the Lord and listen to God's word. Personal prayer and the active contemplation of the presence of God in daily life are the foundation on which effective preaching rests. A homily is not a speech. It is not a collection of propositions, insights, or dogmas. A homily is the fruit of prayer. It is a testimony to the experience of the Church. It is the presbyter's witness to the presence of God in the midst of human life, here and now. Preaching which is truly prophetic must come from a prayerful encounter with God.

The contemplative life of the priest embraces the people served, and indeed the whole world as well. If the living word is to touch those listening at the core of what is most real, the priest must seek to know and understand life as it is. The human person stands at the heart of the life of the Church, as Pope John Paul never tires of saying. Because of this, the pastor is called to be a life long student of humanity. While not assigned a role in economics, politics, the arts, or even family life by ordination, the effective pastor studies and contemplates all that touches the lives of those he serves. The parish priest who is out of touch with the daily realities of the laity is of no earthly good to them. This is tragic indeed, since the laity must find and serve God in the midst of these daily realities, not in some other world.

Having said this, let's turn our attention again to the area of focus which belongs most properly to the priest—the word of God and the experience of God in the midst of human life. The task of the preacher is to bring God's word to human realities in insightful and effective ways. More accurately, it is to reveal God as already present in these realities by preaching, celebrating sacraments, leading prayer, and through the witness of a converted life. The priest is to be a bridge builder who links the human and the divine. To do so effectively, he must know the terrain on both ends of the bridge, without forgetting his unique role as one sent by God to guide the process of building the bridge.

A properly focused spiritual life plays a key role in the ability of priests to build bridges for the people they serve. Effective priests know how to live on both ends of the bridge. Priests who live too much on either the divine or human end of the bridge without linking the two in their own lives will not be effective parish priests. They will be perceived as either naively otherworldly and monkish, or pitifully worldly and humanistic. The spirituality of the parish priest is embodied best in the presbyter who is totally captivated by Christ and the ways of God's grace, at the same time that he enters into the realities of daily life as an intelligent participant for the sake of the Gospel. To be helpful spiritual guides for the laity, the major tensions between the world and the Gospel, and this life and the next, must be addressed in the spirituality of priests before priests offer insight to others.

Each week the Church asks the whole community to reflect on the readings that are proclaimed in the Sunday assembly. I see these readings as my principal encounter with the word of God in the recurring cycle of the Church year. Building a whole week of prayer, study, and reflection around these readings has had an immense impact on my spiritual growth. I have found that when the readings speak to me, addressing issues in my own life, they most often address similar issues in the lives of those in the assembly. To preach effectively I have had to move beyond a study based style of homily preparation to a process of personal encounter with the word in prayer. Homily services sometimes provide stories, illustrations, or secondary insights. They also provide a studied and accurate understanding of the text which is crucial. Yet, the main thrust of my homily almost always comes from having prayed with the word in the midst of my own struggles, and among the people I serve.

Fulfilling the prophetic role as preacher for which I was ordained usually begins on Monday morning when I turn to the Scripture readings for the coming Sunday and pray with the gospel for the first time. The word "pray" is very important. My immediate purpose is not homily preparation, as such, but inviting the word into my heart so that I may hear what the Lord is saying to me. On Tuesday morning I go through the same process of prayerful listening to the word, this time with the first reading for the coming Sunday. On Wednesday I turn to the middle reading. On the remaining days of the week I repeat the process, returning to the gospel on Thursday. What I see myself doing is putting the readings into the crock pot of my heart and letting them stew there throughout the week, confident that something surprising and good will emerge—and it does!

Often, nothing happens while I am praying. Regularly enough to rule out coincidence, insight into the Scriptures comes crashing in on me while I am actively involved with the people of the parish. Whether it be while listening to them reflect on the Scriptures or the challenges of their lives, or watching them share their gifts, or entering with them into the news of the day, God often speaks to me more strongly in the midst of the lives we share than in prayer itself. I am confident, though, that this sensitivity to God's self-revelation in daily life would not happen without a major commitment to quiet pondering of the word each day in prayer. Personal prayer is the place where I become pregnant with the word. Ministry is the place where God's word comes to birth in the midst of human realities. While interacting with God's people it grows to maturity, inviting me to conversion by its powerful impact on daily life.

God's word is most powerful when it is proclaimed in the assembly. Insight and grace are joined to the act of preaching in a way that surprises and challenges both community and preacher. Having lived in the midst of the community, having prayed and shared ministry there, the preacher speaks an incarnate word that is timeless and universal. At the same time, the word is tailored to this community alone. The preaching of the pastor of the community has added potential to be powerful because of his role as member and leader of the community. Jesus said: "The sheep hear the shepherd's voice. When he has brought out those that are his, he walks in front of them, and the sheep follow him because they recognize his voice" (John 10:3-4). Proclamation of the word in the Sunday assembly is one of the primary ways that a pastor exercises leadership. Both preparation for preaching and the experience of proclaiming God's word week after week in the assembly are a golden highway to conversion and holiness in the life of the priest. The homily is about the embodiment of God in human life. The homilist is blessed in the very act of preaching as he stands at the intersection of the Scriptures, his personal experience, and the experience of the community he serves. From this distinctive vantage point, the priest proclaims what he sees and is transformed by what he proclaims.

But there is more, much more! The homily is addressed to a community of prophets, not to passive listeners. The purpose of the homily is to fan into flame the prophetic Spirit in the assembly so that God's word will be announced by everyone everywhere. Clear instruction and clever presentations are important, but far from the adequate goal of good preaching. The homilist seeks to lay bare God's saving activity in the world as that activity continues in the Church today. The community that listens is also the Church called to proclaim God's gracious reign in words and deeds. The priest who is a good teacher or an entertaining speaker has only begun to experience the power of his prophetic role. The presbyter who proclaims a prophetic word himself, but continues to be the lone prophet in the community has not yet reached the goal of the ordained prophet. Preaching hits the mark when it quickens a community of prophets, consecrated to be such in baptism.

Priests are called to surrender to the power of God's word as they see that word come alive in the witness of the assembly. Many of those who listen to the word are transformed by it, sometimes with astonishing impact on the preacher. The community becomes a mirror reflecting the proclaimed word back to the preacher and challenging him to go more deeply in his own response to the word. I am often amazed at the way God speaks to me through the people who have listened to me preach. One day when I was in a snit about something, as I sometimes am, an old man came up to me, took my hand and said: "Father, you have to remember that God loves you, and nothing else really matters." It is a great grace to have the word I have spoken return to me, enlarged and deepened by the wonderful faith of the people who listen.

Good preachers recognize the limits of their own prophetic role and long to see the prophetic word extended far beyond their reach in the lives of all who hear. A truly prophetic pastor refuses to replace the prophetic role of the laity with his own. There is a time and a place for preaching and witness by the ordained, and there is a time to encourage and support lay people as they fulfill their prophetic role. The wise pastor knows that while he has the high pulpit, the laity have the larger prophetic role. If God's word is to reach the ends of the earth, the appropriate time for lay people to exercise their prophetic role is the vast majority of the time and in the most far reaching array of places. The presbyter's role is crucial in instructing, supporting and activating the laity, but then the priest must get out of the way. One of the greatest challenges we face in parish ministry is how to deal with an educated and empowered laity. If the laity are to exercise their prophetic role well, the ordained must do more than talk to them about it. Priests must expect great things from them, support them and trust them.

I told a social action group in our parish that I would preach the Gospel, I would offer them the teaching of the Church, and I would give some practical examples that I thought might be helpful, but I would not try to define how the Gospel applied to their world of home and marketplace. To do so was their grace and calling. I told them that I would go with them to state legislative hearings to support them, but I would not speak, because that was their grace and calling. Once I was serving in a small rural community where the teenage accident rate was unusually high and seemed to be on the edge of being suicidal. I started to talk to the assembly about communication in families, and the way that they supported and showed affection to their children. They were not being very communicative or affirming with me, suggesting that this may also have been the case in their homes. Many liked my homily examples about family life and asked me to say more until one day I refused to speak on the subject further. I told them that I had said what could be said from the pulpit. Now the saving word that needed to be said had to be proclaimed and lived by them at home. I could not replace family members in expressing what parents and children needed to say to one another. In fact, by continuing to speak on the subject in church, I was giving them an excuse for not doing what God expected them to do at home.

The prophetic spirituality of the pastor is based in prayer. We should have no illusions or make no excuses about this; it is only by listening carefully to the Spirit of God that the pastor can be sensitive to the movement of God in the community and be discerning about whose prophetic calling is being challenged in a given situation. The interaction between ordained and lay prophets in the prophetic mission of the total Church lies at the heart of presbyteral spirituality. In this interaction priests learn to listen to God, to speak and act in God's name, and to be acted upon by others who have a prophetic role in the Church.

Vatican II made a conscious choice to call its treatise on the ordained priesthood *Presbyterorum ordinis* (the Order of Presbyters). The priestly role of the presbyter had so thoroughly preempted this ministry that the most common name for the presbyter was priest, and the spirituality proper to the presbyterate was called priestly. Vatican II had a much broader vision of the identity and spirituality of the presbyter. This in no way compromises the fact that the presbyter finds the origin and fulfillment of his ministry at the altar, in the same way that the Church finds the source and summit of its life in the Eucharist. Everything the presbyter does leads toward the Eucharist, and everything the Church aspires to flows from the Eucharist. Presbyters are most fully who they are called to be as pastors, prophets, and priests in the Sunday Eucharistic assembly. This threefold ministry attains its highest purpose in leading the Church into the mystery of the Lord's saving love. Through their ministry as priests, presbyters plunge the assembly into the mystery of the Lord's cross in so powerful a way that the community becomes a living image of the dying and rising Christ. The Eucharist is the supreme act of worship. It offers to God the praise and thanksgiving of those who have experienced the transforming power of Christ's love in their lives. Thomas Aquinas taught that the primary effect of the Eucharist is the unity of the Church. The Eucharist exists for us, not for God. God is worshipped and glorified in the transformation of the human race into the image of the risen Christ.

The Eucharist is about the Church becoming something beautiful for God. This conviction, proclaimed so powerfully by Mother Teresa of Calcutta, is a good place to begin our consideration of the Eucharistic spirituality of the priest. Mother Teresa will not allow her sisters to go anyplace where there is no priest. Her reason for this tells us something about the root and foundation of her life and ministry: Without a priest there is no Eucharist, and without the Eucharist there are no Missionaries of Charity. She says: "Our lives are woven with Jesus in the Eucharist, and the faith and the love that come from the Eucharist enable us to see him in the distressing disguise of the poor, and so there is but one love of Jesus, as there is but one person in the poor—Jesus" *(Something Beautiful for God)*.

The Church proclaims that the purpose of the Eucharist is the transformation of the worshipping assembly into the image of the servant Christ. On Holy Thursday the gospel account of the institution of the Eucharist is not read; instead the Church proclaims the commandment of service embodied in the washing of the feet. In this way we are taught a deeper meaning of the Lord's words at the Last Supper: "Do this in memory of me." The words "This is my body" and "this is the cup of my blood" give birth not only to a powerful sacramental ritual in which the Lord is truly present; they also issue a command about the way we are to live our lives as a great memorial to the Lord. These Eucharistic words of Jesus are clear instruction about what it means to be a community of disciples in the Lord. A dynamic Eucharistic spirituality translates "Do this in memory of me" into "Be this in memory of me." The transformation of the community through Eucharistic worship gives God perfect thanks and praise. God is glorified in our becoming saints!

In the wake of the council the use of substantial bread as a more adequate sign of our nourishment on Christ became an important concern. Far more important is the realization that the Church itself is the substantial bread of the Eucharist. Mother Teresa has profound insight into the transforming power of the Eucharist in her insistence that in their love for the poor the Missionaries of Charity are something beautiful for God. It is to this kind of Eucharistic spirituality that the Church invites presbyters in the rite of ordination: "Accept from the holy people of God the gifts to be offered to him. Know what you are doing, and imitate the mystery you celebrate: model your life on the mystery of the Lord's cross" (Rite of Ordination of Presbyters).

The fulfillment of the ministry of the priest rests on far more than the consecration of bread and wine into the body and blood of Christ, as awesome as this reality is. The priest is called to preside at the consecration of the Church and its transformation into the Body of Christ. The Eucharistic sacrifice and meal are crucial to this transforming process. St. Augustine reminds us that we become what we eat. Pope John Paul II presents the ministry of the priest as a service to the laity (1990 Holy Thursday Message). That service is rendered most powerfully when the laity realize most profoundly their own priestly identity. The whole Church is called to become a sacrifice of praise and self-giving love to God. Our ecclesial vocation is rooted in the Eucharist, and we continually return to the Eucharistic assembly for renewed empowerment and direction. Jesus is the first fruits of God's reign, the preeminent one to offer himself in sacrificial love, the first to rise to newness of life, the origin of our transformation in the power of the Spirit. Through the ministry of the ordained priest, Jesus raises up a priestly people, recreated in the divine image. A proper understanding of the Eucharistic spirituality of the priest is rooted in the mission of Jesus to the world and the role of the Eucharist in the transformation of the Church. The Eucharist is not only a gift to be offered and a presence to be adored; it is preeminently an empowerment to be lived. The ordained priest who finds himself the sole priest during or after the Eucharist has not yet experienced the full meaning of priestly ordination. A dynamic priestly spirituality invites priests to find God in the Eucharistic action and worship they offer, in the full participation of the assembly, and in the fulfillment of the Eucharist in the life of the community.

In the parish where I serve, we become something beautiful for God in the hospitality we offer, especially to those who are alienated. We are a priestly people in the houses we built for Habitat for Humanity, in our ministry at the food shelf, and in our relationship with our Native American sister parish. We are living out our Eucharistic spirituality in our commitment to the unborn, in our support for family life, and in the gift of the Gospel to all we meet. We are a sanctified and holy people in the worship and prayer which fires our surrender to God's will and kingdom. Through all of these we stand before God as "a chosen race, a royal priesthood, a holy nation, a people set apart." (Sundays in Ordinary Time—Preface I) The ordained priest experiences the wonder and power of God in ministering to this priestly people. In celebrating the Eucharist for and with the assembly, the priest is touched by the reign of God embodied in the community and by the powerful effect that the Eucharist has in the life of the Church. The presence of Christ in the Eucharistic elements, the presence of Christ in the ordained priest and the presence of Christ in the priestly community of the baptized are interrelated and inseparable realities. The parish priest's primary avenue to God lies in living out these interrelated dimensions of Christ's presence in the Church. The unique way that presbyters share in the priestly ministry of Christ enables them to offer a beautiful people to God as the fruit of their Eucharistic service to the Church. This realization is the source of profound spiritual joy.

The total Church is a sign of God's saving love in the world, and within this great sacrament bishops and presbyters are sacrament too. Vatican II uses the phrase *in persona Christi caput ecclesiae* to describe the unique sacramentality of the ordained priesthood. The council does not say that the bishop or presbyter is another Christ because the Church has only one Messiah and leader. It affirms an even more awesome understanding of the ordained priesthood: the ordained act *in Christ's person as leader and head of the Church* because the Good Shepherd is present in their ministry in a true sacramental presence. The bishop or presbyter is not Christ's vicar or replacement. The priesthood is a sacrament through which Jesus continues to hold his own place as the Church's shepherd, priest, and prophetic leader. When the full impact of sacramental theology is understood, the concept of vicar seems to be a diminishment, not an enhancement, of ordained ministry. In a similar way the great sacrament of the Church is the living presence of Jesus in the world, not Christ's replacement until he comes in glory.

The priesthood is not every sacrament nor the most important sacrament in the Church. It is a unique and powerful manifestation of the Good Shepherd's presence in the Christian community, here and now. In other words, the priesthood is not primarily a function or a role; it is sacramental presence. While describing the presbyter as the *presider* at the liturgy is accurate, and expecting priests to have the skills necessary to fulfill their role is crucial, the ordained person is much more than a well-equipped functionary. The sacramental intuition which lies at the heart of the Catholic understanding of the Church insists that the priest is a sacramental person whose presence has an impact on the community which cannot be reduced to function. For example, the presbyter presides *in the person of Christ the head of the Church* even when apparently doing nothing at a particular point in the liturgy. The community and its ministers interact, even then, in relationship to Christ the head sacramentally present through the one who presides.

Because priests are living signs and real presence of Christ the shepherd in the community, personal holiness is crucial to their credibility. They impact the community not only by fulfilling the requirements of ritual but also through their own transformation into the image of the Shepherd they represent. As congregations grow in size, and the number of priests continues to decrease, the importance of understanding priests as pivotal ministers who influence the life of the

Church through sacramental presence, symbolic actions, and personal witness will increase. A sacramental understanding of the ministry of the priest emphasizes the symbolic character of priestly identity and action. Priests are not called to do everything; they are empowered to represent Someone. Through their symbolic words and actions they challenge and empower the total community to come to full stature in Christ.

This sacramental spirituality of ordained ministry invites priests to a holiness that authenticates their role as shepherds, prophets, and priests in the Church. To be the sign they were ordained to be, priests must be people of prayer, unifiers, listeners, leaders with courage, conviction, and vision who are able to deal with giftedness, confusion, and conflict, and much more. A priest becomes holy by handling the issues encountered in being a good shepherd today. Most days I spend much of my time dealing with tension and conflict in a very rich and diverse faith community. On those days I grow in grace and holiness by listening, soothing, challenging, supporting, and unifying those I seek to serve. Becoming a good shepherd is a long conversion process. The grace already present in ordination must be claimed in the unfolding of daily life.

A sacramental spirituality invites the ordained to look at the symbolic nature of their actions, along with the quantity of their hard work. Let me give an example. I am pastor of a 98 percent white, upper middle class, suburban parish. One day during the liturgy a little black girl broke away from her father and ran up to me as I sat in the presider's chair. I picked her up and sat her in my lap, where she was quite content to be, and went on listening to the readings. When the time came for the gospel, I carried her back to her dad. I said nothing, but it was apparent to all in this overwhelmingly white congregation that a little black girl felt comfortable enough to walk into the sanctuary in the middle of Mass and approach the priest. And the priest knew her well enough to pick her up and embrace her as a father would embrace any child. Expending very little energy, I had pulled this child into the heart of the Church, claiming her as our own. I don't have to talk about racism always in order to combat it. I may not need to start new programs either. Often all I have to do is be the sign I was ordained to be, and let my action or gesture be a witness to the Good Shepherd's presence in the community. I am convinced that the priest is a sacramental person whose words and actions echo loudly in the life of the community. When I was a student in Rome, some friends came from home for a visit. I had gotten them very good tickets for a papal audience, but they wanted none of it.

They said that they didn't need any more papal triumphalism and oppression. They were practicing Catholics all right, but not much impressed with the official Church. They went to the audience only
because I insisted. They came back transformed and glowing because
Pope John Paul had spotted some handicapped teenagers and had
gone over to them, knelt in front of their wheelchairs, and embraced
them. Much of our best preaching is done through symbolic action.
Sincere expressions of kindness may well win us a hearing for the
harder things we have to say. Our gestures are empty, though, when
our words don't also express the compassion of Christ. Priests must
use this sacramental understanding of ordination to work smarter, not
necessarily harder, as the demands upon them increase. Prayerful
priests are moved to humility, thanksgiving, and ongoing conversion
by the mysterious and surprising ways that Christ reveals his presence
and care through their ministry as shepherds of the community.

The priest exists for the sake of the laity. This teaching of Pope
John Paul that I cited earlier struck home for me as I began a parish
mission in a neighboring parish. Having been introduced by mistake
as a Jesuit, I responded by saying: "No, I am a diocesan priest. The
charism of diocesan priests is the mission and spirituality of the laity.
That is why I am here today." I was surprised by the forcefulness of
my own words. I had long envied the newly rediscovered charisms of
religious men and women and often felt like a nondescript lowly
workhorse as a diocesan priest. What should have always been obvious hit me like a lightening bolt. Diocesan and other parish clergy
have a unique charism that places them at the heart of the mission of
the Church. Not only are they called forth from the laity to be priests
but they also choose to continue to live among lay people, to lead
communities of lay men and women, and to focus their ministry on
the mission and spirituality of the laity.

The significance of this lay-focused presbyteral charism is immense when the emerging role of the laity is taken seriously. There
was a time when being a lay person meant second-class citizenship in
the Church and being in the world represented a compromised kind
of discipleship. Being holy for the lay person often meant riding on
the shirt tails of the clergy or being associated with the spirituality of
a community of religious. With the advent of Vatican II, two things
happened. First, the Church reevaluated its mission to the world. Not
only did the Church refocus its energy outward toward the salvation
of the global human family, but even more significantly the Church
proclaimed that it was in dialog with the world, both influencing and
being influenced by the worldwide human community. Once the

Church had reaffirmed its mission to the global community and to the transformation of all that is authentically human, the role of the laity changed dramatically. Suddenly it was clear that the members of the Church who were most in the world and the most skilled and responsible for its transformation were lay people.

In the milestone declaration *Christifideles laici,* Pope John Paul redefines and affirms the mission of the laity in this way:

> For the lay faithful, to be present and active in the world is not only an anthropological and sociological reality, but in a specific way, a theological and ecclesiological reality as well. In fact, in their situation in the world God manifests his plan and communicates to them their particular vocation of "seeking the kingdom of God by engaging in temporal affairs and by ordering them according to the plan of God" (#15).

Lay people seek God and become holy by being in the world and fulfilling their mission there. All at once the laity have moved from the passive position of the folks on the sidelines, to the active position of storm troopers, people on the cutting edge, ministers of the Church deeply engaged in Christ's work of loving and transforming the world. The Church and the world meet most spontaneously among the laity. The reign of God and secular affairs converge in the lives of lay people. Without the ministry of the laity it would be impossible for the Church to fulfill its mission to the world. In an outward looking Church the laity have an essential role, and the clergy who choose to live among them as their servants have great responsibility. When we understand the ecclesiology of Vatican II and the theological development which has occurred in its wake, saying that the charism of the diocesan or secular clergy is the mission and spirituality of the laity is no small thing indeed!

The situation of the laity and that of the secular clergy have much in common. Both seek to be in the world without being worldly. Both seek God in the unpredictability of daily life. Both find their spirituality focused on the Sunday liturgy, contemplation in action, care for families, weddings and funerals, the rearing of children, care for those in need, and active engagement in their cultural and social environment. In the years since the council, lay people have struggled to identify a spirituality that is appropriate to them and their mission in and to the world. The parish clergy have been involved in a similar quest. Diocesan priests and the people they serve have much to teach one another because, despite the differences in their responsibilities, their pursuit of God shares a common milieu. Monastic charisms and those of other religious communities offer eschatological perspective, precious insights, and needed support to parish priests and lay communities on their secular journey. I have learned theology and the Spiritual Exercises from the Jesuits, and I have been guided in contemplative prayer among the Trappists, for this I will be forever grateful. Yet, there are some things that only those who are committed to a spiritual life in the midst of the ups and downs of secular realities can teach one another. It is one thing to seek God in an environment ordered around religious concerns. It is a very different experience to find God amid the disorder and distractions of a world that often does its best to shut God out. In this, the parish clergy and the lay faithful understand one another. The spirituality of the diocesan priest comes to birth and is nurtured among the laity and in many ways maintains the features of lay spirituality.

To serve the laity well, priests must be life long students of lay people and their world of family, culture, economics, and politics. The other worldly priest may well be a saint, and at the same time be of little help to lay people in the pursuit of their mission to the world. While not called to have his own family, or to engage in business, or to be involved in politics, the priest who is ignorant of these things will be seriously handicapped in his ministry to lay people. In repeating this I realize again that the spirituality of the diocesan priest is more complex than I originally imagined. Not only must the parish priest know the things of God well, he must also know human realities well and understand how the two come together in his own spiritual life and in the lives of the people he serves.

Collaboration is one of the hallmarks of parish ministry today. At first sight, collaboration appears to be new and innovative, the product of studies in effective leadership and psychology. If our commitment to collaboration rests on pragmatic values alone, we will not be drawn deeply enough into the graced dynamism that is to transform our lives. We are committed to collaboration not only because it works better but primarily because it better reflects the inner life of the God in whose image we are made. Over the centuries the western Church has preferred an intellectual or speculative approach to the mystery of the Trinity. Three persons in one God was a puzzle to be solved and explained. The Trinity was the great mystery to be accepted in faith, even when it appeared to be a logical contradiction. Sermons on the Trinity often centered on making what appeared illogical less so. The spirituality of the western Church often encouraged devotion to the individual persons of the Trinity, ignoring the dynamic relationship among the divine persons and within the being of God. In prayer we often thought of God simply as God. The

Trinitarian consciousness of the average Roman Catholic has been rather low, even when their commitment to the doctrine of the Trinity has been very high. Too often, God has been either a monolithic God for the western Christian, or three independent God-persons whom we affirmed to be one.

The Trinitarian consciousness of the eastern Church permeates the liturgy and spirituality of the people. Father, Son, and Holy Spirit is a ceaseless mantra that keeps the image of the Trinity always in public view. More importantly, the eastern Church sees the Trinity as a holy mystery to be emulated and lived, not a puzzle to be solved. The life of the Church is to reflect the image of the Trinity. Just as God is a communion of love in which three equal persons share in one saving mission in different but interrelated ways, so too the Church is a communion of equal persons sharing in one mission in diverse but interrelated ways. The way we see God has a profound effect on the way we conceptualize and live out our ministry. A consciousness of God which was for all practical purposes monolithic—the lonely old being in the sky—contributed to a ministerial consciousness in which priests lived out their ministry and exercised authority in monolithic ways. The full internalization of the dynamism of our Trinitarian faith is crucial to an ecclesial spirituality based on ministerial relationships. Our reason for collaborating grows out of our understanding of the inner life of God and the empowerment of grace. If grace is a share in God's life, and God is Trinity, can we be anything other than collaborative if we are being faithful to grace?

Two things in my office express my vision as pastor. The first is a round table at which we sit as equals in leadership and in ministry. There is no doubt that I have a unique role and authority as pastor; at the same time that there is no doubt that we sit at the table as equal persons who share in one saving mission in diverse and interrelated ways. It is helpful to remember that the Gospels present Jesus saying: "I and the Father are one" (John 10:30) at the same time he says, "the Father is greater than I" (John 14:28), and "all authority in heaven and earth has been given to me" (Matt 28:18). Authority within the inner life and mission of the Trinity is seen in different ways at different times. On the wall above the round table there is an icon of the Trinity. As parishioners, staff and pastor, our task is to embody the grace of the Trinity and to witness to the power of Trinitarian grace in transforming a fragmented world. Trinity lies at the heart of how we see God and how we see our mission in a vibrant ecclesial spirituality.

In the quest for God celibacy can be a way of life which isolates the priest from those he serves, or it can be an opportunity to meet

God and people in a less cluttered lifestyle. Long before it became a monastic charism, St. Paul recommended celibacy as a way to simplify life for the sake of God's reign (1 Cor 7:25-35). The emptiness which celibacy creates in the heart of the priest can give birth to a cold and distant man, or the empty room inside can become a place of hospitality where God is welcomed and the people of the Church are gathered. In some vocations celibacy is focused on a life beyond this one. For most diocesan priests the call to celibacy is much more incarnational. Celibacy is not about avoiding human attachments, intimacy, and love. On the contrary, the celibacy of diocesan priests opens the way to a broad range of ecclesial relationships in which the reign of God is experienced here and now. Mature celibate parish priests are enriched and made holy as they experience the unique way in which God and people make a home together in their hearts. To be effective, the presbyter must keep the poor and empty space within him from being filled with possessions, addictions, and self-centeredness, so that it remains a fitting gathering place for the Church.

In describing the relationship between Jesus and the Church, Mother Teresa uses the image of the vine and the branches (John 15:5). In doing so, she reminds us that all the beauty and fruitfulness of the vine is on the branches. Jesus loves us so much that he empowers us to be his beauty and fruitfulness in the world. While the pastor has a far different importance in the life of the Church, there is a sense in which Mother Teresa's image applies to the parish priest as well.

In concluding this essay I would like to acknowledge the enormous debt I owe to the people and staff of St. John Neumann parish in Eagan, Minnesota, where I am privileged to be pastor. They are something beautiful for God. They are my fruitfulness and my joy. The blessing and the challenge of serving them and being served by them is a powerful grace for me. I thank God for them always.

2

Using the Wrong Measure?

Kenneth E. Untener

You'd have to know Clem Kern to appreciate fully this story. He was a legend in Detroit, as was Holy Trinity parish where he was pastor for very many years. Located in old "Corktown," people of all kinds came from all directions.

A seminary faculty member interviewed Clem as background work for a course she taught on the spirituality of diocesan priests. Looking back on his forty-six years of priesthood and talking about his own spirituality, he said this:

> When it comes to prayer, I didn't do as well as I should have. I think religious order priests do much better. I used to say the breviary for two days at once. I'd start a little after 11 p.m., and by the time I finished it would be just after midnight, so I'd say the office for the next day. It was sort of two for one. As for other kinds of prayer, I didn't do so well on that either. It was hard to find a way of doing it that would be regular like it was in my seminary training. I guess my prayer centered on the Eucharist. The Mass always meant a lot to me. I also tried to see God in the people I served and to live for God. But I could have done better on my prayer life.

Clem was a holy man. In centuries past, before there was a process for canonization, he would have been a saint by popular acclamation. He ministered to the poor and down-and-out (beautiful and humorous anecdotes abound), and he ministered to the rich and to everyone in between. He was gentle yet strong, faithful to the Church yet innovative.

20

Here was this holy, kind, good man, ministering as well as I've ever seen it done, saying that his spiritual life was not so good.

Something doesn't fit.

Different Models of Holiness

We have long taken for granted that religious life is the fullest expression of Christian holiness. It is out of reach of most people, but we can all participate in it in different degrees. Those who cannot do all the things included in this basic model (laity, diocesan priests) were to do as much as they could and settle for a lower level of holiness. For example, Augustine said that, all things being equal, the mother of a dedicated virgin would *ipso facto* have a lower place in heaven than her daughter. She followed the lesser way.

Which brings to mind something else that doesn't fit. I remember, with embarrassment, how I as a young priest sometimes tried to help lay people develop a deeper spirituality. When they asked for help, I would talk about spiritual exercises, mostly prayer. I would help them commit themselves to a pattern of spiritual exercises and regular prayer (usually the form I had learned—meditation). They began with great effort, because they wanted to "be the best you could be," and after some months usually failed. There were streaks of success, but these were followed by days in a row when they did poorly. They kept trying, but for most it didn't fit. Finally, they stopped coming for help, or if they came, we talked of other things.

If I had been honest with them, I would have told them that my efforts at prayer were much the same as theirs. Now, after giving diocesan priests' retreats for over twenty years, I know it is much the same for most diocesan priests.

What is the problem here? Are all these lay people and diocesan priests mediocre Christians?

These people may have a deep spirituality, but we have the wrong starting point, are making the wrong assumptions, and asking the wrong questions. Things do not fit, not because the people are improperly formed, but because we are trying to pour them into the wrong form. The starting point for any examination of spirituality is the person's relationship with God, not a particular model of spirituality.

It's something like marriage. You cannot measure a good marriage by using one model of marriage, no matter how ideal or good that model may be.

Here is a true story of an elderly couple and their relationship to one another. Old Joe died when he was ninety-one. Eleven months later his wife, Pauline, died. In her last months she said that she just couldn't live without him because they had shared every thought and now life was so empty.

Some of the grandchildren would smile to themselves and, although they believed her, say, "You shared everything? When?" If you watched them all day long you would see few words exchanged. After finishing his chores Joe liked to read (even though he'd only been through the fourth grade), and it seemed as though he read every moment he was in the house (it was before television). Meanwhile Pauline was busy about little household things. In the evening they were together in the living room, he reading and she knitting. Hardly a word, maybe no word, was said.

The same scenario happened every evening: Around 9:30 she'd ask if he would like a glass of milk, and he would answer, "That would be fine," as though it was something new. Then he would ask if she would like to play a game of pinochle, and she would greet this suggestion as though it were something they hadn't done in a long time. They would play two games of pinochle, and he would always win. She would tilt the table so the cards went on the floor and say, "Dad, you pick them up, I'm going up to bed." He did, and she did.

Their relationship was a good one. They had their own ways of sharing things, their own "communication system". Much of it was non-verbal. They even had their own ritual (the glass of milk, the pinochle game, the cards on the floor).

Now imagine someone doing research on marriage and coming to this couple to examine their relationship, and bringing his or her own model as a presupposition. The model might be one of a younger "modern couple" in an urban setting. Imagine asking the couple questions like these:

> Do you have good verbal communication? Do you make sure to discuss things with one another on a regular basis? In these discussions, are you able to express your honest feelings, especially when there is conflict? Besides mutual friends, do you have your own relationships with people who are distinctively your friends? Do you occasionally take separate trips? Have you ever participated in marriage enrichment programs? Do you discuss some of your conflicts and struggles in marriage with other married couples, or with a counselor? Are you able to communicate with one another about what you like or don't like in your sexual relationship? Have you experimented to find different ways to achieve sexual fulfillment?

How would Joe and Pauline respond to these questions? Well, they would probably look to the person with a certain respect, acknowledge that they don't do most of these things, and conclude that "we don't have one of those real good marriages."

You cannot measure a marriage by using one model of marriage, no matter how ideal or good that model might appear to be. The starting point is not a model of marriage, but the relationship. Then you discover that this old couple has a very deep relationship, with excellent communication (without regular and lengthy verbal exchange), separate "space" in their lives (without separate friends or trips), continuing growth (without enrichment programs or counseling), and a sexual relationship that brought bonding and healing (without verbal discussion and/or experimentation). To begin with the categories that belong to a particular model is to miss the mark.

Diocesan priests have been measured by a model of spirituality that can make them appear second-rate. Lay peoples' lives have been measured by a model of spirituality that makes them appear second-rate. Something doesn't fit.

A Shift After the Fourth Century

It was not so from the beginning. The early Christians and their leaders practiced the same "ecclesial spirituality." There was no other model.

As time went by, other models developed. By the end of the third century monastic communities had formed from among the laity. Pastors still followed the ecclesial spirituality of the laity. However, something curious began to happen. When efforts were made to reform the "diocesan priesthood," there was a tendency to urge these priests to follow the models of spirituality developed by those in monastic and contemplative communities.

Diocesan priests were increasingly called upon, as far as possible, to model their spirituality on those who lived in prayer, asceticism, poverty, chastity, obedience, and community. One thinks of Pope Gregory the Great, Augustine, Basil, Gregory of Nazianzan, the cathedral canons (who lived in community and sang the office at the cathedral).

The model, the starting point, took a wrong turn.

Religious could cut away many things from their lifestyle that the diocesan priests found central to theirs. Religious communities could and did arrange their work around their prayer and *horarium*, with prayer the priority. Priests in pastoral work, on the other hand, found that the times and place of prayer needed to adapt to the demands of pastoral work. The *horarium* revolved around ministry to others, which could not always be scheduled in advance.

Religious orders found that direct relationship with God governed relationships with others: silence among the brethren or sisters was a given at certain times of day, maybe most of the day. Asceticism was designed and common to all, regular, and reasonable. Priests in pastoral work often enough found their days governed by crises, with unpredictable overwork at times, and then sudden maybe even extended lulls.

Most often the pattern of the priest's life today as formerly, is at best somewhat erratic: three funerals in one week and none for the next four, a flurry of meetings at the beginning of Advent and Lent, and none right after Christmas; two golf days in a row and none for the next month. Regularity in anything, even meals, falls apart sometimes. If the ideal is a regular schedule, regular time for prayer, regular asceticism (or even exercise), regular community, (even regular meals), they cannot manage it.

It turns into the regret, "I'm not praying as I ought." Or, as Joe and Pauline would have said regarding their way of life, "We don't have one of those real good marriages."

Another Frame of Reference

The starting point, the assumptions made regarding the perfection of charity, and finally the consequences of this starting point and these assumptions were simply wrong, and this has carried over to our own day.

With another starting point, other assumptions for the perfection of charity, there will be other consequences, other models of spirituality and holiness. Authentic spirituality has a thousand faces.

If the relationship with God is the starting point, as with Clem Kern, then however one attains it, the relationship can be good, even excellent. Clem's holiness was not of the monastic sort that he so admired. He was ascetic, but not in the monastic pattern. He spent almost nothing on himself, nor on luxuries. Clem let money come into one hand and as quickly slip out of the other. Casually he'd drop on my desk a check that someone had given him for two hundred dollars with the words, "I'm sure you can find some use for this." I'd think, "I'm sure you can, too." On the other hand, he spent hundreds of dollars on one evening, taking the seminary faculty to the top of the Renaissance Building in Detroit for a magnificent dinner, in honor of a librarian who had just been fired. He golfed with Jewish friends at the most expensive country club in Detroit. And he often enough picked up drunks off the street and drove them somewhere for a night's lodging. At his funeral there was an interesting assortment of the very rich and powerful and the very poor and powerless. Like Jesus, he was at ease at the banquets of the rich and powerful, and—quite freely spoke there about the poor who were also his friends. And he loved the rest of us who were somewhere in between.

Clem's spirituality was simply ecclesial. He was a disciple of Jesus by his actions. He loved the Church and the people of God, whether they were Church goers or not. And he had a profound respect for the poor.

Simply Ecclesial

I do not like the phrase "lay spirituality," which implies that it is a certain brand or offshoot. Theirs is the original spirituality—the spirituality of the Christian community, the fundamental spirituality of every book of the New Testament. Lay people have access to the total riches of the Church. Before the coming of monasticism the spirituality of Christians was simply ecclesial. It was founded in discipleship of Jesus, securely rooted in the community where the word was preached, Eucharist shared.

The spirituality of the diocesan priesthood is also ecclesial spirituality, the original spirituality. To be sure, the diocesan priest lives out this spirituality from a special perspective, as leader, presider, pastor, in this ecclesial community. All who live ecclesial spirituality have a certain modality because of the circumstances of their lives. Ecclesial spirituality for the priest includes preaching the good news to which he listens, presiding at Eucharist where he is also participant, being a member of this community that he also pastors.

The relationship with God remains key. Without some continuing conversation in a relationship, you lose your friend; you lose your wife or husband; you lose your God. The depth of relationship equals the depth of communication. If I do not have a conversation "going" with God, then when I have free time I will find something else to do with it. Just because I have more time doesn't mean I will use it to turn to God.

If the communication is ordinarily there, I will return to it repeatedly in many varied patterns. Over the years we have to learn to be creative in our relationship with God, just as we do in human relationships. People who have good marriages find ways to vary the patterns. They sometimes spend quality time together, take vacations, days off, time away from children.

For some priests, centering prayer each day is the best way to spend quality time with God. Retreat times can be quality time away, and a good chance to deepen our relationship with God, and talk with others seriously about what is central in our life and ministry.

Adding on to busy lives usually does not work. What does work is taking what is already present in our lives and turning that into the ongoing conversation. There are the do-able things, like preparation for homilies, Sunday Eucharist, ministry to our parishioners and others, the sacramental moments. Instead of being part of the "job," these can, with a bit of effort, be good conversation times, not only with people but with God. This is to make what we do daily and best the heart of our spirituality.

Spirituality is more than prayer. Spirituality is a vision of reality, a world-view, a way of looking at things. It includes my way of viewing God, but also the world, others and myself. It includes my beliefs and my ideas, but also my behavior, not only toward God but the world, others and myself. Spirituality is never simply in the head. It is also my behavior. Finally it includes my openness to transcendence, a willingness to let people, the world, God, transform me.

Disciples of Jesus Christ

For diocesan priests, as with other Christians, discipleship is central to our ecclesial spirituality. Diocesan priests belong to the community of the disciples of Jesus Christ. We face the same struggles as every lay person, and we live in the same world they do.

Attempts to reform diocesan priesthood by modeling it on religious life have been mis-directed. We need, as does every lay person, to build a spirituality that is ecclesial, with the modality of the circumstances of our own life.

Diocesan priests on retreat seem constantly to be making resolutions to re-do their schedule, and find time for patterns of spiritual exercises that they have been looking for since they left the seminary. We would do better to take the pattern that is there (if one can call our schedules a pattern) and find ways to build into it an attentiveness to God that runs from morning till night.

Clem Kern was a holy priest. Joe and Pauline did have "one of those real good marriages." Diocesan priests, through their pattern of life—not in spite of it—are called as are all in the Church, to the summit of holiness.

3

Ruminations of a Canonist

James H. Provost

Despite what some might read from the appearances, secular priests who are canon lawyers do need spirituality. We need it perhaps more urgently than most! Working in a tribunal, chancery, or in my case at the moment, in an academic setting, we are somewhat removed from the direct feedback that often seems to sustain our brother priests in other ministries.

In the twelve years I worked in the tribunal, only once or twice did a petitioner write to thank me for a decision; but I am sure they thanked the priest who worked with them at the parish level. To me, this is the way it should be. My role as a canon lawyer has been to minister to priests and others who are on the "line." I have seen my ministry as one of "staff," or as a minister to the ministers.

The idea was not my own; rather, it came from a very unexpected quarter. On my way to study canon law after a year in a parish, I stopped at my old seminary. Only a few students were around; vacation was not yet over. The vice-rector was watching the house. In those days, it seemed to be of the nature of the office of vice-rector that he was not a popular man in the house. So when, against the jibes of my friends, he spoke in my defense, his comment stuck with me. He pointed out that I was preparing to become a minister to priests, a man in the back room whose job it was to make others look good as they preached the Gospel and ministered more directly to the needs of the people.

I have not hidden in a back room, but my experience as a priest has been one of administration, of facilitating, of technical support, and at times of helping to articulate the vision and life of the community. Where is the spirituality in all this?

St. Paul has a kind word to say about the charism of administration. He lists it just after "helpful acts" and before "various kinds of tongues" (1 Cor 12:28)—not high on the list, but a charism nonetheless! Charisms are gifts of the Spirit. They are intended for the benefit of others, but they carry with them a certain tone or coloration for the spirituality of the one who is called to carry out the charism. A person who has the gift of healing, for example, can be quite moved (and humbled) by it, causing the person to walk in greater fear of God. So with someone called to administration; if it is indeed a gift, as St. Paul says, it is a humbling experience to discover the Spirit at work in such ordinary activities. And yet that has been my experience.

Perhaps this also fits with the incarnational dimension of the Church. Christ is the Word become flesh; the Church continues his mission in the world—not separate from the world, but right in the middle of it. We are a visibly structured, institutionalized Church, which constitutes an outward sign instituted by Christ to give grace. To be involved in administration, whether parish or diocesan administration, is not to be foreign to the spiritual heart of the Church, but to help make it effective in our time and place.

Two other realities have given tone or color to my life. The night before the closing session of Vatican II, together with other young priests who served as ushers (we had the more elegant Latin title of *assignatores loci*, but nonetheless ushers in the council hall) during the fourth session of the council, I attended an audience with Pope Paul VI just for our group. He came into the room tired; I remember thinking how insensitive his aides were, letting him have saliva settle on the corners of his mouth. But his words to us were from his heart. The council was concluding, he said, but the work was just beginning. We, young priests that we were, would have to carry on the task of implementing the council. When I reflect on this experience even today, it strikes me how much he was reaching out to us, how well he understood it would take a long time and a lot of work if the renewal, and not just the rearrangement called "reform," were to take hold in the Church.

Vatican II has formed the agenda of the Church during my lifetime as a priest; it has formed not only my agenda, but my spirituality. The insight, sensitivity, creativity, whatever one calls the work of the Spirit during the sessions of the council, continue to challenge me to go beyond the comfortable and convenient, and to seek the Spirit calling us to become what we truly are. The very work of administration is one dimension of doing this; and as Yves Congar pointed out in writing about reform of the Church, it has to work its way into the warp and woof of the institution if reform is to be genuine and long-lasting.

The second coloration which has affected me is the sense of authority as service. It has not always been easy for me to appreciate this, and sometimes one or another priest friend has been truly a friend, reminding me to get off my high horse. But the more I work in the Church, and the more I observe at various levels of church life, it becomes apparent that the authority which moves people's hearts is the one which truly works as service.

The flip side of the coin, however, is that the one who provides service also gains power. The secretary of a union, of a political party, of any number of groups, winds up with a lot of power just by providing a service everyone comes to rely upon. So the temptation of power, for me one of the most serious temptations faced by Christ or by the Church down through the ages, is a very real one in my own life. I find I do not have to seek power, or be power-hungry; power just gets generated by doing things for others, so it is important to learn to live with power and to turn it into energy for others.

In light of these influences on my life, I will divide my ruminations on the spirituality of the diocesan priest into three sections: spirituality for a time of change; spirituality for a Vatican II Christian; and some "rules" of spirituality for a secular priest, at least as seen by one who is a canon lawyer.

Spirituality for a Time of Change

Nearly twenty years ago I made a thirty-day retreat. Not your usual Jesuit-directed retreat, but thirty days in a Trappist monastery where I was introduced by a very understanding and patient abbot to the riches of our Catholic spiritual tradition. In one sense, I felt cheated that this did not come sooner in my life, rather than the mind-numbing (and at times body-numbing) hours spent in chapel before dawn during seminary days, and the helter-skelter approach of various well-intentioned confessors ever since. On the other hand, the riches were always there; it was I who needed to change, to pause and discover the resources which mark our tradition.

Change has been the hallmark of our time, and for me ever since my ordination in 1963 it has been a characteristic of the Catholic Church. There have been the surface changes people talk about all the time—whether in liturgy, or in dealing with parishioners, or in organizations and meetings, and so on. But the change I mean here is deeper. There has been a change in what the sociologists call "place."

When the surface changes took place, people felt they did not know their place—whether literally, as to when to stand or kneel, or where we were in the liturgy participation sheets; or figuratively, as how to address a priest (do I call you "Father" or "Jim"?), or when it was proper to speak out loud what was on everyone's mind but was not being spoken by church leaders.

This has affected us as priests. We, too, have trouble knowing our place in some situations, whether in the sanctuary or on the street. As a master of ceremonies for many years, it was my job to help priests find their place at major ceremonies; as a chancery official or canon law teacher, it has been and still is my job to help priests find their place in the changing organizational structures of canon law.

But it is not easy for someone in administration to know his place either, and this becomes more complex as bishops change, as other staff change, and as one's own base of support shifts. For me, the changes which occurred in my personal situation as well as in the wider Church led me to search for some still point, some anchor, in a sea of change. The Trappists helped me discover medieval English contemplatives and the Zen method of meditation.

Finding the still point of God's presence deep within me is never easy. There is too much "noise in the channels" of someone engaged in an active life which can distract from the Center which is always present. It takes regular returning to that Center, whether in a retreat, or preparing a homily, or in the quiet moments in a Eucharistic celebration. Sometimes it is even more urgent when a crisis has arisen, and it is time to take action on something administratively!

I know that even in times of change the Spirit is present and working, but it is not uncommon for me to feel I am in the dark as to where the Spirit truly is leading. Whether it is some inconsistency in church policy, a difficult decision which I know is not going to be received warmly, a crisis I am asked to help with as an advocate for one side or another—I can feel a darkness of anxiety, frustration, even wondering what the Church is really going to become. Sometimes this darkness reminds me of the experience of mystics who spent much more time in attending to the Lord than I find myself spending. Yet I know that it is in reaching into the middle of a very difficult situation and ripping it open that I will discover God, for the Lord is present everywhere, even when that "where" is very upsetting to me personally or to the way I understand the Church ought to be.

In a time of transition, another help has been a sense of history. It gives perspective to realize that today's crises are not new, nor are they necessarily putting an end to the Church's vitality. When secular events pile up into a sense of helplessness it is useful to put them in historical perspective; the same is true with church experiences—our "crises" are often but a continuation of various tensions which have been with us since the Apostles.

Another perspective I have found helpful in a time of transition is the awareness of the ecumenical dimension of Church. What we experience as Catholics is not unique; many other religious groups are going through similar changes, and some are coping better than others. In dealing with transitions I have also found the Lord works in secular as well as religious resources. Some very enriching and supportive experiences for me have come from attending workshops, seminars, or other learning experiences designed for a secular, rather than a religious audience.

Perhaps one of the underlying transitions we are experiencing is precisely this interaction of Church and world, of the religious and the secular. If the Church is not something existing in the abstract, a kind of world outside our world, but rather exists in our everyday experience in the here and now, then it is in our everyday lives that Church takes place. So with spirituality, I do not find it located in a separate space, but rooted in the earthly work of administering, teaching, and struggling with the very human dimension of church life. This forms the bulk of my prayer, of what I can converse about with God, and also the location where the Spirit is touching my life whether I am attuned to it or not.

Spirituality for a Vatican II Christian

As I mentioned earlier, Vatican II is for me the center of my experience as a Catholic and as a priest. It has formed the agenda of my ministry, and also of my perspective on God's working in our world. This is not to take the council uncritically; but it is, I hope, to take the council seriously as the sign of our times, the place where God's Spirit has broken into our troubled history in a very special way.

1. The Challenge of Renewal

The council was called to bring about renewal in Christian life. To achieve that renewal, it had to address certain reforms of church life which seemed to be hindering a genuine renewal in Christian living. We still seem to be working out what those reforms will mean in practice, and it is personally frustrating to see the clear intentions of the council placed into question, nuanced into oblivion, or openly rejected. How does one who is committed to renewal cope spiritually with half-hearted reforms, or efforts to dismantle reforms already in place?

It is not easy, I confess, and forms one of those areas in my life where I have to struggle to find the Spirit at work. Some obvious steps can be taken: to focus continually on the renewal, which is God's work, and which will take place in God's time; to recognize the limitations of any institutional structures, and to be modest in expectations about what can be achieved in any reform; to accept the genuinely human, and therefore political, dimension of the Church, and to recognize in this the very sign of Christ's incarnation continued in the Mystical Body. I try these; usually they work, but at times the darkness is not far distant.

2. Priestly Identity

Another aspect of the council which touches my life quite directly concerns my status as a "cleric" in the Church. Two quite distinct movements have taken place: the change in the relationship of priests and lay people, and the change in the terminology (and understanding) of who we are as ordained "presbyters."

a. Priests and People

The recognition of the dignity and importance of lay persons in the Church did not pose a major problem for me. When I was first ordained, I made one of the early Cursillos in my diocese along with several laymen from the parish where I was stationed. We were all enthused about the experience, and they came to the rectory the next week to discuss how they might become more involved in parish life. We really did not have much for them to do—count the collection, usher at Mass, join the Knights of Columbus. While these were worthwhile activities, they did not harness the commitment and desire to have a more dynamic way of expressing their faith which the Cursillo stirred up.

Once the council addressed the role of lay persons, the possibilities for such dedicated lay persons opened up considerably. They are not second-class citizens, occasionally called on to share in the hierarchy's apostolate, but genuinely Christian faithful whose calling it is to continue the mission of Christ in the world. As one called to serve, I find it rewarding when I can assist them in discerning the ways they can accomplish this mission in the context of their daily lives, as well as when lay persons experience the call to a more full-time service as expressive of their Christian commitment.

Working with lay people who are engaged in full-time work in the Church, however, and also with lay religious who are perhaps even more sensitive to this issue, it has become apparent to me that the danger of clericalization lurks constantly in the background. "Clericalism" is the expectation of special treatment just because of one's status. I helped with a study sponsored by the Conference of Major Superiors of Men on this topic; as the final report pointed out, clericalism is not restricted to the ordained. Working with people who are attending to this problem has increased my own sensitivity to such "expectations" in my own life.

But what really does distinguish a priest from a lay person? Where do I experience in my own life that "difference in kind and not just degree" mentioned in the Constitution on the Church (no. 10)? Canon law says to look at the sacramental dimension (can. 207, §1). It is the sacrament of orders that makes the distinction. From the Christian Family Movement and Marriage Encounter (not, sadly, from my work on the marriage tribunal) I have come to a better appreciation of what it means for married people to "live" their sacrament; at the same time, this regularly challenges me to discover what it means to live my own sacrament of holy orders. Otherwise, it seems to me the "difference in kind" between priest and lay people is an empty shell.

Living the sacrament of orders only pushes the issue back one step; it does not solve it. When I was first ordained, what I could do as an ordained priest, and what a lay person could not do, included a number of functions that today we take for granted will be done by lay people. As a priest in administration rather than in a parish, I have been challenged as what is "mine" as an ordained priest has shrunk, and what is "ours" as baptized Christians has grown. More and more of what used to be considered the clerical prerogative in chancery and tribunal, and in other administrative roles, is now done by lay persons, and usually with as much if not more spiritual commitment and professional competence.

The effect of the sacrament of orders, however, is not primarily in "functions"; it has to be at a more spiritual depth. Two dimensions of this have been helpful to my understanding of what it means for me to be a priest. One is the ministry of witness; the other is the ministry of "ordering," helping to assure order in the community.

All Christians are supposed to bear witness to Christ. The witness I experience myself giving as a priest, however, seems to be a witness of presence. It is both my being present to various people, whether as individuals or groups, and the Presence which is somehow rooted in my understanding of God. God is not an angry tyrant demanding minute observances, nor does God seem to be adequately expressed by "love" (with due reverence for John's epistle); for me God is more mystery, such as the prophet Elijah experienced in the "tiny whispering sound" at the mouth of the cave (1 Kgs 19:12-13). Being a priest involves being sensitive to God's mysterious presence, and being an accepted agent for articulating that presence to others in many different settings.

The ministry of "ordering," or facilitating order in the community, is perhaps more immediately felt than the witness of presence. As an administrator I have often experienced this, as well as suffered its absence. The same is true as celebrant of a sacrament or other liturgical action. It is not only in the correct performance of the rites that this ministry is effective; it also calls for a sense of the community, setting a tone for the celebration, and resonating with the Spirit present in the participants.

This is more a "work in progress" than a completed spirituality, at least for me, but it represents a stage in one priest's approach to spirituality for a Vatican II Christian. The council did away with the 1917 code's notion that priests were "holier" than everyone else and affirmed that holiness is the same for everyone. So the spirituality, the pilgrimage to holiness in which we are engaged, is not a separate road for priests and for lay persons; it is one road, on which we travel together, but each with our distinct gifts, roles, and responsibilities. Failure to witness, to be a sign of the Presence in our midst, sloppy celebrations or poorly prepared homilies—these are topics for examination of conscience, for they give the lie to the sacrament of orders in my life.

b. Presbyter

The council reintroduced the language of "presbyter," although this does not seem to have caught hold institutionally in our country until the American translation of the Code of Canon Law. I am still exploring what "presbyter" adds to my spirituality as a priest.

When I was first ordained, there was a great camaraderie among the priests of the diocese, or at least among priests of distinct age groups. But there was also a superficial dimension to that relationship, found more in shared drinks and days off, and sometimes in heated discussions of what was starting to come out of the council. Later, with the introduction of Jesus Caritas fraternities and a deeper awareness of how much I am responsible for my brothers in the presbyterate, I gained a new insight into the deeper bond we share as priests of a diocese.

As a diocesan priest many miles removed from my diocese, I feel all the more the importance of this bond. I think this is also true of priests within the diocese, as the number of clergy diminishes and each of us is asked to take on more isolated assignments. It challenges me to arrange my time so I am able to be present to and with my brother priests whenever possible—and for me, this implies travel, as well as being open to the priests with whom I serve in academic life, and the priests who are students here.

A cross in my life has been the agony of other priests who are in difficulty. Sometimes it is the vocation crisis of a priest I know, someone I respect, or a colleague of one sort or another. Helping with petitions for laicization is a technical task I can perform, but one which also burdens my heart. At other times it is a conflict between a priest and his bishop, caused by the priest's own misconduct or by a superior's misunderstanding or worse. Acting as an advocate takes the professional skills I have been taught, but it also calls on spiritual resources for which I have to reach pretty deep. And it takes a lot of prayer and trust in the Lord to deal sometimes with the callous disregard by some officials for the sacrament of orders and the dignity of a fellow priest.

3. Dealing with Tensions

The last remark brings me to the spirituality of dealing with tensions. How to keep one's spiritual balance while being caught in the cross-fire, or worse, being one of the poles of a tense situation? It seems to me three factors have been helpful: a sense of justice, a sense of compassion, and a sense of fidelity.

Social justice is an important dimension of the Church's teaching; indeed, it is sometimes referred to as the Church's best kept secret! But justice as such is a key biblical theme, and a proclamation of justice has to ring true within the Church if the Church's teaching is to be credible in the world. This is a common enough observation, but I find it difficult to put into practice. Even in my own work, institutional considerations can take precedence over what seems to be a genuinely just solution to various situations. It becomes even more difficult to handle when injustice seems at times to permeate the very procedures and structures which a canon lawyer must deal with.

It is easy to let one's sense of justice become dulled, to bank the fires in one's belly which should lead to a strong reaction to injustice, in order to accomplish what little we can do in this life. But that does not seem to be a satisfactory answer to me. It is, I suppose, a question of where one's ambitions lie. I learned a number of years ago that if one is to be ambitious for justice, other ambitions—whether for advancement, or recognition, or a relaxed life—have to be given up. Even so, these other ambitions have a way of worming their way back into one's life in unexpected ways, and a self-examination on ambition for justice proves a regular challenge.

Justice by itself can come across as insensitive, even harsh. A sense of compassion has to be joined to justice. This strikes me when I hear confessions, or counsel someone about a marriage case, or work with a priest in trouble, or advise a diocese on some difficult problem. It is not enough to know the law, or even to work out a just solution; compassion for what people are experiencing is so central to the witness of Presence which marks me as a priest.

I do not find it easy to be compassionate in every situation, I must confess. I am often pressed for time and may give a brusque response, or can seem insensitive to someone who catches me off guard. It has been a great gift to have someone call me on this, to remind me of the importance of compassion in a large institution like the Church. It has also been a great gift to be the recipient of compassion, which comes at times from such unexpected quarters.

On a larger scale, I am continually discovering what is for me new about the pain of so many in the Church. What do I mean? I have not had to walk the path of pain I find many others walking in our Church, people whose lives are broken and find little understanding from canon law. Divorced and remarried people who hear the message (whether intentional or not) that they ought to leave the Church; women who experience a call to ministry, and who are very competent in doing it as they lead parishes, but who are told they are easily replaced; parishioners whose children have never known a non-alcoholic priest; victims of abuse from the pulpit, to say nothing of victims of sexual abuse by trusted church figures (and not only clergy); and so on. For so many of these people the system offers little if any acceptable response. To be a representative of that system as a church administrator, or to be someone who trains canon lawyers for such ministry in the future, calls for a heavy dose of the spirit of compassion if we are somehow to remain true to the Master who came to call sinners and to heal the broken hearted.

It is here that a sense of fidelity pushes me. For to what is a priest to be faithful? The law, or the Lord? Hopefully, to both, for the law should be faithful to the Lord. But this is not always so evident on a first reading. When I was involved in diocesan administration and priests would ask me what the law said they could do in a particular situation, I would try to reverse the question. What did their pastoral sense tell them was the appropriate thing to do? Had they tried it, examined it, figured out where the problems were as well as the benefits? After all that, when they had a good sense of what worked pastorally, then we could go to work on what the law would do to protect and support their pastoral care.

But this is not always the approach we take in the Church, nor is it often recognized as the preferable one. Too often it is fidelity to the law which is required as a first step. But the law is meant to serve the good of souls, not vice-versa. A sense of fidelity, it seems to me, means taking seriously that the "supreme law of the Church" is the salvation of souls (can. 1752) without, however, disregarding our tradition or the wider communion in which we live.

Fidelity also means fidelity to the council. Is this fidelity to the text (the letter) of the council, or what that text tried to express (the spirit)? I know there are differing views on this. For me, it is not possible to remain faithful to the council, which called for a careful reading of the signs of the times not just in the 1960s but in the 1990s, if all we do is repeat the words of the council. On the other hand, in my own teaching and preaching it is clear that even the words of the council remain a closed book to too many people (and priests?) today.

Beginning to teach canon law after twelve years of practice, and fourteen years after the council itself ended, gave me an unexpected opportunity to revisit the council, to rediscover its text and spirit, and to search anew the implications for our lives as a Church. This has reconfirmed my commitment to the conciliar message and the need for fidelity to the work of the Spirit in our midst, even when we are misunderstood for this or when we must stand in disagreement with practices or decisions which go against that message.

Rules for a Secular Priest's Spirituality

By "rules" here I do not mean the spiritual rules of a religious order (like the *Rule of St. Benedict*), or the rules and commandments of moral behavior, or even the rules of a somewhat regimented life akin to what we experienced in the seminary. For a canon lawyer, the "rules of law" are short statements or aphorisms which serve as a memory bank for how to interpret the law on a practical basis.

When I speak of "rules" for a secular priest's spirituality, particularly for those of a secular priest who is a canon lawyer, I hope to synthesize some of the guidelines or directions that have been useful in my life as a priest, and which may prove helpful to others.

1. Preach to myself first.

I like to preach. It is part of the actor in me. But I approach preaching with some trepidation. In preparing a homily, I read the assigned Scriptures several times, looking for the theme or thread that ties them together and for the emphasis that is appropriate to the season, feast, or program of the community with whom I will be celebrating. Invariably, there is something there which strikes a chord in me; it speaks to what is happening in my life, to my mood, my concerns, my joys. This becomes even stronger when in the act of preaching I start paying attention myself, realizing that I am seeing connections or emphases which call for a response in my own life. The first person I preach to has to be myself.

2. Think with the Church.

The thinking of the Church is not necessarily the latest document from the Vatican or the most recent pronouncement by a bishop or group of bishops; it is not always the result of popular theological reflection or the current piety. The Church's thinking has deep roots, a great breadth of "catholicity," and a richness of lived spirituality. To think with the Church is not to be trapped in a narrow perspective or the latest fad; it is to be able to accept the wonderful, messy family that we are as Church, and to appreciate the marvelous diversity that is our genuine tradition. To think with the Church avoids carping at whatever is new or different, rejects being cynical about an unpopular statement by a higher authority, and challenges believers to reflect again on what truly is our heritage.

3. A good confessor is hard to find.

This cuts both ways. For me, it is not easy to find someone with whom to celebrate the sacrament of reconciliation on a regular basis, or even an irregular one. A priest who will take my sins seriously, address my spiritual emptiness, and challenge my superficiality, is a real treasure. I have been graced with such priests in my life, although it takes work to discover them, or at least to move myself to seek out their services.

But it is also true that when people come to me to receive the sacrament of reconciliation, they are looking for a good confessor, and for them it is equally hard (or maybe harder if they do not have the mobility with which I have been blessed) to find a good confessor. Which means I am on the spot every time I hear confessions, to provide them with the best service I can. The rewards for me are great when the Spirit touches someone's heart, and they truly experience

God's mercy. The burden is all the greater, then, when I fail to put all God has given me into my role in the sacrament.

4. *Celibacy is not for sissies.*

In the seminary I was probably too young to appreciate what celibacy was going to demand. I had several older classmates who struggled before subdiaconate; for me, it was part of the package. Over the years, though, I have come to appreciate what the Church's discipline requires. It is not for sissies. The loneliness that haunted the poetry of a priest classmate, published posthumously, haunts me. The vulnerability of priests accused of sexual misconduct reminds me how vulnerable any of us is even to false accusations. The usual temptations of single persons—to good food, travel, and so on—are temptations in my life.

If the perfect and perpetual continence required of a priest are going to be for the sake of the kingdom of heaven (can. 277, §1), then it has to be more than just a convenient way of life. It has to produce fruit at least in tenderness and compassion, availability and sacrifice, which are hallmarks of married persons. It also has to have some sort of sign value, which today is not readily seen by our contemporaries (or perhaps by my own family!). Celibacy, which safeguards this continence, is a yoke and burden which only Jesus can make light.

5. *People count more than money or power.*

I do not recall who first gave me this insight, but it has become for me a key to understanding Christ's message. He was not embarrassed to deal with the rich and famous, to eat with the powerful and well-connected, but people are what counted for him.

The message is not meant only for his time, or only for our preaching about the Christian's role in the world. It has a central application internal to the Church itself. People—the faithful, the men and women who struggle to live a gospel life each day—count much more than the money and power that come a priest's way. I know this in my heart; my conscience, however, is not always at ease on this one.

6. *Don't push the river; it flows by itself.*

A wonderful Zen saying, this has stuck with me ever since I read it on a book's title. How much of our lives are spent pushing the river—not even pushing against it, just trying to push it along! The "river" here can be anything: God's grace, the life of faith, the Christian community, the hierarchical structure of the Church. The

Pelagian temptation has to be faced anew each generation: is it really the Lord's work, or have we taken it over?

I find this also helps when I get frustrated about prayer in my own life—usually, what seems to be the lack of it. Yet I know that prayer is a constant conversation with God, and letting God get a word in once in a while is more important than constantly trying to carry on the conversation myself. Contemplation has taught me this, but it applies just as well in the conversation with God which takes place as I go about my daily activities. I do not have to push it; God carries it if I but let him.

7. Use the power you have.

Talents give people a unique power. Charisms are empowerments by the Spirit. Positions of service empower the community, and in their turn develop a kind of power on the part of the servant. We all have some form of power. What is the use of the power struggles that take up so much of our energy—struggles within families, within rectories, within academic faculties, with the Church at large or the church written small— if we do not use the power we already have?

If all Christians would utilize their existing power to bear witness to the Gospel, to do one act of real charity a day, to take one step for justice a week—what effect we would have as a people! Where does it start, if not with my own "power" in being present and in providing service?

8. Illegitimi non carborundum.

"Don't let the bastards wear you down" is how this was translated in the '60s. It still applies today. Of course, we vary in whom we identify as the *illegitimi*. But for anyone attempting to live as a Vatican II Christian, committed to renewal in the Church, there is a tendency to grow weary, to get worn down just by the inertia so prevalent in any group, and so all the more prevalent in a world-wide Church.

I get worn down when I take the work on as my own, rather than as Christ's work; when there is so much personal investment in a plan, a project, a program, that it becomes more important than the spiritual good it is designed to promote. Then I discover myself as one of the *illegitimi*!

9. Law is for life, not life for law.

Jesus' saying about the Sabbath is a constant reminder to canon lawyers of what we are all about. The early Christian community struggled with the relationship of the "Law" with the new "Way." The struggle is not over. We can even make of our law a shadow of that former Law—or is it, the former Law is now taken as the shadow presaging the coming of our canons, the true law issued by Christ's vicar?

When canon law becomes more important than life, then it loses touch with its spiritual roots. This is not only an institutional temptation; it can become a very real, personal temptation for a church official, an expert in the law, a teacher of the law.

10. Salvation of souls is the supreme law.

I will bring these ruminations to a close with the same point made by the people who revised the Code of Canon Law when they drafted the final canon. All the rest of it—the structures and procedures, the rights and obligations, the rules and regulations—all are secondary to what is truly primary in the Church, the salvation of souls. If ever there was basis for an examination of conscience (and perhaps not just a canonist's conscience), is this not it?

4

Tenders of the Word*

Donald B. Cozzens

From a pastoral perspective, the most pressing issue facing the Church today may well be the quality of priestly leadership. In terms of immediate impact on both the day to day faith life of the baptized and the Church's mission to evangelize, the issue of priestly leadership is arguably of greater significance than the diminishing numbers of priests and seminarians, the role of women in ministry, the ordination of married individuals, obligatory celibacy, or the election of bishops. No matter how one ranks the quality of priestly leadership on any scale of Church priorities, it is clearly a matter of concern for the vitality of the Church in whatever age the Church finds itself. At the heart of any discussion of the quality of priestly ministry is the authenticity and maturity of the priest's spirituality. It remains the fundamental issue undergirding his preaching, presiding, pastoral care, facilitating, and administering. While pastoral skills can be taught, they remain techniques unless rooted in a vibrant spiritual life.

Spirituality, that elusive quality of soul that dwells on the borders of mystery and grace, resists definition. Nevertheless, something should be said at this point to focus our discussion on the nature of the spiritual life of the diocesan priest. Spirituality, in its broadest context, refers to the human experience of being connected, both in reality and mystery, to that which is ultimate.[1] Although there are as many different spiritualities as there are human beings, the various ministries and sacramental identities that shape the ecclesial dimensions of Christian life allow us to seek out a spirituality that is appropriate to the diocesan priest.[2] The search, however, needs to be

*A major portion of this chapter appeared as "The Spirituality of the Diocesan Priest" in Donald J. Goergen's, ed., *Being a Priest Today,* Michael Glazier (The Liturgical Press) 1992, Collegeville, Minnesota.

grounded in the understanding that priestly spirituality is fundamentally Christian spirituality. Karl Rahner has observed that "priestly spirituality is not (at least, not primarily) a kind of extra to a normal Christian life, but (while, of course, determined by the concrete life task of the priest as distinct from other Christians) the spiritual, Christian life of a Christian purely and simply."[3]

We may speak, then, of Christian spirituality as "the living out in experience, throughout the whole course of our lives, of the death-resurrection of Christ that we have been caught up into by baptism."[4] These understandings of spirituality take us beyond the notion that spirituality is reducible to holiness, though holiness remains an essential and fundamental component of the spiritual life. We have come to understand spirituality as encompassing the whole of one's life in relationship to that which is ultimate. In the life of the Christian, it is the concrete experience of grace and healing in the paschal mystery, the daily dying and rising, the daily experience of communion and alienation, of virtue and sin, that constitute our redeemed lives in Christ. Spirituality may be thought of as the Christian's existential experience of the mystery of grace and his or her attempt to reflect upon that mystery and to name it. In this sense, spirituality appears as the context or environment that reveals one's life as graced relationship to God and others in Christ and the Holy Spirit. Our discussion, then, of the spirituality of the diocesan priest is an examination of the specific context and environment that constitute his life and unfold, through his decisions and commitments, lifestyle and ministry, his transformation in the death and resurrection of Christ.

Three Preliminary Issues

Three issues have appeared on the horizon of the diocesan priest's life that have shaken his confidence and challenged his sense of self. They have, at the same time, like strong winds buffeting a small boat, disrupted his spiritual orientation. I am referring to the issues of identity, intimacy, and integrity. Each requires some discussion before we can address our central concern, the spirituality of the diocesan priest.

Identity

While some priests deny concern about their priestly identity, most concede that this issue hangs over their heads like a storm cloud, robbing them of the confidence they once knew and rendering them awkward and self-conscious in certain parish and social situations. Postconciliar priests know of the competing theologies of priesthood:

those grounded in the classical approach, which emphasize the onto-logical character of priests, and those influenced by the historical method, which place the ministerial priesthood in the context of the Church's call, rooted in baptism, to be a priestly people. When they gather with their brother priests, they are able to discern with little difficulty more or less where each man stands on this issue. It surfaces in their remarks and attitudes about ministry and women and the issues that affect their lives. They are aware of the attention Vatican II gave to the episcopacy and diaconate, in contrast to the limited treatment accorded to the ministerial priesthood. For the most part, they have greeted enthusiastically the theological developments that have expanded the role of the laity and situated the origin of all ministries in baptism. While a renewed theology of priesthood is emerging, it has been held in careful check by Vatican authorities. It appears that a contemporary theology of priesthood would necessarily raise certain controversial issues such as the ministerial use of inactive and laicized priests, a married clergy, and the role of women in ministry.

Nevertheless, priests are greatly encouraged by the candor of the 1988 document issued by the Bishops' Committee on Priestly Life and Ministry, *Reflections on the Morale of Priests*. Among the concerns they identify as having a negative impact on the morale of priests is that of "differing perceived ecclesiologies." These different ecclesi-ologies, as we have noted, generate different theologies of ministry and priesthood, which in turn cloud the issue of presbyteral identity. The document on morale quotes an observation made in the 1982 publication *The Priest and Stress* that underscores the impact of differ-ent and competing ecclesiologies. "The priestly profession is one that must work within an ecclesial community that is polarized. Sometimes vastly differing notions of faith, ecclesiology, law and ministry are to be found within the same rectory. This is a cause of tension, especially when the individuals must not only work together but share common living arrangements. . .When a mentality of self-righteousness on ei-ther end of the theological spectrum exists, a debilitating wear on the person whose responsibility it is to try to forge some common under-standing results."[5]

Another development obfuscating the identity of the priest is the expansion of ministries called for by the Second Vatican Council and explicated in Thomas O'Meara's 1983 study *Theology of Ministry*.[6] For most priests ordained prior to or shortly after the council, ministry meant priestly ministry. The explosion of ministries described by O'Meara has changed all that. While most priests welcome the new and expanding ministries gracing our Church, they experience a need to reflect upon their own priestly ministry, their relationship to the new ministries, and the concomitant call to collaboration. Those who work with ordained ministers know that their response to the expansion of ministries in the Church is anything but consistent. Some have readily adjusted to their colleagues in ministry while others have felt threatened and anxious. There is no doubt that the priest's identity has been dramatically called into question by these new ministries. O'Meara writes:

> Many challenges to present and future priests come from an expanding and diverse ministry. Since Vatican II, the identity of the priest has become more active than static, more diaconal than sacral, more diverse than routine, more communal than solitary and monastic . . . . Today priestly identity comes not only from sacramental leadership but from communal and ministerial leadership.[7]

Commenting on the studies of the priesthood commissioned by the American bishops and published in the early 1970s, Andrew Greeley suggests that there has been "a loss of nerve, a loss of discipline, a loss of sense of identity in the priesthood."[8] That a loss of nerve and identity is common in today's priesthood is supported by the low job satisfaction found among associate pastors and the reluctance of priests to recruit candidates for seminary training.[9] The causes of this apparent loss of nerve and identity, I believe, go beyond our differing theologies of priesthood and the expanding ministries of our Church. Alongside these ecclesial phenomena, the secular nature of our society questions the meaning and relevancy of religion in general and celibate priesthood in particular. In a secular environment priests are regularly perceived as marginal figures who are considered briefly and with amused detachment. The message is patronizingly clear: While society still requires that a certain respect be shown the clergy, it is doctors and lawyers, business persons and politicians, scientists and bankers, who play the important roles. The peripheral role of the priest has apparently dampened his spirit and eroded his confidence. Yet Greeley and others report that priests remain enormously important to Catholics in general as well as to society as a whole.[10]

The very secularity of much of American life has led to a crisis in meaning and to the loss of a sense of mystery and reverence—all issues of spirituality. It can be argued that never before has the role of the priest, rabbi, and minister been more urgently needed in our society than it is at the present time. While poets and novelists also address the questions of meaning and mystery, priests, in particular, should be at home here. Unfortunately, many are not. A good number of priests

appear to be in retreat, striking the pose of either the reactionary le-
galist and moralist or of the nondirective therapist championing a
pseudo liberalism and relativism that makes sincerity the only criterion
for ethical behavior. Have they somehow lost touch with the passion
of the Gospel, with its mystery, paradox, and meaning? To the extent
that this is true in some priests, they, indeed, have lost their nerve.
The reclaiming of the priest's nerve, that is, his sense of mission, as
well as the discovery of his postconciliar identity, are issues intimately
associated with a spirituality properly his own.

Intimacy

Perhaps no turn of phrase has more aptly and succinctly captured
the spirit of our age than the title of Philip Rieff's book *The Triumph
of the Therapeutic.*[11] While the extent of therapy's triumph may be dis-
puted, it is clear that it has had its day. It is easy to observe the influence of the therapeutic in our schools, courtrooms, and churches.
Our fascination with the insights of contemporary psychology, I believe, has been generally beneficial. The therapeutic mentality has fos-
tered healing for the broken and wounded and encouraged more
creative and fulfilling life-styles. Not only has it had a profound impact upon education, law, and religion but also upon family life and
management theory, indeed, upon almost every aspect of society.
Psychology and the social sciences in general rightly take credit for
their contribution to the holistic emphasis seen in medicine, psy-
chotherapy, and spirituality. Developmental psychologists, in identifying the stages we ordinarily pass through in our psychosexual, ethical,
and faith lives, have furthered our understanding of the complexity of
human and spiritual growth. On the other hand, the downside of the
triumph of the therapeutic has led some to view spirituality as but another means to personal fulfillment. The reality of grace, the profound relational character of spirituality, the centrality of ritual and
symbol, are easily dismissed or overlooked when spirituality suffers
such a reduction.

I believe that the human soul has two basic longings: It longs for
intimacy and for transcendence. So strong is its hunger for these two
realities that failing to find authentic intimacy and transcendence, the
soul will turn to pseudo or plastic forms. For example, often what
motivates individuals to pursue promiscuous sexual encounters is the
unrequited hunger for intimacy. Sexuality, being a major paradigm for
union, is readily confused with authentic intimacy. If authentic experiences of transcendence go unmet, pseudo states of transcendence are

brought on by the use, and often an abuse, of alcohol and other chemicals. Individuals graced with a vital spiritual life regularly experience intimacy and transcendence in their lives. Priests, through their life of prayer and service, their almost daily contact with ritual and symbol, readily meet their souls' hunger for transcendence. Intimacy, for the celibate priest, is another matter. Failure to develop authentic celibate relationships of intimacy has led both to spiritual and vocational crises in the lives of countless priests.

Authentic human intimacy is a hallmark of the mature and healthy adult. The capacity for mature and honest relationships is also critical for a sound and mature spiritual life.[12] While the issue of intimacy is problematic for society as a whole, it appears to be especially troublesome for priests. The psychological and sociological studies of the American priesthood commissioned by the National Conference of Catholic Bishops and published in the early 1970s found that priests were not as mature as their comparably educated male counterparts. "The ordinary men who are American priests are bright, able, and dedicated. A large number of them are underdeveloped as persons with a consequent lack of fully realized religious and human values. . . . They could be far more effective personally and professionally if they were helped to achieve greater human and religious maturity."[13] Though these studies are now dated, there is no evidence to suggest that their findings do not hold true today. To the extent that priests tend to be emotionally underdeveloped and immature, the issue of intimacy will remain problematic to both their spiritual and personal lives.

There are large numbers of priests whose legitimate intimacy needs remain unknown to them. Aware that something is missing and often unable to name that which is missing, they wrestle with their souls' restlessness and discomfort. Prayer is intensified, spiritual directors are consulted, retreats are made—but the vague yet persistent feeling that something is missing disturbs their peace of soul. Whenever this state of soul exists, the celibacy issue looms large. What is missing is judged to be wife and children and the archetypal comforts of family and home. While this may indeed be the case for a good number of priests, for many others it is more an issue of a fundamental human need not being met: the need for intimacy. Individuals with a capacity for intimacy are mature adults who have come to accept both their goodness and their limitations. They have both a deep sense of their own self-worth rooted in the pervading presence and mystery of God's grace and a quiet confidence in their abilities and achievements. They possess both the courage and skill to make appropriate self-disclosure, without which intimacy remains impossible. This capacity for authentic intimacy shapes the context and influences the depth of an individual's spiritual life. Priests who have acknowledged and addressed their intimacy needs as mature, celibate men enjoy a spiritual life quite different in tone and texture from that of their brothers whose intimacy needs remain largely unfulfilled.

Furthermore, the capacity for intimacy determines the priest's conceptualization of God and readies him for the experience of God's presence and love in his life. He becomes aware of God's "affection" for him—the experience of which allows him to pass through loneliness into solitude. Aware of his fundamental rootedness in God's loving presence, he discovers a spontaneous ability to relate intimately both to himself and to those few friends and family members that constitute his core community of support. Without this ability for appropriate intimate relationships, the spiritual life of the priest is seriously handicapped and his psychological life will be restricted and unfulfilled. Not only does the priest's spiritual and emotional life suffer, his ministry and in particular his preaching will be sterile and only minimally effective.

The human condition makes intimacy a challenge in any age and culture. It appears to be a particularly vexing problem in our age. Technological breakthroughs as well as the materialistic and individualistic values of contemporary society have underscored the need for human connectedness and intimacy without facilitating their achievement.[14] Faced with the same difficulties confronting his brothers and sisters in society, the priest carries the added burden of the identity crisis discussed above. Without a healthy sense of identity, the achievement of authentic intimacy becomes heroic. The spiritual vitality of many priests today is a tribute to their heroic surrender to grace and their trust in a provident God who knows well their human needs and longings.

Integrity

The final preliminary issue to our discussion of the spirituality of the diocesan priest is that of integrity. While there is a good deal of denial here, priests, in moments of honesty, concede that it is possible for them to sell their souls in their service to the Church and to God's people. The vast majority of priests prize their loyalty to the Gospel and to the Church whose mission it is to serve that gospel. They also strive to be obedient to the gospel and to the Church. Their loyalty and obedience to the Church, however, are not without complexity. They know it is not to be a blind and unthinking obedience and loyalty. Their challenge is to be true men of the Church and at the same time their own men. This fidelity to Church and conscience implies a certain tension in the life of the priest. The anxiety engendered by this tension is inevitable. Sooner or later, every priest struggling for personal integrity feels it. Because he believes the Church enjoys the abiding presence and guidance of the Holy Spirit, and because he trusts the integrity of Church leaders, there are relatively few issues of personal integrity that surface in his life. However, when they do surface, they indeed become issues of conscience. While he knows well the central role played by an informed and faithful conscience in the life of the Christian, the cognitive dissonance that follows upon what his own experience of priesthood and ministry tell him is in conflict with Church discipline or teaching is nonetheless painful. So painful, in fact, that some priests adapt an attitude of unthinking obedience and loyalty in order to escape the discomfort of being in tension with the Church they love. The consequent diminishment of personal integrity compromises the authenticity of their spiritual lives. They become, quite unwittingly, "kept men" who expect to be taken care of because of their supposed loyalty and fidelity to the institutional Church.

The antidote to this compromise in integrity is the courage to think. But thinking, the priest discovered in the seminary, can be dangerous. It may easily lead to uncertainty, and uncertainty in turn evokes anxiety. To flee the existential anxiety of human life by embracing in a nonthinking and nonreflective manner the religious truths, traditions, and customs of his faith is to compromise his integrity. The priest, then, must not only read in the areas of theology, Scripture, and the human sciences; he must think about and reflect upon his lived experience as a human being, Christian, and priest. His faith is meant to be integrated into the fiber of his life, for failing to do so blocks his ability to minister as a mature person of integrity. He may preach the Gospel, but his congregation senses that he has yet to live it.

The task of achieving and maintaining the priest's integrity is often compounded by his family of origin. If he comes from a dysfunctional family or enters the seminary and priesthood with serious authority issues, his personal integrity often appears to be under constant attack by the most reasonable expectations and directives of his superiors. The nature of the priest's relationship with his mother and father becomes a reliable indicator of the degree of difficulty he will encounter in his quest for personal integrity. Without a sense of personal integrity, the priest's spiritual life evolves into nothing more than sentimental exercises that serve to quiet the disturbing eruptions of his bad conscience. The guilt of his bad conscience often goes unrecognized for, in his own eyes, he is a good priest, clearly obedient to his Church. Where this is the case, the priest may suffer from clinical depression resulting from his repressed or denied guilt. The implications for his moral and spiritual life are evident.

Towards a Spirituality of the Diocesan Priest

Presbyteral spirituality, as all authentic Christian spiritualities, involves the disciplined self-surrender to the saving power of the paschal mystery. The context and environment of the priest's ministry and especially the distinctive character of his priestly ordination allow us to speak of a spirituality that is proper to the diocesan priest. Yet the specific character of presbyteral spirituality should not be exaggerated. Robert Schwartz observes that the spirituality of priests is essentially the spirituality of the Church. "Although shaped and formed by a distinctive role among the people of God, at its most basic level presbyteral spirituality is ecclesial. The priority given to the image of the people of God in *Lumen gentium* affirms the ecclesial spirituality common to all, making ministerial priests more like the people they serve than different from them."[15] With this caveat in mind, we turn now to the spirituality of the diocesan priest.

Before Vatican II the diocesan priest's spirituality was grounded in what was understood to be his ontological status as a priest of the Church. This status conferred upon him powers that were held in awe by believers and at least respected by nonbelievers. His priestly identity was concomitant with his power to consecrate, forgive, anoint, and bless. With these powers came the responsibility to lead a holy life befitting his presbyteral status. The celebration of Eucharist, praying the breviary, the rosary, and other devotions were the source and fuel of his spirituality. Serving the poor, visiting the sick educating children, instructing converts, and preaching to his people also became mainstays of his spiritual life. While undeniably ministerial, his spirituality was focused on the ascetical and devotional aspects of the inner life. He said his prayers so that he might be a good priest and serve his God and people well.

A shift in emphasis has occurred since the council. The origins of the shift surely go back to the early decades of our century, which witnessed the beginnings of the modern liturgical movement, if not beyond. The shift is more developmental than disjunctive, for it builds on the traditional staples of priestly spirituality. It enjoys, nonetheless, a distinctive character that continues to evolve and emerge. In the past, the priest prayed in order to preach. Now, following the insight of Abraham Heschel, it may be claimed that the priest preaches in order to pray.[16] He understands the inherent mutuality and interdependence between his ministry and spiritual life. The decision to pray is arguably the most important decision the priest makes concerning his spiritual life. At the same time, the decision to exercise priestly ministry is equally central to his spirituality. The decisions to pray and to minister both serve the spirituality of the diocesan priest, for they are the form and structure of his life in grace. The emerging spirituality of the diocesan priest, therefore, may be thought of as a dialectical spirituality that is rooted in his life of faith and prayer and at the same time shaped and forged by the exercise of his ministerial priesthood. It is in the latter pole of the dialectic that we discover those characteristics that allow us to speak of a spirituality proper to the diocesan priest.

The function and scope of priestly ministry has been significantly reshaped over the past twenty-five years. Postconciliar research in the areas of ecclesiology, ministry, and priesthood have generated in turn issues and questions relating to the spirituality of priests. The conciliar document *Lumen gentium*, for example, reclaimed the traditional understanding of the Church as mystery and as the people of God.[17] In the Counter-Reformation era, the Church perceived itself as the center of God's saving plan for the salvation of the world. Now, in the conciliar era of Vatican II, emphasis is placed on the Church as servant to a graced and redeemed humanity. This retrieved understanding of Church focuses attention on the Church as a people-centered community rather than as a priest-centered one. The priest in turn is regarded as one who serves a people-centered community, a very different emphasis from that of the priest-centered Church.[18] In a people-centered Church, while the ministry of the priest continues to hold a central and unique place in the life of the community, it is exercised as one ministry among other ministries.[19] In a Church understood as the people of God, the priest functions as servant of God's people and as one whose ministry is exercised in cooperation with and interdependent upon other diverse ministries in the Church.[20] Since Vatican II, the priest's ministry is less solitary and more communal and as much diaconal as sacral.[21]

In a recent article on the priesthood, Michael Himes reflects on the diaconal and episcopal dimensions of ministry:

> Catholics have long been accustomed to speak of a universal priesthood in the church, a priesthood of all the faithful. I am suggesting that, as

there is a universal presbyterate, so too there are a universal episcopate and a universal diaconate in the church, an episcopate and diaconate of all the faithful. All are called to the episcopal function of maintaining the unity of the community. All are called to the presbyteral function of responsibility to and for the word. All are called to the diaconal function of direct service to those within and outside the community. The vocation to these universal ministries is given in baptism, which is the principal sacrament of ministry.[22]

Himes' insights into the universal episcopate and diaconate have significance for both the morale and spirituality of the diocesan priest. There is no question that the diocesan priest is called to be a servant of God's people and to work to further justice and peace. Also, it is clear that the priest participates in the episcopal ministry of furthering the unity and mission of the Church. His primary ministry, however, remains his sacral service "to and for the word." Whenever the priest overidentifies with either the diaconal or episcopal ministries, he risks both the loss of focus in his ministry and his identity as priest. Furthermore, his morale is lowered when he is expected by others or himself to be equally invested in the diaconal and episcopal ministries while being fully committed to his ministry as priest.

These significant developments in our understanding of Church and the ministry have elicited a new style of presbyteral ministry. No longer the final word on all parish matters, the diocesan priest, as servant-leader, is a facilitator and enabler of numerous and varied ministries within his parish. Though captain of the team, he is not to forget that he remains a member of the team. Instead of issuing directives and orders, the priest is called to a collaborative style of pastoral ministry. There is a certain asceticism in collaborative ministry, in identifying and fostering the ministerial gifts of others, in listening to the concerns of parishioners, in trusting their experiences and vision. Few diocesan priests would deny this. Nor would they deny the *kenosis,* the call to humility and self-gift that is at the heart of servant ministry.[23]

A Spirituality of the Word

A priest is a man to whom the word has been entrusted. He is, before all else, the minister and servant of the word of God.[24] Karl Rahner writes: "This efficacious word has been entrusted to the priest. To him has been given *the* word of God. That makes him a priest. For that reason it can be said it is he to whom has been entrusted the word."[25] *Presbyterorum ordinis* states that "priests . . . have as their primary duty the proclamation of the gospel of God to all."[26] Unless grounded in authentic holiness of life and maturity of personality, this most serious obligation and responsibility of the priest will remain substantially unfulfilled. And so he prays that he might preach. But as Heschel has observed, he also preaches that he might pray. Perhaps the dialectical dimension to the priest's spirituality is most clearly manifested in his ministry of preaching. For not only has the council reminded him of his primordial obligation to preach the gospel, it has at the same time encouraged him to preach at weekday celebrations of Eucharist as well as at the Sunday liturgy.[27] Each day he is encouraged to offer a homily, each day he is shaped and formed by the word of God that he proclaims. This call to daily preaching, I believe, is at the heart of the diocesan priest's spirituality. It requires, day after day, the reading of the Lectionary, prayer and reflection on the readings of the day, and the crafting of the homily itself. Taken seriously, this responsibility to preach God's word becomes the ground and foundation of the diocesan priest's spirituality. Conversely, the call to preach the Gospel at Sunday and daily liturgies becomes an intolerable burden to the spiritually shallow. In Rahner's words, "the word of God in the mouth of a priest empty of faith or love is a judgment more terrible than all versification and all poetic chatter in the mouth of a poet who is not really one. It is already a lie and a judgment upon a man, if he speaks what is not in him; how much more, if he speaks of God while he is godless."[28] To the priest faithful to prayer and reflection, to quiet listening to the voice of God as revealed to him in the events of the day, the call to preach becomes the anchor of his spirituality.

The dialectical dimension is likewise found in the other manifestations of ministry that fill the day-to-day life of the diocesan priest. In his teaching he is taught—not only by the experience of grace and truth he finds in his students but also by the power of the word of liberation, forgiveness, and healing that he shares with his listeners. In his counseling he is counseled. Reminding the counselee of God's understanding and acceptance, he discovers that he, too, is accepted and understood in spite of his own brokenness and human limitations. The graced connectedness that is regularly experienced in the process of pastoral counseling refines the priest's spirit and sustains him when confronted by his own doubts and anxieties. The courage that he witnesses in the lives of his parishioners encourages his own soul to face bravely the responsibilities of Christian discipleship. In visiting the sick, the patient in himself is uplifted. In consoling the grieving, he finds consolation. In his ministry of leadership he finds guidance and direction from those in his congregation blessed with the charism of leadership. In serving the needs of the poor, his own poverty of soul finds relief. While Christian ministry is dialectical in the sense just described, the priest's service to the word of God remains the cornerstone and linchpin of his spirituality. It is especially in his Eucharistic presiding and preaching that his spirit is transformed by the saving grace of Jesus Christ crucified and risen. At the Lord's table, breaking word and bread, blessing cup and covenant, the mark of his priesthood emerges in bold relief.

The spirituality of the diocesan priest, therefore, is a spirituality of proclamation. Through years of faith and formation he has come to personally know the power of the proclaimed word.[29] Through years of being submerged in the human condition he has encountered the power of grace unfolding in the depths of his own life and the lives of his people. His preaching, he discovers, is aptly thought of as the art of naming grace.[30] The art of preaching, the art of naming grace, brings the priest into realms of mystery and meaning. His challenge, he discovers, is to acquire that subtlety of soul and flexibility of intelligence demanded of his craft. Without these qualities, his preaching will be pedantic and lifeless. He may well invoke the name of God while failing to name the experience of God in the lives of his listeners. He may speak of mystery and of that which really matters, but he will speak as one not personally touched by the mystery of grace nor inspired by his soul's thirst for meaning. But let him take seriously the call to preach and he will discover that refinement and passion of spirit common to the poet and mystic.[31]

Before proceeding to the final section of this chapter, I want to remind the reader that the emphasis I have placed on preaching in the context of Eucharist as the linchpin of the diocesan priest's spirituality is not meant to diminish the more traditional mainstays of his spirituality: The Liturgy of the Hours, the celebration of penance, days of retreat and recollection, spiritual reading and direction, Marian devotion—all these sustain the priest in his quest for holiness and, of course, give authority and power to his preaching and ministry.

Prayer and Grace

It has already been noted that the decision to pray is the most critical decision an individual makes in relation to his or her spiritual life. The psalms and lessons of the Church, whether scriptural or patristic, remain an important source of spiritual nourishment for priests and Christians in general. There is a growing awareness, however, that some form of contemplative prayer is vital to the life of the priest.

When priests speak of their spiritual lives, more often than not they speak of a sacred time during the day when they enter into a period of solitude and wordless prayer. This quiet time of waiting on the Lord, of faithful listening to God's spirit, becomes central to their life in the Spirit. It is in silent prayer that the priest, in listening to the depths of his spirit, is able to discover what is going on in his own soul. In these periods of silent prayer he finds the grace to name what it is that he is experiencing at this particular point in his journey. In turn, this spiritual self-knowledge allows him to listen to God from his heart. Not only does he find the direction God wishes him to take personally but he finds himself able to discern what it is that God is asking of him in his ministry as priest. Finding time for contemplative prayer remains a significant challenge for the diocesan priest. The almost unbearable demands upon his time make this challenge all the more difficult. The call to contemplative prayer remains, nonetheless, as imperative for the diocesan priest as it is for the priest in religious life.

Recalling the final words of Bernanos' *Diary of a Country Priest*, the diocesan priest knows that "all is grace." His commitment to prayer and ministry brings him into daily contact with the hidden workings of grace. In his preaching, the diocesan priest proclaims the word of God and in doing so names the grace of everyday living. In terms of his own life, he comes to see that both the pain and the privilege of the priesthood are rooted in grace. The inescapable loneliness of celibacy is graced. So, too, the fraternity of the priesthood is graced. When his preaching stirs hearts and deepens faith, there is grace. When his ministry is ineffective and his words ring empty, there, too, is grace. When his motives are misjudged and his limitations laid bare, it is grace that sustains him. It is grace that sustains everything, and all about is the hidden presence of the Spirit. The priest comes to believe, sooner or later, that grace is "loose in the world."[32] No force is able ultimately to restrain this loving grace loosed upon the world: not the sinfulness of the world, not the sinfulness of the Church, not his own sinfulness. Herein is the source of his hope and courage.

Joseph Campbell speaks of the hero as an individual who "has given his or her life to something bigger than oneself."[33] Indeed, the priest has given his life to something bigger than himself—the gospel of Christ and the building of the reign of God in history. He preaches the word in season and out, when it is joyfully received and when it is cynically rejected. While in need of ministry himself, he ministers to others; while wounded himself, he heals and gives comfort. Though broken in heart and spirit, he reconciles and forgives; though anxious himself, he gives courage and hope to the alienated and estranged. In the name of God and the Christ and the Spirit, he has set out on a journey fraught with dangers and dragons. His quest is to set people free with the freedom and grace of the Gospel and in doing so to renew the face of the earth. The grail after which he seeks is the treasure hidden within the hearts of all men and women: to find their true selves in God, for therein lies their salvation. As the diocesan priest continues to discover his true identity as a member of the people of God with a unique and heroic mission to fulfill, he will discover the spirituality that is properly his own.

Conclusion

The spirituality of the diocesan priest emerges from his ministry as priest and preacher. He prays in order to preach and preaches in order to pray. He prays in order to serve and serves in order to pray. Whatever he does is grounded in the gift of grace, and in the very doing of what priests do, his soul is renewed. It is possible, therefore, to speak of the spirituality of the priest as a *dialectical spirituality*. The dialectical nature of the diocesan priest's spirituality is most clearly seen in his preaching, in his service to the word of God. The encouragement to preach a homily at daily celebrations of Eucharist as well as Sunday celebrations is the major structural development in the spirituality of the priest emanating from Vatican II. For the daily homily demands prayer and reflection, study and contemplation. It calls the priest to acquire the imagination of the novelist and the heart of the poet. The creative act of preaching, in which the word of God transforms preacher and hearer and names the grace of everyday life, serves as the linchpin of the diocesan priest's spiritual life. To preach well and effectively, to be servant-leader to the Catholic community, to evangelize society, is, indeed, a heroic mission—the mission of the priest.

Have we reached a point where it is possible to name the spirituality of the diocesan priest? I am not sure. Robert Schwartz speaks of the spirituality of priests as an ecclesial spirituality.[34] Certainly, he is correct. However, this description can equally be attributed to other spiritualities. The same can be said of *dialectical spirituality*. While *presbyteral spirituality* sounds somewhat pretentious, it is perhaps the simplest and most appropriate term for the evolving spirituality of the diocesan priest. Named or unnamed, we are witnessing the emergence of a spirituality that is uniquely appropriate to the diocesan priest.

Notes

[1]Gerald May states that "spirituality consists of an experienced and inter-preted relationship among human beings and the mystery of creation." *Will and Spirit* (San Francisco: Harper & Row, 1982) 22.

[2]Karl Rahner, *Theological Investigations,* vol. XIX, "The Spirituality of the Secular Priest," trans. by Edward Quinn (New York, Crossroad, 1983) 103.

[3]Ibid., 119.

[4]*Spiritual Renewal of the American Priesthood* (United States Catholic Conference, 1973).

[5]*Reflections on the Morale of Priests* (United States Catholic Conference, 1988) 7–8.

[6]Thomas F. O'Meara, *Theology of Ministry* (New York: Paulist Press, 1983) especially chapters 1 and 6. *and Its*

[7]O'Meara, "The Ministry of the Priesthood in Relationship to the Wider Ministry in the Church," 3.

[8]Andrew M. Greeley, *American Catholics Since the Council: An Unauthorized Report* (Chicago: Thomas More Press, 1985) 115.

[9]Ibid., 114–15

[10]Ibid., 112. Also see James Kelly and Tracy Schier, "Data and Mystery: A Decade of Studies on Catholic Leadership," America (November 18, 1989) 345–50.

[11]Philip Rieff, *The Triumph of the Therapeutic* (New York: Harper Torchbooks, 1968).

[12]See Joann Wolski Conn's *Spirituality and Personal Maturity* (New York: Paulist Press, 1989). Conn notes that "in the biblical vision, spiritual maturity is deep and inclusive love. It is the loving relationship to God and others born of the struggle to discern where and how God is present in the community, in ministry, in suffering, in religious and political dissension, and in one's own sinfulness. . . . Maturity is understood primarily as a matter of relationship"(16).

[13]*The Catholic Priest in the United States. Psychological Investigations* (United States Catholic Conference, 1972) 16.

[14]See John Naisbitt's *Megatrends* (New York: Warner Books, 1982).

[15]Robert M. Schwartz, *Servant Leaders of the People of God* (New York: Paulist Press, 1989) 54. Schwartz continues: "Formed by the same word, nourished by the same eucharist, called to the same quest for holiness and justice, priests and people are able to serve one another" (54).

[16]Abraham Joshua Heschel, *Quest for God: Studies in Prayer and Symbolism* (New York: Crossroad, 1982). Heschel writes, "Preach in order to pray. Preach in order to inspire others to pray. The test of a true sermon is that it can be converted to prayer" (80).

[17]*Lumen gentium,* ch. 2. Also see *Gaudium et spes,* especially the preface. In *Vatican Council II: The Conciliar and Post-Conciliar Documents*, ed. Austin Flannery (Northport, N.Y.: Costello, 1975).

[18]I am indebted to Robert Schwartz's treatment of this development in *Servant Leaders of the People of God,* 5–6.

[19]See Thomas F. O'Meara's "Ministry of the Priesthood and Its Relationship to the Wider Ministry in the Church," 2, as well as his important book, *Theology of Ministry.*

[20]See *The Continuing Education of Priests: Growing in Wisdom, Age, and Grace* (United States Catholic Conference, 1985).

[21]O'Meara, "The Ministry of the Priesthood and Its Relationship to the Wider Ministry in the Church."

[22]Michael J. Himes, "Making Priesthood Possible: Who Does What and Why?" *Church* (Fall 1989) 7.

[23]See *As One Who Serves: Reflections on the Pastoral Ministry of Priests in the United States* (United States Catholic Conference, 1977).

[24]Karl Rahner, "Priest and Poet," Theological Investigations, vol. 3, trans. Karl-H. and Boniface Kruger (New York: Helicon, 1967) 303.

[25]Ibid., 307.

[26]*Presbyterorum ordinis,* in Walter Abbott, *The Documents of Vatican II* (Guild Press, 1966) 538–39.

[27]*Sacrosanctum concilium,* in Walter Abbots, *The Documents of Vatican II,* ch. 2, nos. 52, 155. "The homily . . . is to be highly esteemed as a part of the liturgy itself. . . ."

[28]Rahner, "Priest and Poet," 308.

[29]"The word of God in the mouth of the priest wants therefore, if it is to be spoken rightly, to be absorbed and subject to itself the life of the priestly individual. It wants to be made manifest in him. But then it calls upon the whole man and lays claim to him with everything that is his." Ibid., 313.

[30]See Mary Catherine Hilkert's important book, *Naming Grace: Preaching and the Sacramental Imagination* (New York: Continuum, 1997). This work and her "Naming Grace: A Theology of Proclamation," *Worship* 60 (September 1986) 434–49 are fundamental to a spirituality of proclamation.

[31]See Rahner, "Priest and Poet," 294–317.

[32]See Thomas F. O'Meara's *Loose in the World* (New York: Paulist, 1974).

[33]Joseph Campbell, *The Power of Myth* (New York: Doubleday, 1988) 123. See especially ch. 5, "The Hero's Adventure."

[34]The subtitle of Robert Schwartz's *Servant Leaders of the People of God* is "An Ecclesial Spirituality for American Priests."

5

Paul of Tarsus:
A Model for Diocesan Priesthood

Richard J. Sklba

"Paul and Barnabas appointed presbyters for them in each church and, with prayer and fasting, commended them to the Lord in whom they had put their faith" (Acts 14:23).

For many years diocesan priests, when innocently asked, "What order to you belong to, Father?" would often quickly and playfully respond, "The order of St. Peter, of course!" Their purpose was to assert affiliation with the full Church rather than some more limited ministry, possibly to claim some degree of superiority in an ultramontane fashion, and thus show their identity with the full history of the apostolic tradition over the years. That response, in all candor, contained the subtle put-down and one-upmanship that only a person knowledgeable of the in-house jokes of the profession could catch. Implicit also was the suggestion that all the other religious associations were late comers and somehow second string, no matter what they might be saying of their own historical pedigree or lineage. More recently the ready label has undergone a change. The response might well tend today to invoke St. Paul instead.

Perhaps a reason for the change could be the rediscovery of the local church as the primary point of ecclesial references reflected by the various documents of Vatican II. Earlier seminary textbooks written in the long shadow of the papal definition of Vatican I would probably have implied a different picture. Thus the shift from Peter as a voice of unity among his brethren to Paul the missionary preacher and founder of so many local churches has a certain rootedness in questions of ecclesiology.

Perhaps the change was occasioned by the renewal in biblical studies. In the past four decades seminary formation elevated New Testament writings to fresh preeminence. These studies also underscored the theological role of early Christian faith in the formulation of all the inspired narratives as well as epistles. That means that even accounts that seemed very historical at first glance, for example the Acts of the Apostles, were fashioned to share a theological perspective. Any historical figure described in these narratives could also be viewed as a representative model or type. Specific actions or characteristics are associated with virtually every personality of the New Testament so that each in some way becomes a prototype for a category of minister or believer in the Church.

Yet another reason for the shift from Peter to Paul may be the rediscovery of the impressive similarity between the first ages of Christianity and our own times with all of today's turmoil. This perception is underscored by the reformed Lectionary's determination to bring modern readers and preachers along the early Church's first travels toward the fullness of their faith each year, especially during the Easter season. The annual repetition of these daily readings has produced its own harvest. In any case, the "resourcement" of recent decades on all levels has resulted in a new readiness for diocesan priests to identify with Paul of Tarsus rather than with his Petrine colleague. The contemporary pastor might not be physically stoned by irate parishioners or abused in the myriad ways suffered by the Apostle to the Nations, but the trials and the challenges, especially in the more polarized environment of recent decades, have made that identification understandable and even spiritually helpful at times.

In particular it is the Acts of the Apostles, and the story of Saul/Paul's escapades therein, that have been striking for many modern diocesan priests. The quest for a daily homily during the weeks after Easter, and the startling similiarity of the events recounted with the efforts of his own ministry, have provided new energy and fresh insight for many a thoughtful priest-student of the early Church. A sense of "Been there! Done that!" is more frequent than ever before. The "Judaizers" of old may not abound any more, thanks to a new era of interfaith respect and cooperation, but virtually every group opposing Paul's ministry has found contemporary counterparts of remarkably vociferous abilities, and with equally annoying results.

For that reason it seems valuable to take a fresh look at the treasure named the Acts of the Apostles in order to mine the gold of Paul's ministry and rediscover a potential model for the cusp of a new millennium.[1] If the concepts in the following pages are given a modern day dress at times by reason of the analogy necessitated by any hermeneutical transposition into another age, the effort is intended as clarifying reformulation rather than mere anachronism. At any rate, Paul of Tarsus offers a model and a measure of achievement for yet another set of coworkers with and for the risen Lord.

A Man of Character

The first time a reader encounters Paul in the unfolding drama of the Acts is at the martyrdom of Stephen where a presumably young man, then named Saul, guarded the outer clothing of the angry executioners (8:1).[2] More than a casual bystander, Saul clearly shared the conviction of the crowd in rejecting the perversities that Stephen had been accused of disseminating in Jerusalem. To suggest a lesser importance for the Temple was unthinkable in Saul's eyes, even though his own diaspora experience kept him far away from the daily Temple rituals, and even the more proximate piety of Galilee at that time concentrated its focus on the prayers and blessings of the synagogue rather than sacrifice. The long history of human conviction that error had no rights, and that repression was the ready answer to dangerous opinions, seems to have found a ready supporter in Saul! Such seems to have been Saul's stance when first met in Acts.

So much passion and zeal did Saul possess that he quickly began a campaign of harassment against the fledgling Christian Community, moving from house to house in order to ferret out individuals of Stephen's ilk and to haul them off to prison for their religious crimes (8:3). Obviously a person of action rather than mere sideline speculation, Saul would also seem to have been an individual who carefully played by the rules, for he made sure to obtain full authorization from the office of the high priest himself (9:1f) in order to extend his search for followers of the Nazarene even as far as Damascus itself. He was a team player with great concern to do the job right.

Zealous and committed, with a thoroughness that brooked no obstacle to complete obedience to the will of God, Saul recognized authority and obeyed it totally. It would seem that very few gray areas of ambiguity existed for young Saul, and his personality was sharply defined as strong, clear, and consistent. He possessed integrity and respected authority as well as used it. All of these characteristics find ready verification in Saul/Paul's later letters, but they are already visible from his first appearances in the accounts of Acts.

At the same time, his response to the shattering events on the way to Damascus was a surprising contrast to the elements described above, for he is described as open to instruction and docile toward those who led him into town (9:8). Once having arrived at the home of Judas on Straight Street, he simply awaited further direction. Saul's RCIA journey was rapid, for only three days later, he was visited by an eminent disciple named Ananias who had learned in a vision of his own something of Saul's future destiny and mission. In that vision it was the risen Lord himself who described Saul as a "chosen tool (σκευος)" (9:15), carefully prepared for the task of communicating Christ's name to foreign nations and royal courts as well as the people of Israel themselves.

Exploring Saul's character as it appeared in the subsequent unfolding of Acts, the portrait of a clear-headed, strong-willed, and no-nonsense kind of man appeared. On the island of Cyprus at Paphos, for example, when Saul (who as the text reminds us in 13:9 was also called Paul—or "Shorty" if the latter was a more popular nickname rather than one of family origin) vigorously confronted Elymas, the magician, calling him "a son of the devil, fraud and impostor" (13:10) and promptly struck him blind. Paul's personal (not necessarily physical) presence was so commanding, and his speech so authoritative, as to be confused at Lystra with the Greek god Hermes himself (14:12)!

That same Paul was so annoyed by the chatter of the soothsaying, fortunetelling slave-girl who kept following him on the way to prayer each day that he whipped out a spontaneous exorcism (16:18) and thereby created an enormous commotion at Philippi, even ending up in jail as a result! When the magistrates recognized their terrible legal blunder in administering a public beating to a Roman citizen, and depriving him of due process before the law, they attempted to facilitate a quiet and quick departure. Paul refused such a resolution and insisted upon a public apology and exhortation (16:39)! He stubbornly persisted in his desire to go to Rome (19:21), proudly proclaimed his habit of speaking the full truth without waffling (20:20.27), and refused to be intimidated by the threat of chains and trials in Jerusalem (20:23).

It was in anger that Paul responded to Ananias, the high priest, who ordered a guard to slap him on the mouth (23:2). Moreover, Paul's entire family must have shared a certain spirit of courage and conviction, for it was his own nephew who came forward with the news of a planned ambush and assassination (23:16). Paul refused to offer a bribe to Felix, the Roman governor, in exchange for the freedom he deserved without special payment (24:26), and by King Agrippa's own admission might even have been set free had he not so stubbornly demanded to have his case heard by the emperor himself in Rome as was the right of a Roman citizen (26:32).

Such is the character portrait of Saul/Paul in the Acts of the Apostles. Such therefore might also be the model proposed by Acts for anyone summoned by God through the Church for the first foundation or the subsequent pastoral care of Christian congregations: strong, zealously committed, forthright, conscious of personal dignity, not easily swayed yet docile to the will of God as made manifest and passionately committed to do the right thing no matter what the cost. This was certainly not a non-directive Rogerian at work!

Personalities engaged in effective priestly or pastoral ministry today vary enormously. The blind zealot is never sufficiently respectful of anything other than ideology, and therefore ultimately fails in such a vocation. The person of deep conviction, however, unhampered by whining self-pity or temporary setbacks, and possessing a strong confidence in the power and call of God is the ideal candidate for ministry in any age. The model provided by Paul for diocesan priests today is the possession of some basic convictions, strong enough to form the center of one's existence, and important enough to die for. Furthermore, a willingness to work long and hard is a trait clearly possessed by Paul who supported himself by tent-making rather than impose on his hosts during the missionary journeys (18:3). That capacity for hard work is also part of the model provided by Paul for priests today.

A Man of Prayer

Paul's character seems to have been rooted and fashioned by prayer from the very beginning, at least as he is presented in the pages of the Acts. In later epistles to early Christian communities, he insisted that he had zealously embraced the traditions of Judaism (Gal 1:14) and had apparently been educated as a devout and practicing Pharisee. The ritual of daily prayers known to that movement would have been his as well.[3]

Immediately after the account of Paul's traumatic encounter with the risen Christ, he was led by the hand to the home of a disciple in Damascus. There he began his own triduum of prayer and fasting (9:9) as he awaited divine disposition of his case. Fasting in Judaism was the sign of profound sorrow, loss, and penitence. The acknowledgment of personal sin usually accompanied the practice, ever since the days of lament over the destruction of the Temple and the admission of popular guilt for that punishment. To be engaged in that practice must have implied a stunning realization on Paul's part of personal arrogance and sinful stubbornness. That passivity didn't last very long, though presumably the prayer was an enduring reality in Paul's life, for after his baptism (9:18) and (Eucharistic?) meal, he was quickly out in the synagogues of Damascus vigorously proving that Jesus was indeed the Christ (9:22). The example of prayer combined with intense activity remains valid for the contemporary priest, especially if their private and public prayer is somehow rooted in the cycle of festive seasons and annual cycles of celebration.

Later on, after completing his mission with Barnabas of bringing relief to the famine stricken disciples in Judea (11 :30), Paul returned from Jerusalem to Antioch and joined the group of early Christian leaders entitled "prophets and teachers" (13:1): Simeon Niger, Lucius the Cyrene, and Manaen. There, while engaged in the people's work of worship (literally λειτουργουντες) and fasting, the Holy Spirit set them apart for a special work. Whatever the precise mode of discernment may have been, Saul and Barnabas continued in their prayer and fasting, received the imposition of hands from representatives of the community, and departed for the seaport of Seleucia and sailed for Cyprus (13:4). These rituals evidently accompanied the quest for the divine will and disposed the suppliant for accepting its manifestation however demanding.

An openness to God's Spirit was one of the marks of Phariseeism that taught the way of holiness for daily life and was not content with merely the written laws as was the case among the more traditional Sadducees of the priestly classes. Whatever the method of determination, it was that same Spirit that forbade their speaking the word in Asia (16:6). A constant openness to the demands of the Spirit was the hallmark of a person who made God's will a matter of paramount importance in life. It is clear that the prayerfulness of Paul was not restricted to mere recitation of words, however traditional and sacred. Prayer for Paul was posture before the Mystery of God's will.

Paul's prayer was not individual and isolated only, but regularly sought the company of others in the synagogues when he traveled, or in the locations used for the purpose by devout Jews of the day. At Philippi, for example, Saul exited the city gates on the Sabbath and found a prayer place near a river (presumably for the ritual purification required of the devout each Sabbath, cf 16:13).

Without attempting to exceed the data or suggesting mystical gifts of extraordinary nature, Saul is listed as having visions on three occasions after his inaugural vision on the way to Damascus in Acts. First at Troas Alexandriae, a vision of someone summoning them to proclaim the word in the province of Macedonia (16:9), led them to cross the Hellespont into strictly European territory for the first time, and thereby arrive at Saul's beloved Philippi. Later at Corinth after a great deal of acrimonious argumentation with some of the Jewish synagogue leaders, Paul was encouraged by the Lord in a vision to speak clearly and forthrightly without fear (18:9). Somehow he never seemed the wilting lily type and would scarcely need a prodding to break silence; nevertheless the promise of Divine presence and deliverance from harm was sufficient to keep Paul actively teaching in that city for a year and a half (18:11). Finally in Jerusalem after another tumult at the Temple, Paul was allowed to address the Sanhedrin council.

In that context he took advantage of the bitter division in doctrine between Pharisees and Sadducees and provoked a near riot so that he had to be taken by force of the military to the barracks for his own physical safety. There the following night the Lord appeared and ordered him to bear witness in Rome itself (23:11)!

Paul's faith was clearly and confidently in the God of his ancestors, as he stated so clearly before the court of the Roman governor Felix, with a faith that embraced everything laid down by the law or written in the prophets (24:14).

In prison or in court, in synagogue or solitary isolation, Paul is repeatedly described as entering the presence of God, purified by prayer. This was the source of his unfailing spiritual focus and the origin of his energy for the Name. Thus the model provided by Paul for diocesan priests today is his sustaining fidelity to prayer at the center and source of all his work.

Community Member

In spite of the singular impact of Paul upon the early churches and the entire subsequent history of Christianity, Paul was no Lone Ranger. His entrance into the Jesus movement was at the invitation of Ananias and accompanied by the imposition of hands, which symbolized the hovering presence of the Holy Spirit and a concrete welcome into association with the work in question (9:17ff). His immediate baptism was clearly his formal initiation into the community of faith, and the reference to being strengthened by food may have Eucharistic overtones, again a profoundly social introduction to the very community he had attempted so vigorously to destroy only a short time beforehand.

Throughout the rest of his life Paul returned regularly to the synagogue gatherings for prayer and preaching about the resurrection of Christ: in Damascus (9:20), in Iconium (14:1), in Corinth (18:5), and regularly in Ephesus (18:19 and 19:8). Proud of his Hebrew heritage and Jewish associations over the years, he instinctively returned to that community's rhythm of life and prayer whenever he entered a new city.

Barnabas presented Paul to the apostles in Jerusalem on his first visit after the transforming events in Damascus (9:27), and it was the leaders of that community who sent him off to Tarsus for his own safety. The very same may well have been responsible for sending Barnabas to bring Paul back. They had an urgent need for the services of a qualified and effective teacher, and that put Paul back into the midst of the Antiochian community once again (11:26).

It was as a team that Paul and Barnabas were sent out, first to de-liver the relief gathered in Antioch for the victims of the Judaean famine (11:30), then on a more general mission to the diaspora (13:2). Paul's association with the prophets and teachers of Antioch placed him among a group of focused ministries (13:1) from which he and Barnabas were set apart by the Spirit. It's consoling for anyone who may have experienced rough waters in team situations to learn that even Paul and Barnabas had their falling out over John Mark (15:37-40), and new team configurations were formed of Paul with Silas and Barnabas with John. Undoubtedly one of the basic reasons for the pairs was obedience to the customary practice of requiring two witnesses for any legal testimony, but pairs they were, and joint bear-ers of several responsibilities over the years.

In the key issue for the primitive Church, namely the binding force of the full Mosaic Law, it was Paul and Barnabas again who were sent to Jerusalem for consultation (15:2) and subsequently sent back to Antioch to implement the decrees of that first council (15:23). In another situation Paul joined forces with Aquila and Priscilla at Corinth (18:2). Paul seems to have transcended gender differences when needed, as for example in his acceptance of ministerial partner-ship with Lydia, the merchant of dyed goods (16:13-40), or the wel-coming of several women of high standing in the communities of Thessalonica (17:4) or Beroea (17:12).

These delegations were never isolated or severed from the com-munity or the work of the churches of that day. In fact, at major junc-tures in the story, the author of Acts makes clear that the ministry of Paul and Barnabas required a final report and assessment by others than themselves. Whether it was a specific task or a more general proclamation of the word of God (15:35), some evidence of fidelity was expected. Thus we find strategically located expressions of ac-countability for their ministry, first to the community of Antioch upon the conclusion of their first missionary journey (14:26-28), and then to James and the elders in Jerusalem after the completion of the third journey (21:17-20). The result is yet another element to the model provided by Paul for diocesan priests, namely, a commitment to work in close association with others, men and women alike, for the sake of the Gospel.

Witness to the Resurrection

Although the pages of Acts are filled with individual concrete actions and events, some more comprehensive plan seemed present, at least in the mind of the human author, from the very beginning. Immediately after Paul was struck blind on his way to Damascus, and Ananias chosen to give the first individual convert instructions in history, Paul was somehow designated as a chosen instrument of evangelization to carry God's true Name to nations and rulers as well as to the children of Israel (9:15). Initially the message was given the generic title of "Word of God" (13:5.7; 15:35). Elsewhere with growing precision, that message was described as encouragement (13:15; 20:1f), the good news of God's fulfilled promises (13:32), Jesus as the Christ (18:5), the gift of the Holy Spirit (19:4), and the kingdom of God (19:8; 28:31). Needless to add, these are also the themes for contemporary daily homilies given across the nation, depending on the texts of the day, the season of the year, or the needs of the congregation.

Nevertheless, the focus of Paul's witness, stemming no doubt from his very first encounter with the risen Lord on the way to Damascus (9:5), was Jesus victorious over death and sin. When confronted by the accusations of the entire Sanhedrin in Jerusalem (23:6), or when confronted by those of the high priest and elders in the court of the Roman governor at Caesarea (24:21), Paul was quick to assert that it was for believing in the resurrection of the dead that he was on trial. Not only was that true, of course, but it was also a clever way of dividing the house, for that particular doctrine was vigorously held by the Pharisees and rejected with equal conviction as a modern innovation unfounded in the Scriptures by the Sadducees.

The indisputably Pauline epistles insist on the resurrection as the enduring reference for Paul's witness, a fact confirmed by the perceived failure of more elegant rhetorical efforts at the Areopagus in Athens when Paul concluded with a flourishing proclamation of that event (17:22-31). A "God who raised from the dead" was the name of the God that Paul was destined to bring to the nations, and his very personality with all its passionate convictions, were placed at the service of that great event.

Any diocesan priest who claims the Apostle Paul as model today has to possess a similar driving conviction regarding the centrality of the Resurrection in all his pastoral practice.

Agent of Conversion and Change

Upon entering any city or town Paul and Barnabas first turned toward the synagogues of their people. The context of prayer and study there was very familiar to them, and the certain availability of people presumably willing to discuss the issues of faith is what brought Paul to town in the first place. There on a regular basis the Jewish men of town, together with sympathetic persons not quite ready to take the final step of embracing Judaism completely, gathered for discussion and worship. Paul chose to be in their midst, arguing from the very Scriptures they read (17:11), that Jesus was the promised Christ (18:5). The explanations and arguments were many and often repeated, for there was a scandal in his message (17:32). Moreover, the possibility that the Gentiles could have equal rights to the inheritance, or that obedience to the Torah was thereby marginalized, was offensive. It took a great deal of time, patience, and prolonged goodwill to repeat the message so often in order to be finally heard.

As such Paul and Barnabas were ministers of conversion and change of heart about the mysterious plans of God. They spoke of forgiveness of sins in Antioch in Pisidia (13:38). They expounded the four basic requirements of Christian ethics as determined by the council: abstinence from idolatry, from blood (which might be equated with respect for life since life was imagined as uniquely present in one's life blood), from strangled meat (which might be equated with the rejection of violence), and unchastity (15:29). To highlight these as pre-eminent rather than the more traditional Jewish non-negotiables of circumcision or sacrifices required a major change of mind among Paul's listeners. More recent experience of implementing conciliar decisions serves to remind contemporary readers that not everyone is equally delighted with such decisions. Undoubtedly there were very vocal groups who resisted the change vigorously and made the ministry very difficult!

Similarly, however, in summarizing his work for the elders of Miletus, Paul referred to the basic acts of repentance before God and faith in the Lord Jesus Christ (20:21) as fundamental to the faith he proclaimed. More traditional and familiar expressions of basic realities were put aside. The moral implications of such doctrines underscored a renewed passion for justice and self-control (24:28) and repeated insistence on change of mind (26:16.20). This was no easy task for the preacher.

Because such transformations took time, Paul and associates stayed for long periods at any number of communities, as for example, three weeks at Thessalonica (17:2), a year and a half at Corinth (18:11), three months in the synagogue at Ephesus (19:8), followed by two full years of lecturing in the hall owned by Tyrannus closer to the old harbor of Ephesus (19:10), two years in Caesarea (24:29) and two years in Rome (28:3).

During that period of time Paul was often confronted by angry individuals whose basic livelihood had been threatened or decreased as a result of his preaching. The owner of the slave girl in Philippi was certainly outraged over the loss of income when his divining slave girl was exorcized into freedom. Demetrius and the silversmith union were enraged over the discrediting of mighty Artemis of the Ephesians.

All of this occurred because Paul was convinced of his calling as an agent of change of heart. That is one way of defining the vocation of a diocesan priest as well, and the assignment to a particular community for a longer period of time is a realistic appraisal of the time necessary for even the beginning of such a change in the thinking of a parish congregation.

Servant of the Community

The figure of Paul as presented in the Acts is that of a person dedicated to serving the communities of faith in Christ. His work with Barnabas at Derbe, for example, was summarized as making many disciples (14:21). Enlarging the local community by preaching, and deepening the faith of its members, was one form of service in which Paul was preeminently successful. In returning to towns previously evangelized like Lystra and Iconium, they concentrated on strengthening the spirits of the newly baptized and encouraging them in perseverance (14:22). That effort to strengthen the resolve and commitment of their early converts was a point of reference and concern elsewhere in Acts as well (cf 18:23).

The reader is informed that Paul and Barnabas made it a point to appoint elders (πρεσβυτεροι) for every church so that the stability of designated leaders, possessing authority and linked to the first apostolic preachers of the faith, would be guaranteed (14:23). The triumphant return of Paul and Barnabas from the Council of Jerusalem, with news of the decision that confirmed and authenticated their teaching

regarding Gentiles and the Mosaic Law, was yet another example of
their service to the community of Antioch (15:30-35). It was to the
elders of the church of Ephesus, summoned to the port city of
Miletus, that Paul directed his final words of encouragement and
counsel (20:17-38).

It would not seem an exaggeration or an example of exegetical
fancy to see a sacramental aspect in the manner in which Paul and Silas
dealt with their converted jailer at Philippi. When the jailer discovered
to his amazement that the prisoners had not fled after the earthquake
had loosened their shackles, he sought instruction in the new faith of
his captives and washed their wounds. (After all, genuine instruction
in the faith always leads to acts of charity!) Afterwards he and his entire household in turn were washed in baptism, followed by a meal
(Eucharist?) in the context of great rejoicing (16:29-34). Any celebration of the rituals of the early Church strengthened their faith and
served to unite the newly regenerated people into the life and ministry
of the local Christian community. One can't help but wonder how
Lydia and her circle handled the welcome for the local jail keeper and
his family!

Churches were served and strengthened by the addition of the
more affluent as well as the poor. Paul welcomed members of high social standing at Beroea (17:12) and preached to the well educated in
Athens at the Areopagus (17:22-31). In his primary concern for the
health and well-being of each community, Paul remains a unique
model for diocesan priests. His missionary journeys found him serving a succession of individual congregations, one after the other.
While residing in each, his whole being was apparently absorbed in
the task of unifying them and deepening their faith in Christ Jesus.
His own comfort or convenience was subordinate to the work for
which he had been called by Ananias so many years before. He served
each community vigorously and energetically, then handed it over to
the responsibility of the elders who succeeded him. The example for
diocesan priests who move from one assignment to another, renewing
their zeal to the best of their ability with each unpacking of the suit-
case, is obvious.

Colleague in Suffering

The abuse and mistreatment received by Paul and his associates by
way of response to the Gospel ranged from the sophisticated mockery
of the Athenians (17:32) to the stoning at Lystra so severe as to be
thought dead (14:19), and the physical beating and imprisonment at

Philippi (16:23). At Jerusalem he was dragged out of the Temple precincts by the crowd that fully intended to kill him and would have done so had not the Roman soldiers garrisoned there intervened (21:30-32)! Repeated attempts to assassinate him kept him under Roman arrest for his own protection and safety (23:12).

One of the most astonishing things about the arrangement of the material in Acts relates to the events of the first missionary journey. A sequence of city visits serves to illustrate the point. Paul and Barnabas were driven out of Antioch in Pisida by a coalition of synagogue leaders and prominent citizens who were jealous of Paul's success with the Gentile community and upset with the turmoil caused by the large numbers of people entering their synagogue to hear the new preacher (13:50). Therefore Paul and Barnabas went on to Iconium where they were attacked and stoned (14:5). Then they moved on to Lystra where, as noted above, Paul was stoned and left for dead (14:19). The sequence was hardly very positive nor successful.

The source of utter amazement stems from the fact that Paul got up, brushed off the dust, and marched back into Lystra to resume his teaching before being so rudely interrupted (14:20). Moreover, the text calmly notes that he marched back to those very same towns of Lystra, Iconium, and Antioch in Pisidia (14:21) that had treated him so shabbily and rejected his message so definitively. He went back! He would not go away. Even though he repeatedly turned to the Gentile community when some of the Jewish synagogue leaders rebuffed his efforts, as in Antioch (13:46), Corinth (18:6), and Rome (28:28), he still refused to give up and returned again and again to synagogues in each town as a logical starting point for his mission. His words of encouragement for each of the faithful communities in those towns were accompanied by the announcement that it was "through many tribulations we must enter the kingdom of God" (14:22)!

Once again the portrait of Paul's ministry becomes a model and example for diocesan ministry today. One hardly returns to contentious, mean-spirited parish committees or councils with Paul's calm conviction that they are the portals to the Kingdom! Neither does one pull up roots easily and move on to another town, even when the call of the Gospel is fairly clear and the needs of the people substantial. Paul experienced the asceticism of serving and leaving, repeatedly starting all over again in a succession of communities and trusting that someone else would build on his work without worrying if things he worked so hard to establish were changed. That is the special type of poverty demanded of the diocesan priest today. Paul stands as a model and a challenge. A priesthood without stress,

opposition or resistance of any sort doesn't lead to the kingdom of
God—at least not in Paul's judgment!

Epilogue

The uniqueness of Paul—by way of his personality, heritage, opportunity, talent, interest, and ability, as well as his unrepeatable moment
in the history of Christianity cannot be duplicated. The larger lines of
his portrait, however, make him an extraordinarily valuable icon of pastoral ministry for priests today. Undoubtedly a similar case might be
made for lay pastoral associates working in contemporary parishes as
well, but they are not the specific focus of this collection of essays.

A careful study of the Acts reveals the portrait of the man Paul as
presented by Luke the historical theologian of the Church for all
times. They may have been colleagues and friends. Regardless, Paul is
patterned after the image of Peter in the first twelve chapters of Acts,
and both are deliberately and carefully fashioned as similar to Jesus
himself. From a literary standpoint Paul's shadow is completely en-
compassed by that of Jesus who spoke the word of God in power.
Paul's shadow also falls upon all successive generations of preachers
and church founders. His contribution toward shaping the type of
priest pastor needed in a renewed Church, especially as delineated in
the Acts of the Apostles, remains a valuable measure of effectiveness
for all ages.

Therefore Acts ends with the stirring announcement that Paul
brought his work to its destined completion, welcoming all who came
to him and preaching the kingdom of God (28:30). At the very center of the only civilization he knew, Paul taught about the Lord Jesus
Christ openly and unhindered. That's the paragon of diocesan priesthood in every age.

Notes

[1] Recommended for further study is the six volume series entitled *The Book of
Acts in Its first Century Setting,* edited by Bruce Vawter and in the process of publication by Wm. B. Eerdmans.

[2] It is strongly recommended that the reader take time to review the actual text
of each citation from the Acts in order to appreciate the full implication of the inspired text for the issue in question.

[3] Though the Talmud prescribes benedictions for rising, dressing, washing,
and any act of preparation for normal daily activities, critical scholarship cannot
determine with precision the exact date of the oral traditions behind the texts, cf.
Berakhot 60b.

6

Personal Symbol of Communion

Denis Edwards

As I look back on my own story as a presbyter of the Archdiocese of Adelaide, I find a number of distinct spiritualities and theologies at work in different periods of my life.

The spirituality in which I was formed in the seminary was that of the priest as the *alter Christus*. The spiritual formation program at its best could be described in terms of the title of Abbot Marmion's classic book *Christ the Ideal of the Priest*. This, of course, had a great deal to be said for it.

In practice, however, it was a partial kind of spirituality, one that was concerned with "spiritual exercises" rather than the whole of life. Life beyond spiritual exercises was dealt with through the idea of growth in virtue. There was much emphasis on the virtue of obedience. What was communicated was a muscular, ethical approach to life, with little emphasis on the human and the inter-personal, on God's gracious invitation into love, or on the Gospel.

This spirituality was accompanied by, and inter-related with, an underlying theology of Church in which the ordained minister was central in every way. Theologically, canonically and practically, the ordained ministry was identified with the Church and its mission. We were trained to have the answers. It was a clericalist spirituality. The presbyter, the *alter Christus,* brought Christ to the community. There was no problem of meaning or identity because the ordained ministers had authority, status, and respect in the Catholic community.

Even as I was imbibing this spirituality it was being undermined by Vatican II. A radically different pattern of thought was at work in and through the council. This new direction of thought found expression in the language used by Bishop Emile de Smedt of Bruges in his criticism of the first draft of the Constitution on the Church. He challenged the draft's "triumphalism," its "clericalism," and its "juridicism."

By the time of the vote on the third and final text, on November 21, 1964, a highly significant decision had been made. The chapter on the People of God was to be the second chapter of the constitution. It was to follow immediately after the first chapter on the mystery of the Church and its sacramental and trinitarian nature. The chapter on the baptized People of God was thus given priority over the chapter on the ordained ministry. Ordained ministry was now situated within a theology of the Church, and the Church was understood as the whole baptized community. This structure was to be reflected in the revision of the Code of Canon Law. Clearly, baptism into Christ has priority over ordination.

In the theology of Vatican II, it is not only the ordained minister but the whole baptized community which manifests to the world the Light of Christ, the *Lumen gentium*. It is not the ordained minister, but the whole community which is the sacrament of salvation, the face of Christ to the world. This effectively puts an end to a spirituality of the ordained minister as *alter Christus* to the Church. The Church itself is the sacrament of Christ.

In the light of this radical shift, we are still struggling with our understanding of the theology and spirituality of the presbyter of the diocese. One way of framing the issue is to say that the clericalist view of things saw the ordained as central, and then asked: What role is left over for the baptized believer? In fact the question was often asked: How do the laity participate in the "mission of the hierarchy?" Since the council, the question becomes: If the baptized really are the Church, what is the distinctive role of the ordained within this community?

One important attempt to answer this question emerged for me in the early years of ministry when I was involved with lay apostolate groups, such as the Young Christian Workers Movement. I still remember my astonishment and the sense of learning something radically new when, as a seminarian, I was exposed to young workers reflecting on their working lives and finding the call of God at the heart of the issues that confronted them at work. The review of life, with its see, judge, and act method, the reflection on the Gospel, the mission of worker in the workplace, the beginnings of social analysis—all of this was a liberation in terms of a workable spirituality.

By and large, however, it went along with a theology of distinction of roles, where the role of the "laity" was to transform the secular environment and the role of the ordained minister was to take responsibility of the church arena. This distinction, which can be found in some of the documents of the council, is at odds with the deeper theology of the council which refuses to allow the baptized to be relegated to the "secular" sphere. Rather, this theology insists that the baptized have one vocation to discipleship, which involves commitment in every aspect of life, including their life as members of the Church. Post-conciliar documents made it clear that, by virtue of baptism, they are called in certain circumstances to take on ministries in the Church.

This broader theology of ministry leads again to the question: What is distinctive about ordained ministry? Some would answer this question in a functional way. They see the presbyter as defined by the ministries of word and sacrament. Preaching is certainly central to the ministry and spirituality of the ordained minister. Vatican II has said that "it is the first task of priests as coworkers with the bishops to preach the Gospel of God to all people."[1] But while preaching is a primary function of the ordained minister, it is not, and ought not be, restricted to the ordained.

Many would understand the priest's identity as constituted by the call to preside at Eucharist. But while the Eucharist is closely linked to the presbyter's vocation, it seems to me that it is not an adequate focus for understanding the unique ministry of the diocesan presbyter. On the one hand, it is clear that in the early Church the presbyters did not preside at the Eucharist. And on the other hand, many of us today experience ourselves very much as presbyters even when not preaching or presiding. In my own time of study at The Catholic University of America, I attended daily Eucharist at Caldwell Hall for two years, an experience I valued greatly. But in those years I presided and preached only occasionally. Yet I was very aware that I belonged to the Archdiocese of Adelaide, that I was a presbyter of that local church, that I was studying on behalf of and for that church. Although the Eucharist is central to my existence as a Christian and as an ordained minister, my identity as a presbyter of a local church is not in any way dependent on how often I preside at Eucharist.

It seems to me that the identity of presbyteral ministry is found somewhere else than in the functions that the presbyter performs. What is needed is an overarching theological vision of the ordained ministry that provides a perspective in which important functions, like preaching and presiding at Eucharist, can be understood.

It seems to me that the theological identity of the diocesan presbyter has to do with being a person who is publicly identified with a local church. I will argue that this ministry is about belonging to a local diocesan community, in union with the bishop, as a public sign and agent of the unity in diversity of that local church. I will argue that the local church is fundamentally the sacrament of divine relationships inculturated in a local geographic area. This will involve reflection on God as radically relational and on church as the sacrament of relationships.[2] The presbyter is the public sign of unity in diversity in such a church.

The Church as Sacrament of Relationships

The foundations for a relational understanding of God can be found in chapter 14 of John's Gospel. There we find Jesus saying: "On that day you will know that I am in my Father, and you are in me, and I am in you"(14:20). The disciple is to be caught up in this dynamic network of relationships. The being-in-one-another of Jesus and the Father reaches outwards to embrace human beings: "Those who love me will keep my word, and my Father will love them, and we will come to them and make our home with them" (14:23).

The mutual relationship between Jesus and the Father is not isolated in an inner-divine world, but is the basis for the Johannine understanding of divine indwelling in the community of disciples. This demands a new attitude on the part of the disciples towards one another—"I give you a new commandment, that you love one another. Just as I have loved you, you also should love one another" (13:34; 15:12, 17). This mutual love is the sign that the community of Disciples offers to the world.

These same themes reappear in Jesus' prayer of chapter 17: "As you, Father, are in me and I am in you, may they also be in us, so that the world may believe that you have sent me" (17:21). Again, the outward, ecstatic structure of trinitarian communion is made clear. The mutual indwelling of Jesus and the Father reaches out to include human beings, who in turn are to witness to divine communion to the world. Jesus prays "that they may be one, as we are one, I in them and you in me, that they may become completely one, so that the world may know that you have loved them even as you have loved me" (22-23).

The oneness of God is here understood as a communion between the Father and Jesus. It is a dynamic, relational unity of persons in love. It is an ecstatic and inclusive communion which draws us creatures into the radical unity between Jesus and the Father. The Trinitarian role of the Spirit is not yet made fully explicit, but it is clear that it is through the work of the Spirit that the faithful are brought into the divine communion of love (14:15-24).

The Cappadocians, Basil (c.330–79), his brother, Gregory of Nyssa (c.330–95) and friend, Gregory of Nazianzus (330–389), made major contributions to the development of the relational understanding of the Trinity. Their first crucial contribution was their use of the substantial word "hypostasis" for the Trinitarian persons. This gave a radically new weight to the idea of a person. In their theology, everything springs forth from Persons, above all from the First Person who is the Unoriginate Origin. Their second contribution was to identify what distinguishes the three Persons in their mutual relations. They understood the divine Persons as distinct only in their mutual interrelations. In every other way the Trinity is completely one and simple.

The divine Persons exist in their interrelationships. This means that God's being must be understood as fundamentally and radically relational. Walter Kasper points out that this implies that "the final word belongs not to the static substance, the divine self-containment, but to being-from-another and being-for-another."[3] The heart of reality is not to be understood primarily in substance terms but as Persons-In-Mutual-Relations.

John Damascene (675–749)first used the word *perichoresis* to describe this Trinitarian communion. *Perichoresis* describes the being-in-one-another, the mutual dynamic indwelling of the Trinitarian Persons (John 10:30; 14:9; 17:21). It comes from *perichoreo,* meaning to encompass. It is to be distinguished from *perichoreuo,* meaning to dance around, but the image of the divine dance captures something of the vitality of the idea of *perichoresis.*[4] The word describes the mutual and reciprocal relations of intimate communion between the Trinitarian Persons—a communion which is so radical that there is only one divine nature.

Diversity and unity are not opposites in this type of communion. Rather true individuality increases in this kind of mutual presence in love. *Perichoresis* expresses the mutual giving and receiving of love between the divine Persons. It expresses the ecstatic presence of one to the other, the being-in-one-another in supreme individuality and in unimaginable freedom. Each Person is present to the other in a joyous and dynamic union of shared life.

In contemporary theology there has been a turn to this relational and interpersonal approach to the Trinitarian God. There is a return to a more Eastern view of the Trinity, which instead of beginning with the divine unity, begins with the divine Persons. Walter Kasper, combining insights from the Cappadocians and the Western tradition, particularly Richard of St. Victor, comes to an understanding of the Trinity as a communion of Persons, as a "unity in love."[5] Orthodox

theologian John Zizioulas writes that the being of God can be understood ontologically only as "communion."⁶ God's being exists as an
act of communion. God's ultimate reality is located not in substance
but in personhood, in the freedom and ecstasy of persons in communion. Catherine LaCugna argues that the essence of God is relational
and personal, that "God's To-Be is To-Be-in-relationship, and God's
being-in-relationship-to-us *is* what God is."⁷ God exists as diverse persons united in a communion of freedom, love, and knowledge. If the
essence of God is relational, then this points towards an ontology of
relation.⁸ The very foundation of all being is relational.

Tony Kelly sees God as the "absolute Being-in-Love." For him
"The Be-ing of God is a life of communion," and this means that "the
ultimate ground of our existence is intrinsically relational."⁹ Ultimate
reality is relational, and the emerging universe is ever coming into
being out this divine communion of dynamic Love. Elizabeth
Johnson develops a feminist theology of the Trinity in Wisdom categories, as Spirit-Sophia, Jesus-Sophia, and Mother-Sophia. She too
understands the Trinity as a perichoretic communion of radical equality and mutuality, imaged on the model of friendship. She sees the
Trinity as totally shared life at the heart of the universe.¹⁰

If the divine being is radically relational then this suggests that
created being is fundamentally relational. As Walter Kasper, John
Zizioulas, Catherine LaCugna, and Tony Kelly point out, a relational
theology of God suggests a relational worldview and a relational ontology or metaphysics. An ontology of substance gives way to, and can
be included in, an ontology of relations. Trinitarian theology suggests
a metaphysics centered on dynamic relationships. Ultimate reality is
understood in terms of personhood and ecstatic, self-transcending
communion. Being is understood as being-in-relationship.

This theology of God as Persons-In-Mutual-Communion is what
gives shape to our self-understanding as church. Our mission as
church is to be a sign and an agent of the divine relations of mutual,
equal and ecstatic love that are at the heart of the universe. The
Church is this message. The Church's being is communion. Its very
being is mutual relations. The Church is the sacrament of relationships, called to witness to the relational God. This is the grace that the
Church is to be for the world. According to Vatican II, "the Church
in Christ, is in the nature of sacrament—a sign and instrument, that
is, of communion with God and of unity among all men and
women."¹¹ Quoting Cyprian, the council sees the Church as "a
people brought into unity from the unity of the Father, the Son and
the Holy Spirit."¹²

The Church gives symbolic expression to the perichoretic relationships of equal and mutual love which are the dynamic heart of reality. It manifests that we and the whole universe spring from these divine relationships in the divine choice to create and that the universe exists at every moment only in relation to this divine *perichoresis*. It witnesses to the fact that this Trinitarian God has chosen to enter into saving and gracious relationships with us in the outpouring of the Spirit and the incarnation of divine Wisdom in Jesus of Nazareth. It shows that we human beings are not isolated beings but fundamentally relational creatures, needing always to be inter-related with other human beings, with other creatures and with the divine persons. It symbolizes that through divine grace our call and destiny is to be caught up, with other creatures, in the dynamism of perichoretic love.

If the Church is to give witness to divine relationality, to relations of mutuality and equality, then this has implications for every aspect of church life. It gives shape to a theological understanding of the role of the presbyter in the diocese.

The Presbyter as Public Sign of Communion

The presbyter is the sign and agent of the unity, the unity in diversity, of the local church, and in and through this the sign of Trinitarian relations of mutual love.

It is the bishop who, according to the teaching of the Vatican II, is "the visible source and foundation of unity in a local church." And the bishops together, as members of the college of bishops and in union with the bishop of Rome, "represent the whole Church in a bond of peace, love and unity."[13] For the local church, the bishop is the sign and agent of communion, and through the bishop the local church is united in communion with other churches.

The identity of the presbyter is related to that of the bishop. It is an essential dimension of the identity of the presbyters to be coworkers with the bishop in a local church. It is also part of their identity to be part of a community of presbyters. The council teaches that the presbyters of a local church, in union with the bishop, have a corporate identity. They form a *presbyterium*.[14] We are told by the council that in each local assembly the presbyters "represent in a certain sense the bishop" and take upon themselves in part the bishop's "duties and solicitude."[15] They "make present" the bishop in the individual assemblies of the faithful.[16] They "render the universal Church visible in their locality."[17] The presbyter, then, is called to be a sign and instrument of communion, as an extension and representative of the unifying role of the bishop in the local church.

The presbyter as personal sacrament of communion is closely linked with the Eucharistic meal which is the great liturgical act of communion. In the Eucharist the Church accomplishes an eschatological act. The gathered assembly becomes a reflection of the eschatological community. It becomes an image of the Trinitarian life of God. This eschatological communion which we anticipate and taste in the Eucharist involves not just human beings but a communion of all God's creatures in God.

John Zizioulas points out that in terms of human existence here and now, this eucharistic experience means: "the transcendence of all divisions, both natural and social, which keep the existence of the world in a state of disintegration, fragmentation, decomposition and hence of death."[18] The Eucharist is an event of radical inclusivity and of radical relationality. A Eucharist which discriminates between races, sexes, ages, professions, and social classes violates its eschatological nature. It fails to be the sacrament of communion. The Eucharist is the event of eschatological relationships experienced in anticipation. It is an expression of Trinitarian love, and the act in which the Church tastes the life of the Trinity. In this act the Church finds itself challenged to live its nature as communion through the orthopraxis of inclusive love.

The presbyter is called to witness to this inclusive love as a public symbol of the relational Church and the Trinitarian God. This witness embraces both unity and diversity. The Church is not a group of like-minded people, but a unity forged by the Spirit of God from diversity. In his recent address to the Faith and Order Commission of the World Council of Churches, John Zizioulas said:

> The structure of the local Church must be such that two things would be simultaneously guaranteed. On the one hand, unity and oneness must be safeguarded. No member of the Church, whatever his or her position in it, can say to another member, "I need you not" (1 Cor 12). There is absolute interdependence among all members of the community—which means that, simultaneously with unity and oneness, there is in the Church diversity. Each member of the community is indispensable, carrying his or her gifts to the one body. All members are needed but not all are the same; they are needed precisely because they are different.[19]

The diversity of communion embraces differences of race, sex, and age, differences in wealth, power, and social standing, and also differences in spiritual gifts. The presbyter is a sign of unity but not of uniformity. Catholicity, involving the celebration of difference and radical inclusivity, are both part of a Trinitarian approach to ordained ministry.

Such a Trinitarian approach to ordained ministry can overcome the distortions that occur both when the theology of ministry is centered only on Christ, as well as when it is centered only on the Holy Spirit. A purely Christocentric approach can tend to understand ordained ministry as a ministry "from above," and as ministry over the Church community. A purely Spirit-centered approach to the theology of ministry can tend to see ministry as a ministry "from below," and as a ministry which springs only from the community.

A truly Trinitarian theology of ordained ministry will understand ordained ministry, like the Church itself, as coming both "from below" and "from above." Ministry is the work of the Holy Spirit and of the risen Christ. Christ is present in the Spirit. Christ is present in the community. Ministry flows from the Spirit at work in the community and it also springs from the risen Christ. To see the presbyter as representing Christ standing over against the community is to distort ordained ministry. To see the presbyter simply as the arbitrary creation of the community is also to distort ordained ministry. What is needed is a Trinitarian view of ordained ministry as both springing from the community which is inspired by the Spirit of God, and as commissioned to the community by the risen Jesus.

This Trinitarian theology of ministry not only transcends the dichotomy between Chistocentric and Church or Spirit-centered theologies. It also transcends the dichotomy between "functional" and "ontological change" approaches to the theology of ministry. Its emphasis is neither on function nor on ontology, but on symbol. It sees ordination fundamentally as a symbolic change. And what is symbolized is radically relational. Ordination publicly sets a person aside to be a symbol and agent of the Church's communion.

A Relational Spirituality

What all of this means for me is that, as a diocesan presbyter, I now see my own spirituality as fundamentally relational and communal.

The God that the Church is called to give witness to and to celebrate is a communal God, a God who is friendship beyond all comprehension. It is clearer to me than it used to be that my life of prayer is a matter of always being drawn into this dynamism of giving and receiving, this constant movement of shared life. My own spirituality is becoming more and more Trinitarian, more consciously a being led by the Spirit, a following of Jesus and a being directed towards the One who is Unoriginate Origin, Fountain Fullness, Source of all Being, Father and Mother to all creation. One of the delights in becoming more conscious of this kind of Trinitarian spirituality is the discovery that it is already there in the liturgy—even if the language is far from inclusive and in need of reform.

I now see my day-to-day ministry as a presbyter in relational terms. This ministry is a call to be present with people as a witness that they belong to the community of the local church, and that they belong to the communion that is God. I see my role as presbyter as helping to build authentic experiences of ecclesial community in all kinds of ways. It involves encouraging all the acts of others that are directed towards building community within the Church and beyond the Church. It involves pointing to the deeper meaning of our communion through preaching the Word. Finally and centrally, it involves celebrating our participation in the divine eschatological communion in the Eucharist.

A Trinitarian approach to ministry is necessarily collaborative. It will involve modeling community in various ways, particularly through various kinds of team ministries. A theology of the ordained ministry that centers on Trinitarian communion will support a spirituality that is radically critical of all forms of clericalism and pyramidal thinking. It's guiding idea is that of mutual and equal relations. It is empowered by a vision of perichoretic love.

It follows that such a spirituality and lifestyle is collaborative, empowering and inclusive. It suggests that the criterion of mutual and equal relations is fundamental for our lives and ministries as presbyters.

In such a communal and egalitarian context, the exercise of power undergoes a transformation. Here Bernard Loomer's insights into the nature of power are particularly helpful. He distinguishes between unilateral power and relational power.[20] Unilateral power is the power to exert influence in order simply to advance one's own purposes. This kind of power operates only in one direction, seeking to increase one's own influence or status. Relational power, by contrast, is the capacity to both influence others and be influenced by them. It involves the capacity to receive other people's insights, and to take account of their feelings and values. Relational power frees one to act cooperatively, to be influenced, without being threatened and without losing one's identity and freedom.

Loomer sees Jesus as "at the bottom of the hierarchy of unilateral power," but at the "apex of life conceived in terms of relational power."[21] Relational power is power "from below." It is non-violent, participatory, and empowering. It reflects a leadership which is faithful to the Gospels where all forms of dominating power are forbidden (Mark 10:42-45) and where only the leadership of the servant is allowed (John 13:1-15). More and more I see that one of the crucial tests for the fidelity of presbyteral ministry is to ask whether power is exercised unilaterally or relationally.

A communal life-style and ministry can only be authentic when it is sustained in the freedom that comes in solitude and prayer. But it needs to be supported, as well, by the sense of a close connection with the bishop, and with the presbyterium of the diocese. In my own case I have found it necessary, and a great grace, to meet regularly with other presbyters in a small group for review of life, prayer, and celebratory meals. I have found, as well, that I need to live in community— an option that is not possible for everyone in the present structures.

As my sense of God as Communion-in-Love has grown, I have found that my own friendships with women and men are more and more central to my spirituality and my being. These friendships matter more than ever before. They express and participate in ultimate reality.

Relationships of mutual love constitute the Church's message. They are the very being of the Church. Those of us called to presbyteral ministry in a local church are public signs and agents of these relations of mutual love. It seems to me that this is what fundamentally gives shape to our spirituality. We are the visible signs and agents of the Trinitarian communion which is the very being of the Church.

Notes

[1] *Presbyterorum ordinis,* 4

[2] In this section I am following a line of thought developed in "The Church as Sacrament of Relations" in *Pacifica* 8 (1995) 185–200. The trinitarian theology is further argued in *Jesus The Wisdom of God: An Ecological Theology* (Maryknoll, N.Y.: Orbis Books, 1995).

[3] Walter Kasper, *The God of Jesus Christ* (London: SCM, 1983) 280.

[4] Bonaventure translated *perichoresis* into Latin as *circumincessio,* from *circumincedere,* meaning to move around. It suggests an active moving around one another—a kind of divine dance. Other writers used the word *circuminsessio,* from *circuminsedere,* meaning to sit around. It suggests more the divine presence to one another in repose.

[5] Walter Kasper, *The God of Jesus Christ* (London: SCM, 1983) 264–316.

[6]John Zizioulas, *Being as Communion* (Crestwood, NY: St Vladimir's Seminary Press, 1985) 17.

[7]Catherine LaCugna, *God For Us: The Trinity and Christian Life* (Harper-SanFrancisco, 1991) 250.

[8]*God for Us,* 243.

[9]Tony Kelly, *An Expanding Theology: Faith in a World of Connections* (Newtown N.S.W.: E. J. Dwyer, 1993) 158. For the foundations of Tony Kelly's trinitarian theology see his *The Trinity of Love* (Wilmington, Del.: Michael Glazier, 1989).

[10]Elizabeth Johnson, *SHE WHO IS: the Mystery of God in Feminist Theological Discourse* (New York: Crossroad, 1992).

[11]*Lumen gentium,* 1.

[12]*Ibid.,* 4. Since the council it has become more and more clear that "the ecclesiology of communion is the central and fundamental idea of the council's documents." This quotation is from the *Final Report* of the Synod of Bishops (1985). See *Documents of the Extraordinary Synod of Bishops* (Homebush, N.S.W.: St. Paul Publications, 1986) 35

[13]*Lumen gentium,* 23.

[14]Ibid, 28.

[15]Ibid.

[16]*Presbyterorum Ordinis,* 5.

[17]*Lumen gentium,* 28.

[18]John Zizioulas, *Being as Communion,* 255.

[19]Metropolitan John (Zizioulas) of Pergamon, "The Church as Communion" *St Vladimir's Theological Quarterly* 38 (1994).

[20]Bernard Loomer, "Two Kinds of Power," *Criterion* 15 (Winter 1976) 12.

[21]*Ibid,* 28.

7

Priestly Spirituality:
"Speaking Out *for the Inside*" [1]

William H. Shannon

When I was asked to write this chapter, my first instinct was to turn to Thomas Merton, whose spirituality has so deeply affected me and my own writings, to see whether or not his writings had anything to offer on the subject. While he was a priest, Merton never exercised the ministry of a diocesan priest. He lived out his priesthood as a monk. Still, there is a universality about his writings that moved me to turn to him to see what I might discover.

What came to mind almost immediately was a letter he had written to *The Saturday Evening Post* on December 18, 1966. At that time the *Post* carried a regular column which offered readers the opportunity to express their views on various subjects. Called "Speaking Out," it was a "by invitation only" column, and in 1966 the one who extended the invitations was senior editor, John Hunt. In December of that year he wrote to Thomas Merton inviting him to do a guest article for the column. The topic he asked Merton to write about was monasticism and the monastic way of life: hardly a surprising request, since Thomas Merton was easily the best known monk in America.

But Merton had other ideas. He felt he had things to say to the readers of *The Saturday Evening Post* that were more important than information he could give them about the monastic life. Any *Post* reader who wanted to know about monasticism could find plenty of material in a good encyclopedia.

He wanted to speak with the *Post* readers about the interior dimension of human life: a dimension of depths and interiority which is present in everyone but unfortunately discovered only by a few. Merton wanted "To Speak Out" all right, but, as he told John Hunt,

"For the Inside." He realized, from his own life experience prior to his entry into the monastery, how easy it is to block out that inner reality and live almost entirely on the outside, never even suspecting the depths of reality that are within. The predicament of such people would be somewhat like the position of the people of Europe before the New World was discovered. Europe was the only world they knew; yet all the while there was a whole other world, full of new and marvelous things waiting to be discovered. It was there, but they were totally unaware of its existence. When at last they discovered it, all sorts of new adventures were open to them.

In a somewhat similar way, people who only know life's externals are cut off from a realm of their own reality—life on the inside—that offers new and exciting experiences, far surpassing those of a life lived mostly on the outer surface of reality. Merton's strong desire to offer the *Post* readers a vision of these "new and exciting experiences" prompted him to try to override Hunt's suggestion for an article about monks and write instead an article with the title "Speaking Out *for the inside.*"

Hunt, who had his own ideas as to what readers might want from a well-known monk, was not impressed, it would seem, by the alternative Merton had proposed. At any rate, as far as I have been able to discover, Merton's proposal was not accepted. He did not appear in the pages of *The Saturday Evening Post.*

After explaining what he would include in the article he had in mind (the complete letter to Hunt may be found in the fifth volume of the Merton letters[2], Merton concludes by saying: "This is rather tough and will demand a lot from your readers." "My suggestion," he continues, "is: frankly admit the toughness and unpalatableness of the subject and treat it as it is. Some may be hit hard, most will remain indifferent."

His words were hardly calculated to "sell" his idea to the editor. I have had enough contact with editors to know that they don't want material that is "tough and unpalatable," much less stuff that most readers would "remain indifferent" to. In describing his proposed article in such terms , did Merton realize that he was practically writing his own rejection slip? Probably not. It was typical of him that enthusiasm for a topic often blinded him to the fact that something that excited him might not be equally exciting to a general readership.

We might ask the question: "Did Merton make a mistake? Should he have accepted the opportunity to write about monasticism?" Perhaps he should have, because interiority is what the monastic life is all about. He could have written about monasticism and, in that context, "speak out" all he wanted to "for the inside." The reason he did not make this choice, I believe, was his conviction that this probing into one's depths and truly finding the "inside" of ourselves was a task for everyone, not just for monks. In 1966 he was not willing to risk having readers think that he believed otherwise. *Discovering the depths of one's being and finding God there is not a monastic task; it is a human one.*

Having accepted the invitation to "speak out" about "the spirituality of the diocesan priest." I must say I feel a certain affinity with Merton who, when he was asked to write about monasticism, expressed his preference to "speak out" about the quest for interiority which he saw as a human search, not just a monastic one. In a somewhat similar fashion I believe that spirituality, which is a search for true interiority, is not something that is different for priests because they are priests. I would prefer to say that spirituality, in its essential nature, is the same pursuit for the priest as it is for the other "faithful."

I use the term "the *other* faithful" with deliberate intent. For all too long a time we have "clericalized" the priest, and in doing so, have set him apart from those who were referred to as "the faithful." In such a context it is all too easy to see the Church as divided into the priests on the one hand and the faithful on the other (and thus envision a different spirituality for each). My strong conviction that such a division is wrong theologically, psychologically and pastorally is supported, I believe, by a carefully nuanced statement in *Lumen gentium.* It was a sentence that startled me the first time I read it. Speaking of the relationship of priests and people in the Church, it says: "Pastors and the *other* faithful are bound to each other by a mutual need."[3] What had startled me about this statement at first reading was not the content of the statement (which certainly made sense to me), but rather my realization that this is the only ecclesiastical document I know of that includes priests among the "faithful!"

This inclusion of priests among the faithful is an important insight into priesthood. The priest's task is to minister to the faithful. But if he is also one of the faithful (as he truly is), then he has to minister to himself as well. There is a moving passage in chapter twenty of Acts. It describes Paul's tender and affectionate parting from the presbyters of Ephesus who had come to Miletus to bid him their farewells. In an emotion-charged address Paul exhorts them:

> Keep watch *over yourselves* and over all the flock, of which the Holy Spirit has made you overseers, to shepherd the Church of God that he obtained with the blood of his own Son (20:28).

Note that Paul admonishes the presbyters of Ephesus, not only to keep watch over their flock, but also to keep watch *over themselves.* I take this to mean that keeping watch over the flock is a responsibility to be carried out with the realization that they themselves are a part of that flock. If I may give my own paraphrase of Paul's charge to the presbyters: "You must lead those to whom you minister along the way to God. But you must follow that way yourselves." And to me it makes sense to say that the way is the same for all. The spirituality which the priest must cultivate in his own life is the spirituality he must share with the people he serves. Moreover the other faithful will share with him this same spirituality as they live it out in their daily lives. In this way the spirituality of each will be enriched by that of the other.

For there is, I believe, only one Christian spirituality. It is a spirituality rooted in the Gospel and flowing from baptism. At the heart of this spirituality is a deep interiority that alone puts one in touch with what is truly real: the reality of God, the reality of oneself, the reality of all God's creatures. This, I think, is what Merton intended to write about in *The Saturday Evening Post* article that never was. For in his writings on spirituality Merton is constantly pointing to the existence of this marvelous interior dimension of depth and awareness, which—sad to say—all too many people miss, because they systematically block it out by a life almost wholly concentrated on externals.

The poet Rilke defined the plight of contemporary women and men as "always looking out, never looking in." This can be true even of people for whom prayer is an important part of their religious practice. For prayer can be described in two different ways. We may speak of it as "familiar conversation with God." This is certainly a legitimate metaphor for prayer. It is a form of prayer that can help us to get in touch with our inner reality. At the same time I must admit (and probably you must too) that all too often I can engage in such prayer and my mind and heart may be a long ways away from the words I am saying.

But there is another way of describing prayer. There is a form of prayer whose sole intent is to help me reach the inner dimension of my being. Merton speaks of this kind of prayer in an unpublished booklet prepared in 1961 for the Gethsemani novices. He writes:

> Prayer is not only the "lifting up of the mind and heart to God," but also the response to God within us, the discovery of God within us; it leads ultimately to the discovery and fulfillment of our own true being in God.[4]

When we discover God within, we have entered into the realm of mystery. As Merton puts it in his words to the novices: "Prayer is always enshrouded in mystery." He goes on to be even more emphatic (and also more enigmatic): "To pray is to enter into mystery, and when we do not enter into the unknown we do not pray." In fact he adds: "If we want everything in our prayer-life to be abundantly clear at all times, we will by that very fact defeat our prayer-life."

If this sounds strange to some of us, it may be because we have been brought up with a one-dimensional approach to spirituality. We have seen prayer as an outward activity communicating with God in words. We have not sufficiently recognized that deeper dimension, that other way, of prayer, namely, prayer as inward venture: the prayer of quiet and silence, the prayer of interiority, the prayer of contemplation. In this way of prayer we let go of words and concepts and imaginings as ways of relating to God. Instead, we enter into God's own silence in the depths of our being. There we discover and experience God in a relationship so direct that in God we discover our own true selves. There is a brilliant passage in Merton's book *The New Man* that expresses that truth in a profound way:

> The experience of contemplation is the experience of God's life and presence within us not as object but as the transcendent source of our own subjectivity. Contemplation is a mystery in which God reveals himself to us as the very center of our most intimate self. . . . When the realization of his presence bursts upon us, our own self disappears in Him and we pass mystically through the Red Sea of separation to lose ourselves (and thus find our true selves) in Him.[5]

To speak of "losing" ourselves in God and at the same time "finding ourselves in God is simply to put into other words that remarkable truth which is at the core of all true Christian spirituality, namely, "that God is everywhere." When we begin to experience the divine Presence as the heart and center of our interior life, then this amazing truth "God is everywhere," ceases to be merely an article of faith we believe in or a conclusion of reason we assent to. Instead, it becomes a reality of personal experience. It becomes what Merton calls, in the aforementioned letter to John Hunt, a "communion with the Unknown" within us.

But this is only a beginning. Our inner life does not exist in isolation. It is linked with the inner life of everyone else. How can I say that? Because the "Unknown" whom we meet in our depths is the same "Unknown" who dwells in the depths of all of God's people. This is why Merton can say that "communion with the Unknown" in ourselves becomes the basis for "communion with that same Unknown in others" (Once again I am quoting from the letter to Hunt).

These words of Merton are tremendously important for understanding the spirituality of the priest. What they say to me is that in experiencing God in the depths of his being, the priest also experiences each and every one of the "other faithful," for they too are in communion with God. In God priest and people are truly one with one another. The priest is one with each and every one of them and all of them with him. We all meet in God.

Let me make this very concrete. Suppose a priest is greeting his parishioners as they depart from Sunday Eucharist. If he sees them only on the surface of reality, they seem to be individuals, all separate from one another. Yet if he moves to a deeper level of consciousness—that level wherein alone he is able to see reality as it really is, wherein alone he is able to meet the "Unknown" in himself as the same "Unknown" who is in these "other faithful"—he can let go of the "illusion" of separateness. He can see that he and they are one.

As soon as he lets go of the notion of separateness, he recognizes the deepest possible reason for his responsibility to his people, especially those who are in need. His responsibilities to the homeless, the sick, the needy, the oppressed, the marginalized spring from that deep oneness in God that he has with them and with all his sisters and brothers. He must love them as himself, for in a very real way each of them is "his other self." As Thomas Merton said in Calcutta at a gathering of people from many religious traditions: "We are already one. But we imagine that we are not. And what we have to recover is our original unity. What we have to be is what we are."[6]

The equation of Christian social responsibility is this: coming to know God in our own inner selves means coming to know people and coming to know people means getting involved with them and with their problems, their needs, their aspirations. And that involvement takes place in history, in the here-and-now of their lifetime and ours. To quote Merton once again: in a 1966 article in *Commonweal* he articulates a "ministry" insight that grew out of his contemplative experience: "That I should have been born in 1915, that I should be the contemporary of Auschwitz, Hiroshima and the Watts riots are things about which I was not first consulted. Yet they are also events in which, whether I like it or not, *I am deeply and personally involved*" (italics added).[7]

And what of ourselves as priests? If we have really become aware of our oneness with all our sisters and brothers, dare we remain uninvolved in the predicaments that belong to their history and ours? That we and the other faithful are contemporaries of the Persian Gulf War, of the terrible disorder that followed the breakup of the Soviet Union, of the unrest in the Middle East and the terrible bloodshed in Africa and Bosnia, the disarray in politics and the sad picture of politicians more interested in getting reelected than in meeting the needs of a troubled nation—all these are matters about which neither they nor we were first consulted, yet they are matters that somehow we all have to be involved in.

Inner Unity

Interiority, then, is at the heart of any true spirituality. whether we are talking about a lay person, a religious or, as in this chapter, the priest. Taking time to live on the inside will not only mean that the priest will find his own identity in God and his communion with the other faithful; it will also unify his own life. It will give him an inner center, an inner core, from which his actions will proceed. Because he has an unclouded sense of who he is and a clearer vision of what the things are that really matter, he will have a more accurate insight into life and the priorities he needs to set for himself. This inner unity will strengthen him to do better whatever it is he has to do. For *he* will really *be* there in the doing.

That inner unity will give us a consciousness of authentic freedom. The priest whose life is lived from the inside out will be able to stand on his own feet and make decisions of conscience that are his own and not vicarious decisions made for him by someone else. Inner unity brings inner calm. We come to learn that many of the things that once unsettled us, we are now able to take in stride. Whatever directions our lives and ministries may lead us in, we will always know that there is a center that roots our lives, like the center of the spokes of a wheel. As Merton once said: "If we do not live in this center, then everything becomes a rat-race."[8] If, on the other hand, we live more and more at that center, we can go anywhere on the circumference of life's circle in our daily activities, and that center will always be there for us to return to. Yet the center is not a refuge. When we return to it in prayer and reflection, it is not to escape responsibilities, but to be strengthened to deal with them, not to hide from the complexities and absurdities of life, but to be enlightened in ways that enable us to face them. It will be at that center, at that point of inner unity, that we shall be able to discern some kind of a pattern of meaning in our lives. We will know that we are in touch with what is truly real.

This is not to say that life will necessarily become easier, though it will surely be more tranquil. Nor does it mean that there will be no further struggles or that we shall have at our finger tips the answers to all the questions that life may pose. Indeed, if anything it may mean having more questions or at least deeper ones (because we are in touch with life at a deeper level) than those who are content to live simply on the surface of life. Mario Cuomo, three-times governor of New York, in a recent talk put his finger on much of the malaise that is in government today (I might also add "in the Church today," but that would be a whole other type of article). Cuomo said: "How do we resist the lust for easy answers even if they're wrong?"[9]

Earlier in that same year (1966) in which he was in contact with John Hunt, Merton received a request from a man whose task was helping people who needed to make career changes in their lives. Did Merton have any advice that might help such people? Merton, with that remarkable ability he had of going to the heart of issues, suggests that, whatever changes people make in their lives, whether career changes or other changes, there is one basic guideline they should keep in mind. It is simply this:

> We should decide not in view of better pay, higher rank, "getting ahead," but in view of becoming *more real,* entering more authentically into direct contact with life, living more as a free and mature human person, able to give myself more to others, able to understand myself and the world better.

"Becoming more real" is a phrase that occurs frequently in the Merton vocabulary. For him it is another way of saying "interiority." It is a term he frequently uses to describe contemplation.

The importance of interiority, of being in touch with the truly real in the depths of our being, was also the theme of a letter Merton wrote a year earlier in response to a wholly different question. In 1965 the manager of a bookstore at the University of Delaware asked Merton for some words on the importance of reading in college. Merton wrote:

> It seems to me that a man or a woman goes to college not just to get a degree and a good job, but first of all to find himself and establish his true identity. You cannot go through life as a mask or as a well-functioning biological machine (*Witness to Freedom,* 169).

He goes on to warn that we cannot allow ourselves to be shaped entirely by forces outside ourselves. We become real, he says, insofar as "we accept the real possibilities that are presented to us and *choose from them freely and realistically* for ourselves." But to make such choices, out of the overwhelming mass of information and knowledge that college thrusts on one, requires the building of that inner self, that inner truth, which creates a center in us that gives meaning and unity to all we do.

"Therefore," he says, "if a person is going to make authentic judgments for himself, he is going to have to renounce the passivity of a subject that merely sits and 'takes in' what is told him whether in class or in front of a TV, or in the other mass media." True interiority, therefore, is not passivity. Rather it is our response to the God who is present within us, the God who is more truly within us than we are within ourselves. Full awareness of this divine presence is a return to the state of paradise. It is, therefore, God's gift to us, as it was—the Genesis myth makes this clear—God's gift to humanity in the beginning.

There is a problem we all have to deal with. You and I can accept everything I have said up to now about interiority, about the presence of God within. But it might very well be an acceptance that grips our minds only. It sounds great! God within! Bringing unity to my life! Having a center that gives meaning to my life! How wonderful all this is! But our acceptance of it must be more than a kind of intellectual euphoria. If it is to have meaning in our daily living, we need to transfer it from the mind to the heart, from the realm of intellectual knowledge to that of lived experience.

And let us be honest and realistic about this. It is by no means an easy task. Indeed, it is almost impossible for us, if we are over-busy, if our lives are frantic, distraught, and overwhelmed with too much activity. And "frantic," "distraught," "overwhelmed" are probably adjectives that fit the lives of most of us. We do so many things; we are often not really *there* to any of them. Merton has a right-on description of the over-active life. He calls it a state of "semi-attention," "half-diluted consciousness."

We live in a state of constant semi-attention to the sound of voices, music, traffic, or the general noise of what goes on around us all the time. This keeps us immersed in a flood of racket and words, a diffuse medium in which our consciousness is half-diluted: we are not quite "thinking," not entirely responding, but we are more or less there. We are not fully *present* and not entirely absent; not fully withdrawn, yet not completely available.[10]

Quiet time (silence, solitude are appropriate synonyms) must be an essential ingredient of a spirituality of interiority. We need some time without activity, without words, without people. We need these not to escape from activity or words or people, but to get our heads on straight and our hearts beating to the proper rhythms so that we can work creatively, speak wisely, deal with people gently and compassionately. Without some quiet time in our lives, any real interiority will quite simply be out of the question. It is *that* important. As Merton writes in *The Sign of Jonas*: "Those who cannot be alone cannot find their true being and they are always something less than themselves."[11]

Perhaps someone will want to retort: "That's easy for Merton to say. After all he belonged to a monastery whose very name evokes a picture of quietness and silence: monks who (when Merton first went there) never spoke to one another except in sign language." And Trappist life called for more than external silence. The lifestyle Merton had elected required silence of the heart as well as silence of the voice.

Obviously you and I cannot elect silence in the same way and to the same degree as Merton did. If ours cannot be the high octane silence of the monastery, it still remains that we need some quality silence, solitude or quiet time to fuel any kind of in-depth spirituality. Merton speaks of the creative power and fruitfulness of silence:

> Not only does silence give us a chance to understand ourselves better, to get a truer and more balanced perspective on our own lives in relation to the lives of others: silence makes us whole if we let it. Silence helps to draw together the scattered and dissipated energies of a fragmented existence. It helps us to concentrate on a purpose that really corresponds not only to the deeper needs of our own being but also to God's intentions for us.[12]

Some priests find themselves naturally drawn to silence and solitude. They relish the opportunity for quiet time and endeavor to make it a daily part of their lives. They must cherish this as a great grace from God. There are others for whom the atmosphere of silence and quiet which are conducive to interiority is something they have to struggle for. Their natural bent is to be deeply involved in external activities. They find it hard to quiet down and experience God within. Their inclination is to seek God in what they do. This is in no sense reprehensible. In fact, it is a very healthy attitude, for it is an effort to appreciate and in some way experience that "God is everywhere." Yet in order to know that I am finding God in the external activities of life does require some quality time of silence and solitude on my part just to enable me to realize that this is what I am doing.

As I type this text on my computer I can see hanging on my wall a copy of Jean Francois Millet's famous painting *The Angelus*. It shows a man and woman in the fields stopping for a brief moment to recite the Angelus prayer that is traditionally said morning, noon, and evening. Looking at the picture, one sees a church in the far background. You can almost hear the Angelus bell ringing and calling them to this moment of prayer. I am seldom at my computer at Angelus time, but I like to have it there as a reminder to me of that loving God who is indeed everywhere, yet who so frequently seems to elude my consciousness.

One God, but Lots of Ministries

Several times Paul speaks of the unity that exists among the disciples of Jesus. In Ephesians, for instance, he reminds us that there is "one Lord, one faith, one baptism, one God and Father of all, who is above all and through all and in all" (4:5-6). I would like to add: "there is one spirituality." And that spirituality is interiority, that meeting with the Unknown within us and at the same time communion with the same Unknown in others. But Paul makes clear that, in the context of that Christian unity, there are many different ministries (some called to be apostles, some prophets, some pastors and teachers). Yet all these ministries are the work of the *one Spirit* who acts in all. In the preface for Christian Unity in the Roman *Sacramentary*, we sing of the wonders produced by the Holy Spirit.

> How wonderful are the works of the Spirit,
> revealed in so many gifts!
> Yet how marvelous is the unity
> the Spirit creates from their diversity.

Different Ways to the One Spirituality

Having established (I hope), that the essence of Christian—indeed of any—spirituality is interiority, we must recognize that there are many different ways of achieving that interiority. To find the way best suited for a particular individual requires that we look at their character and personality, their life situation, the ministry or role which they carry out in the midst of the community.

How does the diocesan priest live a life of interiority and make use of his gifts to carry out the responsibilities that belong to him by virtue of his ministry? Or to put the question another way, what implications for priestly ministry flow from our unity with the other faithful?

One way of answering these questions is to say that we serve the whole body of the faithful, including ourselves (1) by celebrating the dying and rising of Jesus in liturgy; (2) by teaching, in a variety of contexts, what we believe about God and Christ and Church and the demands of Christian discipleship; and (3) by the exercise of pastoral care and compassion for all God's people and especially for those most in need of it.

Collaborative Leadership

One thing should be very clear to us: we do not carry out our ministry all by ourselves. The leadership we exercise in the Church must be *collaborative:* we plan with the other faithful and with them build Christian community. Inviting their collaboration is not an act of generous sharing on our part of something that belongs by right solely to us. I mention this because the prevailing attitude in the Catholic Church before Vatican II considered the Church's mission as entrusted to the hierarchy alone. If the laity shared, it was "by clerical largess," and not by reason of their membership in the Church. After all, did not Pius XI define Catholic Action as the "participation of the laity in *the apostolate of the hierarchy*?" (italics added) .

Vatican II radically changed this mentality. It stated that "the lay apostolate is a participation in the saving mission of the Church itself. Through their baptism and confirmation all are commissioned to that apostolate by the Lord Himself."[13] In fact, Vatican II went even further in breaking down the clerical divide. It tells us that by reason of this commission from the Lord himself, the laity have a special affinity with Christ and a certain kind of equality with their pastors. In article 32, *Lumen gentium* offers an important ministerial perspective: "The laity have Christ for their brother who, though he is Lord of all, came not to be served but to serve (cf. Mt. 20:28). They also have for their brothers those in the sacred ministry." This designation of the priest as "brother" of the laity is a remarkable switch in language. If we had the courage to adopt the ecclesiological thinking that is behind it, we would move a long way toward removing the charge of paternalism that so many people, especially women, experience from the clergy and find so offensive.

Collaborative leadership is not only sound ecclesiology. It is an effective way of putting the rich resources of the whole Christian community, not just the priest's, at the service of God's kingdom. When I was writing this chapter, I asked a number of people what they would say if they had been invited to write it. One of them, a college professor, said: "Tell them not to look just inside their own number for all the answers and plans. Let them know that there is a lot of life out there among the people, a lot of vital energy waiting to be released into the mainstream of the Church's life."

The deepest reason of all for a ministry that is truly collaborative is not only sound ecclesiology or good practice, but also—and this is a theme that is very much at the heart of this chapter—the contemplative intuition that the pastor and the other faithful at the deepest level of consciousness are truly one. For this reason it makes sense for them to collaborate in helping others to arrive at this consciousness of unity and communion that alone can create true community. Collaborative ministry is a way of enabling all to awaken to God's presence in themselves and in one another with a realization of all that that awakening implies for the building of God's kingdom.

Collaboration in Liturgy

Previous to Vatican II, the role of the priest focused largely on the administration of the sacraments and the promotion of devotion. He was the leader in liturgy, but it was a leadership that could hardly be called collaborative. The "other faithful" who came to the Eucharist might well have felt somewhat like the young boy who was in the school play. The play was about the Genesis story of Adam and Eve. The boy was asked if he enjoyed having a part in the play. "Awe, I don't like it very much," he said. "The snake has all the good lines." I would not want to push the analogy too far, but a lay person *attending* liturgy in pre-Vatican II days might well have said: "The priest has all the lines."

We have yet to appreciate fully the revolutionary change in our understanding of Eucharist brought about by Vatican II and the liturgical directions in which its thinking continues to move us. To understand just how radically different Catholic Eucharist has become, one needs to remember where we have come from.

The theology of the Eucharist that emerged from the Council of Trent and persisted down to Vatican II was clearly that of medieval scholasticism, which spoke of sacraments in terms of matter and form and validity and liceity, minister and recipient. Thus, in the case of the Eucharist the matter was bread and wine; the form, the words of consecration said by the priest over the bread and wine. The priest was the celebrant and did not need the people to have a valid Eucharist. All he needed was bread and wine and the words of consecration that he spoke.

The people were spectators, watching an action performed on their behalf. Some, though by no means all, received Communion. This meant getting something, namely, the Body and the Blood of Christ; but seemingly, this communion with Christ had nothing to do with any kind of relationship, let alone any deep unity, with the rest of the people in the church. It was a "Jesus and me" experience. One of the ways people made this clear was by burying their faces in their hands, to exclude from this exquisite moment all else, including the rest of God's assembled people.

This was the Eucharistic heritage from Trent and the Eucharistic practice until Vatican II. The Constitution on the Sacred Liturgy, as well as the liturgical documents issued after the council to implement the directives of that constitution, produced what can only be called an unprecedented and explosive revolution in liturgical understanding and practice.

Though it would be too strong to say that the Council took the Eucharist away from the priest and gave it back to the people, it would not be too strong to say that it returned the Eucharist to what it had been in the beginning: an assembly of God's people come together to praise God, to hear God's Word and to "break bread" with the firm belief that the Lord Jesus was present among them. It would be quite correct to say that the priest is no longer the central actor in this drama of salvation. That role belongs to the risen Jesus present in our midst through the action of the Spirit and to the assembly of people among whom he is present. Though not the central actor, the priest has a special role: while he is not the consecrator (the Holy Spirit is) he is, by reason of his ordination, the presider who leads the assembly and says on its behalf the prayer inviting God to send the Holy Spirit on the bread and wine and also on the assembly.

In fulfilling his role as presider, the priest should be conscious of the oneness of all who celebrate Eucharist with him. And in order that Eucharist may put all in touch with their own interiority, the presider sees to it that there are substantive moments of contemplative silence in the liturgy (e.g., before the prayers, after the readings, after the homily, at the time of Communion).

The Eucharistic "revolution" brought a radical change in Eucharistic vocabulary. Where we once restricted the role of "celebrant" to the priest, we now speak of the entire assembly as "celebrants." The priest presides over the celebration. Where we used to speak of the priest changing the bread and wine into the Body and Blood of Christ, we now see his role as a humbler one: to ask God to send the Holy Spirit to effect this change, in other words, to ask God to send the Holy Spirit to do for us now what Jesus did at the Last Supper. The words "This is my Body," "This is my Blood," are no longer referred to as the words of consecration, but rather as the words of institution (See, e.g., the *Catechism of the Catholic Church* which uses the words "the institution narrative" [the French text is even more expressive *le recit de l'institution*] #1353). They are a recital of what Jesus did at the Supper that become effective *now* through the action of the Spirit of God.

There is no question that the priest's role in today's Eucharist is a more modest role than it was in the Tridentine liturgy. At center stage in the Eucharist is the assembly, not the priest. Some one wrote to me recently and suggested the following scenario as indicative of a wonderful understanding of Eucharist. A person emerges from Church on a Sunday morning. Someone asks her: "Who celebrated the ten o'clock Mass?" She answers: "Oh, about three or four hundred of us and Fr. Smith presided. It was a great celebration. We truly experienced the presence of Christ and our oneness with him."

This approach to collaborative leadership in worship makes significant demands on us priests as presiders. Our task is to help people who come from varied life situations, with a multiplicity of problems, cares and concerns, to discover and respond to the presence of the risen Jesus in the Eucharistic celebration. We have to be welcoming, encouraging, inviting and sharing. A pre-Vatican II bishop whom I knew used to speak of "reading Mass." We are called not just to the reading of a text, but to the proclamation of a message and that message will always be simply: "Christ has died. Christ has risen. Christ will come again." Our responsibility is to concretize that message for those who celebrate with us.

We are not just leaders at worship who must call forth the full, active, knowledgeable participation of God's people; we are also promoters of a deeper spirituality which more and more people long for: a spirituality that goes beyond devotional exercises to an awakening of a deep sense of that union with God which I have already described as interiority. Among other things, this means learning the value of silence. As I have already suggested, the priest as presider at the Eucharist must bring a contemplative dimension to the celebration of liturgy. Moments of silence in Eucharistic gathering and at other times in the midst of our day's activities, can be a powerful way of helping all the faithful to realize their oneness in the Lord: that they too are the Body of Christ.

Some people do not know how to deal with silence: it almost seems to embarrass them. One of the greatest gifts a priest can contribute to the people he serves is an appreciation of the value of silence, not only in liturgy, but also in daily life. Clearly he can only do this authentically, if silence has become a regular and significant element in his own life. We must realize and help others to realize that there is so much more to life than the fleeting fragments of it that we catch in our words. Life is not an uninterrupted flow of words which is finally silenced only by death. Rather life, if it is true and genuine, develops in silence, comes to the surface in authentic words and returns to a deeper silence. At the end of life we speak our most authentic word of all, our final declaration of who we are in our depths. That word, which is our Amen to this life, ushers us into the eternal silence of God.[14]

All this means that the priest takes on a role that previously was not familiar to us, that is to offer spiritual direction to those who seek to follow the invitation of the Spirit in walking the path that leads to true interiority of life. It also means encouraging some of "the other faithful" to prepare themselves to carry on the ministry of spiritual direction. We may even involve ourselves in the process of that preparation. The more our lives are enriched by a spirituality of interiority, the more will we be eager to awaken in others this sense of awareness of God and the divine presence in their lives. Nor is this awakening a one-way operation. As people share with us the story of how God has been acting in their lives, our own spirituality is enriched by the sharing.

The Priest's Role as Teacher

The primary duty of the priest is the proclamation of the good news. We are called to be teachers: in the classroom, in the lectures we give, in RCIA programs, in adult faith-formation. Among the many teaching functions we perform, the most important is the preaching of the Sunday homily. This calls for much prayer, reflection, study, reading, consultation with the parish liturgy committee and the development of good rhetoric. *The lectionary is our most important book.*

We have at our liturgy a much more sophisticated and educated community than we preached to in yesteryear. To treat lightly our responsibility for the Sunday homily is to fail in one of the principal ways available to us for the promotion of the reign of God. To preach a good homily we need to love the scriptures. A wealth of excellent commentaries is easily at hand. We need to be acquainted with at least some of them.

What should we try to achieve in a homily? I recall a conversation I had with a woman who was deeply committed to social justice. She told me that one day she spoke with her pastor and expressed the hope that he would use his homilies to challenge people more. The priest told her that he felt that the purpose of the homily was to bring comfort to people. We have to ask the question: what form should our homilies take: challenge or comfort? If we look at the preaching of

Jesus, it is clear that he did both. And so must we. We need to communicate a sense of joy in living the Gospel; yet there are times when the Gospel calls us to risk saying the unpopular when we are convinced that it must be said. Jesus took the risk of saying the unpopular and it cost him his life. So did Oscar Romero and so many others before him and since, and they paid the same price.

The teaching ministry of the priest is by no means limited to the teaching that takes place at liturgy. There is the need of instructing the young, the parents of those whose children are to be baptized, those who are preparing for marriage. More than all these, there is the faith-formation that must be a life-time experience in the lives of all the faithful, including the priest. Priests need to keep themselves conversant with the teaching of the magisterium, the reflections of theologians, the many things written today about spirituality. This is in truth a life-journey and today there are many more of the other faithful who will be eager to accompany us on this journey. We are all fellow-travelers.

Our aim in teaching Catholic faith, morals and spirituality is to create in the whole Church a membership that is well-informed and, at the same time, enabled and encouraged to think for themselves. Our teaching must reveal our commitment to the basic unity of faith formulas, moral principles, and spiritual guidelines. The result we look for is conviction, not just submission, commitment, not mere acceptance, maturity rather than simplistic compliance. What we teach must draw on many sources: Scripture, the living tradition of the Church, the magisterium, the teaching of theologians and the experience of the Christian community. Yet in all our teaching, we need to remember, as Merton puts it: "We must announce the Person of Christ, not certain formulae."[15]

It behooves us also to remember that not all teaching in the Church comes "from above." While giving due respect and proper assent to the teachings of the magisterium, we must keep in mind that listening to public opinion in the community of God's people is an important way of hearing "what the Spirit is saying to the churches" (Rev 2:7). The "sense of the faithful" is not extrinsic to the Church's living tradition, but an important formative element within that tradition. We need to value the experience of Christian people striving to live Gospel imperatives in their lives.

The Priest and Pastoral Care

Leaders and teachers, we are also called to exercise pastoral care. Pastoral needs, once relatively easy to define, have become more diverse and more demanding. There are the needs of the handicapped and the elderly. Multi-lingual and multi-cultural diversity calls for special concern and training. People in marriages that are broken or on the verge of breaking have claims on our sympathetic understanding and willingness to help. The number of widowed, separated, and divorced steadily increases. We need to extend compassion to them and at the same time develop the ability to listen to what they have to say to us. How do we help people through an annulment process? What do we have to offer to those who view it as a demeaning process? What do we have to say to people who live in divisive situations and who daily face violence in their homes and in their neighborhoods? And there are the poor, the homeless, the hungry, the marginalized, the victims of our society who have a privileged claim on our ministry. In the Decree on the Ministry and life of Priests, Vatican II said: "Although he has obligations to all persons, the priest has the poor and the lowly entrusted to him in a special way" (art. 6, par. 3).

From my seminary days I recall a talk given by Fr. Leonard Feeney. I don't remember much of the content of the talk, but an aside he made in the course of it has always remained with me. "If you want the people you serve to love and care for you, despite your faults and failings," he said, "be kind to their babies, their brides and their dead." It was wise advice, though his list of crucial moments must not be taken as exclusive. Other moments of crisis, that we cannot always anticipate, will arise in people's lives. What we do for them or to them at these times will have lasting effects. Sensitivity to them and their loved ones in particularly meaningful times in their lives will often affect the feelings they will have about church, about priesthood and even about God. A priest who strives to live a truly interior life will be better able to enter into the sufferings and sorrows of people from the inside, rather than being a sympathetic, but outside, spectator. For his interiority will not allow him to forget his contemplative union with all of God's people.

In speaking about pastoral care, let us not forget that we are still talking about collaborative ministry. The priest is not a Lone Ranger in offering pastoral care. There will be others of the faithful whose caring and nurturing skills may well be far superior to our own. Our task is to tap these resources for the good of the whole body of Christ.

To conclude, perhaps somewhat abruptly, let us not forget either that we are speaking of a ministry that flows, ideally at least, from a deep interiority on the part of the priest (and also of the other faithful). That is why in this chapter, discussing the spirituality of the diocesan priest, I have *chosen to "Speak out for the inside."*

Notes

[1] Portions of this chapter have previously appeared, though in different contexts, in two journal articles of mine: "Thomas Merton: Contemplative Spirituality as Lived Wisdom," in the *Catholic Library World*, April/May/June 1995, and "Eucharistic Revolution," in *America*, May 20, 1995.

[2] *Thomas Merton, Witness to Freedom: Letters in Times of Crisis*, William H. Shannon, ed. (New York: Farrar Straus and Giroux, 1994). 329–30.

[3] *Lumen gentium*, art. 32.

[4] *Selections on Prayer*, unpublished typescript (Louisville: Merton Center, 1961) 1.

[5] Thomas Merton, *The New Man* (New York: Farrar Straus and Cudahy, 1961) 19.

[6] Thomas Merton, *The Asian Journal* (New York: New Directions, 1973) 308.

[7] Thomas Merton, *Contemplation in a World of Action* (New York: Doubleday Image, 1973) 161.

[8] Thomas *Merton in Alaska* (New York: New Directions, 1988) 160. (Hereafter *TMA*.)

[9] "Editorials," *The Nation*, 260, no. 14 (April 10, 1995) 476.

[10] Thomas Merton, *Loving and Living* (New York: Farrar Straus and Giroux, 1979) 40. (Hereafter *LL*.).

[11] Thomas Merton, *The Sign of Jonas* (New York: Harcourt Brace, 1953) 262.

[12] *LL*, 43.

[13] *Lumen gentium*, art. 33.

[14] Cf. Thomas Merton, *No Man Is an Island* (New York: Harcourt Brace, 1955) 261.

[15] *TMA*, 158.

8

A Glorious and Transcendent Place

Robert F. Morneau

Introduction

One approach to the spiritual life is by way of phenomenology, a careful, reflective description of what actually happens within the soul in its attempt to be authentic and loving in its journey into God and community. There are other paths to the understanding of spirituality. One deals with the classics, extracting the wisdom of the mystics and doctors of the Church. Another is a deductive analysis of the magisterial documents, listing principles and foundations for spiritual growth. Yet a third is a therapeutic approach, noting the obstacles in a given time to union with God and one another and being assisted in overcoming them.

But phenomenology is not without its difficulties. What phenomena are we to address and describe within diocesan priesthood: the retired priest who served fifty years, a time cutting across a history of massive transition? The newly ordained associate who is fresh out of the seminary laden with ideals and dreams of the kingdom? The silver jubilarian who wonders if twenty-five more years is possible, given the mid-life tensions? And then there are diocesan priests who are in full-time administration, teaching, counseling, etc. Is there a single spirituality for the diocesan priest, and how can it be described and analyzed with any accuracy?

Despite all these varied circumstances and possible obstacles, I do think that the diocesan priest, whatever his age or situation, is called in a four-fold way to be a listener and a lover, the core of what spirituality is all about. When we get down to the bare bones, "all" that is asked is an authentic obedience and a courageous response to the unique calling and circumstances of one's life. Of course, that "all" is everything and the price is the gift of oneself.

Four paths, not two roads as Robert Frost suggests, lie before the diocesan priest and his task is to spend quality time on each: the pastoral path, the preaching path, the philosophical path, the poetic path. My conviction is that Jesus has led the way and invites the ordained minister to follow. Jesus has integrated these four paths into a single road leading from Bethlehem to Calvary, journeying with the people, proclaiming in word and deed the Good News, seeking truth and wisdom that provides a vision, imaging life in such a way that hope is rekindled and charity becomes the single passion of life. The vocation of the diocesan priest, I think, lies in following Jesus along the road he himself chose.

The Pastoral Path: "Teach me thy love to know"

An oration for the funeral of a priest:

> Lord God,
> you chose our brother N. to serve your people as a priest
> and to share the joys and burdens of their lives.
> Look with mercy on him
> and give him the reward of his labors,
> the fullness of life promised to those
> who preach your holy Gospel.
> We ask this through Christ our Lord. Amen.

A key principle of spirituality is to be clear about its origin. God initiates the relationship that is the essence of spirituality. God chooses a people and enters into a covenant that carries with it privileges and demands. God calls a priest to serve the community and to be an instrument of peace and grace. Spirituality is not Emersonian "self-reliance"; spirituality is not something that a priest does on his own initiative. Rather, it is a response to a unique invitation to serve the people with one's whole life.

That principle having been articulated, we come to the beautiful but demanding pastoral task of a diocesan priest's spirituality: to share the joys and burdens of people's lives. It is an apostolic spirituality with a strong contemplative dimension but not one that is cloistered. Personal presence (as one priest put it, "I go to every dog hanging") is a way of life. Participation in the messiness of the human condition is literally the order of the day.

Sharing joys, the joy of birth, the joy of love, the joy of anniversaries, plunges the priest into the gratuity of God's grace. All is gift and the priest reminds the people, often by word, always by presence, that the Source of the gift deserves our thanks and praise. Nothing is to be taken for granted, nothing is to be assumed as a right. By sharing in the joys of the people those joys are multiplied many times over.

One of the anguishes of this type of spirituality is that one can be invited into the joys of other people when one's own heart is down, even in deep anxiety. Tremendous grace and personal sacrifice is needed to transcend one's own dark situation so as not to dampen the joy of others. Like the actress who has a terminally ill child and who has to continue to perform the comic opera, so the priest is challenged to enter into festivities even when his spirits are laden with pain.

A spirituality of pastoral sharing also embraces burdens. The tragedy of suicide, the wrenching pain of divorce, the news of cancer, the rejection of a parent or child, the hatred within family systems, the scandals that cause disillusion, the violence that shatters innocence—all come to rest at the feet of the diocesan priest on a weekly basis. Not to be overwhelmed by such weighty issues, not to yield to "compassion fatigue," not to quit are challenges that, if accepted, not only do not weaken one's relationships with God and others but strengthen them many times over.

Ministry, this serving of and sharing in the life of the people, is a central avenue by which God speaks to and encounters the diocesan priest. Ministry is much more than doing, it is encounter. Jesus becomes manifest in the hungry and imprisoned, in the lonely and shy, in the last and the least. God's will is done by responding with courage and love to the poor and abandoned, the hopeless and lost, the forgotten and dying. It's a street spirituality, rooted in prayer and worship, but expressed in orthopraxis. It's a spirituality that demands great flexibility and sacrificial generosity. Diocesan spirituality is all-consuming and therefore salvific.

The Anglican pastor, George Herbert (1593–1633), a noble country parson, captures aspects of this pastoral spirituality in his poem "Matins." What is needed most is love—"Teach me your love to know"—for it is charity above all that underlies pastoral duties. Here is the request for love in full context:

Matins

I cannot ope mine eyes,
But thou art ready there to catch
My morning soul and sacrifice:

Then we must needs for that day make a match.

> My God, what is a heart?
> Silver, or gold, or precious stone,
> Or star, or rainbow, or a part
> Of all these things, or all of them in one?

> My God, what is a heart?
> That thou shouldst it so eye, and woo,
> Pouring upon it all thy art,
> As if that thou hadst nothing else to do?

> Indeed man's whole estate
> Amount (and richly) to serve thee:
> He did not heav'n and earth create,
> Yet studies them, not him by whom they be.

> Teach us thy love to know;
> That this new light, which now I see,
> May both the work and workman show:
> Then by a sunbeam I will climb to thee.[1]

Thus the pastoral path of the diocesan priest's spirituality is grounded in the call to holiness, the perfection of love. If serving and sharing is done without a loving heart, little or nothing will be ultimately accomplished. But this is a solid love, often a tough love, not based on feeling alone nor on romanticism. Love is as solid as the cross, as persistent as quackgrass. It flinches at nothing, it cannot be rooted out even in times of drought. Pastoral spirituality is a love for the people unto death. It identifies with the joys and sorrows of a broken world.

In Vatican II's "Decree on the Ministry of Life of Priests," a linkage is made between celibacy and this spirituality of serving and sharing:

> Celibacy accords with the priesthood on many scores. For the whole priestly mission is dedicated to that new humanity which Christ, the conqueror of death, raises up in the world through His Spirit. This humanity takes its origin "not of blood, nor of the will of the flesh, nor of the will of man, but of God." (Jn 1:13). Through virginity or celibacy observed for the sake of the kingdom of heaven, priests are consecrated to Christ in a new and distinguished way. They more easily hold fast to Him with undivided heart. They more freely devote themselves in Him and through Him to the service of God and men. They more readily minister to His kingdom and to the work of heavenly regeneration, and thus become more apt to exercise paternity in Christ, and do so to a greater extent. (#16)[2]

Celibacy becomes inauthentic and can lead to a radical narcissism if priesthood is not characterized by intense devotion to the service of God and people, if the priestly heart is divided among many interests, if one's life is not truly generative. Like any other means, celibacy can be misused and abused. But when embraced as gift and grace, it leads to spiritual depths not imagined by the human heart.

The Preaching Path—"that glorious and transcendent place"

Diocesan priests stand before their people time and time again to proclaim and interpret the word of God. For many the time committed to this ministry is extensive: preparatory reading, study, prayer, writing, preaching itself. Most priests take with great seriousness their call to be preachers of the words, communicators of God's message whether convenient or inconvenient, as St. Paul reminds us. Preaching, according to the poet George Herbert, is a "glorious and transcendent place":

THE WINDOWS

Lord, how can man preach thy eternal word?
    He is a brittle crazy glass:
Yet in thy temple thou dost him afford
    This glorious and transcendent place,
    To be a window, through thy grace.

But when thou dost anneal in glass thy story,
    Making thy life to shine within
The holy Preacher's; then the light and glory
    More rev'rend grows, and more doth win:
    Which else shows wat'rish, bleak, and thin.

Doctrine and life, colors and light, in one
    When they combine and mingle, bring
A strong regard and awe: but speech alone
    Doth vanish like a flaring thing,
    And in the ear, not conscience ring.[3]

It is in "this glorious and transcendent place" that the priest does a number of things: provides the congregation with the words helpful in expressing their faith; helps to interpret life in relation to God's designs and purposes; leads people to a greater unity of faith, hope, and charity; assists a pilgrim people in facing the ambiguities, terrors, and challenges of life; provides reasons why we should praise and thank our God. In another poem Herbert maintains that "praying is the end of preaching."

It is the word of God that forms and sustains the spiritual life of the Christian community. In a special way that word is formative of the mind and heart of the diocesan priest. His spirituality is necessarily scriptural in nature. Part of the uniqueness of his journey to God lies in the following passage: "Every high priest chosen from among mortals is put in charge of things pertaining to God on their behalf, to offer gifts and sacrifices for sins. He is able to deal gently with the ignorant and wayward, since he himself is subject to weakness; and because of this he must offer sacrifice for his own sins as well as for those of the people" (Heb 5:1-3).[4] Much thought over the centuries has been given to the ontological nature of the priest, reflections which at times have been illuminating, often confusing. What is not in doubt is the humanness of those chosen to ordained ministry. Priests are human beings, vulnerable to all of life's vicissitudes. Not only is the priest subject to sin, he too is a sinner like the rest of humanity. The spirituality lived here can be anguishing: ordained for the things pertaining to God, the priest knows himself as inadequate and weak, charged with Mystery and yet so finite. It is only through the grace of Christ and of the working of the Spirit that the priest can hope to fulfill his destiny.

In the ministry of preaching this scriptural passage from Hebrews informs both the tone and message shared with the people. The priest is one with his people, identifying with their weaknesses and struggles, capable of expressing compassion and tenderness, challenging the community and himself to trust in the mercy and providence of God. Arrogant preaching is blasphemous because it is a lie. It flows from an inauthentic spirituality devoid of humility which, if possessed, would ground us in the truth of things.

A second scriptural passage comes from the last supper discourse where Jesus speaks so intimately to his disciples:

> "I do not call you servants any longer, because the servant does not know what the master is doing; but I have called you friends, because I have made known to you everything that I have heard from my Father. You did not choose me but I chose you. And I appointed you to go and bear fruit, fruit that will last, so that the Father will give you whatever you ask him in my name" (John 15:15-16).

Spirituality for the diocesan priest is grounded in an intimate relationship with Jesus Christ. This is foundational. When that relationship is not nurtured by personal prayer, theological study, and constant vigilance, the whole edifice of one's personal vocation is in jeopardy. The Gospel reminds us that this relationship comes primarily from God's initiative. God chose us; we have the freedom to say yes or no. Just as that divine choice is renewed each day, so we must respond to this invitation. The genre of this relationship is more friendship than servanthood, though service will always be one of its essential expressions. The diocesan priest preaches from the position of a loving intimacy with God who also invites the people to a similar intimacy and the vocation to bear eternal fruit.

A third selection from Scripture undergirding the spirituality of the diocesan priest comes from St. Paul's Letter to Titus:

> For a bishop, as God's steward, must be blameless; he must not be arrogant or quick-tempered or addicted to wine or violent or greedy for gain; but he must be hospitable, a lover of goodness, prudent, upright, devout, and self-controlled. He must have a firm grasp of the word that is trustworthy in accordance with the teaching, so that he may be able both to preach with sound doctrine and to refute those who contradict it (1:7-9).

This portrait of bishop/priest sketches the nature of the authentic steward of God's word. Not only must that word be preached, it must be lived. Preaching is difficult since the preacher is never capable of fully living the word, be it love, hope, faith. Yet as long as there is an authentic struggle to not only preach but live the word, the people will be well served. Given the circumstances of the diocesan priest, parish life and all its many and complex ramifications, it is easy to see why St. Paul urges unto the bishop/priest the qualities of hospitality, love, prudence, moderation.

A significant part of the spirituality of a diocesan priest is closeness to the people. Preaching is one means of achieving this bonding, but it must be a type of preaching that is appropriate. Fred Craddock, one of the finest teachers of homiletics in our times, provides an insight that every preacher should paste on the door of the refrigerator:

> If these listeners can leave the service with no sense of having been put down; if their self-worth has been affirmed or restored; if God's love and grace are seen as available realities; if they are convinced that repentance and trust are acceptable to God; if there is more awareness of other persons and more hunger for covenanted life; then even strangers will likely say to the preacher, "You understand us quite well."[5]

Spirituality is about life, life in God. As God has given life to the priest, the life of grace and faith, that same life is to be shared with people. Helping people overcome self-hatred, showing them how to come into God's presence singing for joy, demonstrating that conversion is not only possible but filled with delight, challenging the community to do justice (now!), instilling a hunger for depth and destiny—such is the business of the priest who lives with and among his people. An alternative message must be offered to our people who are inundated with the sad news of individualism, consumerism, and racism.

Every retreat director knows from experience that the conferences given for the edification of the retreatants are also directed first and foremost to the director. George Herbert writes: "For in preaching to others, he forgets not himself, but is first a Sermon to himself, and then to others; growing with the growth of his Parish."[6] The pulpit, "that glorious and transcendent place," is also a painful and lowly geography. Whatever the topic of discourse, the preacher himself is the object of affirmation or confrontation. The preacher himself is bound to his people in a rich and intricate mutuality and together they grow or stagnate. The preaching ministry is highly participatory. The listeners are not inert and passive but are to be alert and responsive. Ultimately it is the Spirit teaching to and through the preacher; ultimately it is the Spirit who opens the ears and hearts of the congregation.

Is it not true that the perfect achievement of our spiritual life is truly dependent on the spiritual life of every other human being? (François Roustang) Even the scientific community and the study of the new physics demonstrates the interconnectedness of all life at every level. The spirituality of the diocesan priest is dependent upon the mature spiritual life of his people, the opposite also being true. Such being the case, an immense responsibility descends on all parties and we are drawn back into the theology of the Mystical Body of Christ. If one person suffers, we all suffer; if one rejoices, we all rejoice since we are members of a single body.

A last word regarding the preaching ministry so essential to the spirituality of the diocesan priest. "As soon as he notices that his thought or sermon shows signs of crystallizing in the order of essence, and is no longer nourished by love encountered existentially—for only love edifies, while knowledge inflates—he should be warned that he is in danger, and recognize a summons to go back to prayer."[7] Like the homing dove, spirituality keeps coming back to its proper roost, love. Preaching must be grounded in love for the people, in love for God. If anything else is its motivating force, the red flags surface, the waterfall is just ahead. Time to get back on our knees—preacher and congregation.

The Philosophical Path: "Is there in truth no beauty?"

For most diocesan priests, several years of philosophy were required before formal theological studies began. Nor was this requirement simply to learn a language system underlying the dense
vocabulary of theologians. Rather, philosophy, that love for wisdom
and truth, contained an intrinsic value. Through metaphysics one was
exposed to a vision of reality; in epistemology, one studied the ways
of knowing, whether inductive or deductive; in ethics, human reason
took a crack at discovering the standards of moral decision making.
Philosophy, whatever its limits and ranging ambiguities, made strong
pursuit of the truth, a truth in which both beauty and goodness dwelt.

Again the poet George Herbert provides some basic questions:

Jordan (I)

Who says that fiction only and false hair
Become a verse? Is there in truth no beauty?
Is all good structure in a winding stair?
May no lines pass, except they do their duty
    Not to a true, but painted chair?

Is it no verse, except enchanted groves
And sudden arbors shadow coarse-spun lines?
Must purling streams refresh a lover's loves?
Must all be veil'd, while he that reads, divines,
    Catching the sense at two removes?

Shepherds are honest people; let them sing
Riddle who list, for me, and pull for Prime:
I envy no man's nightingale or spring;
Nor let them punish me with loss of rhyme,
    Who plainly say, *My God, My King.*[8]

The spirituality of the diocesan priest is grounded in three truths
that have their roots in philosophy, their fruition in theology. The first
truth focuses in on the truth of oneness and unity, more specifically
the oneness between the diocesan priest and his diocesan bishop, the
oneness with the local church. The second truth relates to goodness,
the light of simple goodness that plunges into the world of darkness
and sin with the grace of reconciliation and mercy. Thirdly, the diocesan priest embraces the truth of beauty, the harmony and integration
that links together contemplation and action, adoration and service.

In Vatican II's Dogmatic Constitution on the Church *(Lumen
gentium)*, we find the truth of oneness and unity forcefully stated:

> By her relationship with Christ, the Church is a kind of sacrament or sign of intimate union with God, and of unity of all mankind. She is also an instrument for the achievement of such union and unity. For this reason, following in the path laid out by its predecessors, this Council wishes to set forth more precisely to the faithful and to the entire world the nature and encompassing mission of the Church. The conditions of this age lend special urgency to the Church's task of bringing all men to full union with Christ, since mankind today is joined together more closely than ever before by social, technical, and cultural bonds.[9]

The truth of this ecclesiology is the truth that oneness is the goal of life. Just as we have come from God, we are destined to return to be once again one with him, and one with all of our sisters and brothers. This oneness challenges contemporary philosophies and life-styles that maintain that we are autonomous selves, that individualism is our way of life, each person for himself or herself. Global solidarity is still an ideal in the minds of but a few. Nationalism reigns supreme; parochialism is the pragmatic way of living.

The diocesan priest, spiritual leader of a parish, does not work in isolation. The "Lone Ranger" image, capturing a good chunk of our national history, may be the operative metaphor for some diocesan priests but in the end it simply doesn't work. The diocesan priest is linked ecclesially, theologically and spiritually with the local church and with its appointed leader, the diocesan bishop. The spiritual importance of the Chrism Mass can hardly be over-emphasized. When the bishop and presbytery come together with representatives from each parish to bless the oils, renew commitments, and celebrate Mass, we have the basic ingredients of diocesan spirituality: liturgy of Word and Eucharist, the assembly gathered in song and prayer, the call to service and mission.

A perspective regarding the relationship between the diocesan bishop and his priests is given in *Christus Dominus*, the decree on the bishops' pastoral office in the Church from Vatican II:

> A bishop should always welcome priests with a special love since they assume in part the bishop's duties and cares and carry the weight of them day by day so zealously. He should regard his priests as sons and friends. Thus by his readiness to listen to them and by his trusting familiarity, a bishop can work to promote the whole pastoral work of the entire diocese.[10]

This truth of oneness, the very dream of God for the kingdom, must be understood and lived by the ministers of word and sacrament.

If there is an obvious division between the leadership personnel within the Church, extreme harm is done to diocesan life. This unity is more than just "getting along." It is, rather, a relationship built on a significant degree of trust and affection. It is a relationship centered on a common vision and commitment. The spirituality of the diocesan priest is linked inseparably to the larger life of the diocese and to its designated leader, the diocesan bishop.

The second truth along this philosophical path is that of goodness. In her novel *Middlemarch*, George Eliot notes: "That by desiring what is perfectly good even when we don't quite know what it is and cannot do what we would, we are part of the divine power against evil—widening the skirts of light and making the struggle with darkness narrower."[11] Spirituality is about goodness, about confronting the evils of oppression, injustice, and sin. The diocesan priest works in the midst of the world, challenged to "widen the skirts of light" and reduce the vast darkness that surrounds the lives of so many. One of the anguishes, and paradoxically, one of the blessings, is that the priest has to struggle with the darkness within himself, aware that his potential for doing evil is as great as that of any other individual. The goodness sought must, therefore, be characterized by compassion. We all carry with us our human condition which needs sympathy much more than judgment.

Shakespeare's Portia calls the world naughty: "That light we see is burning in my hall. How far that little candle throws its beams! So shines a good deed in a naughty world."[12] Portia's understatement emphasizes that our world is more than naughty. It is filled with violence and hatred, war and cruelty, indifference and chaos. Yet to be light in the darkness is essentially to follow the way of Jesus, the light to all the nations. The priest is ordained to follow the master, to live a life of discipleship that leads to peace. The light of goodness shines when the priest proclaims the good news of God's love, seeks out and saves those who are lost, shoulders the burdens and joys of others, leads people through (not around) suffering and death into the joy of the resurrection. To make that goodness incarnate, specific, concrete, is a major ingredient in the life of the diocesan priest.

The third truth deals with beauty. Herbert raises the question: "Is there in truth no beauty?" Certainly there is, and in large doses. Hegel maintained that beauty is "the spiritual making itself known sensuously." The great beauty of the spirituality of the diocesan priest is the Eucharist, the invasion of grace by means of the body and blood of Christ. What is more beautiful, what is more truthful than love become incarnate? To celebrate daily the mystery by which the spiritual

(Truth) becomes sensuous is an awesome responsibility. When that responsibility is not carried out well or without joy, things become ugly.

Ralph Waldo Emerson provides some insight into the mystery of beauty as part of the philosophical, spiritual path. Two reflections: "Beauty is the mark God sets upon virtue."[13] "Though we travel the world over to find the beautiful, we must carry it with us, or we find it not."[14] It is virtually impossible to separate the transcendentals. Goodness and beauty are linked by means of virtue. Vice discolors the plan of God, the faces of people. Virtue is illuminous and lightsome, bringing a radiance to our days that can accurately be called beautiful. And if beauty is not in the heart, deep within the soul, no amount of activity or travel will give us access to this grace of harmony and integrity known as beauty. The poet Ruth Mary Fox summarizes these thoughts: "You have drunk deep of beauty—so men say;/ You have known much of love." All spirituality returns to love in which we find all three truths: oneness, goodness and beauty.

The Poetic Path

Poetry is about language, language that is intense, intimate, and often, intimidating. Listen to the poetic genius of George Herbert in his direct dialogue with God:

Trinity Sunday

Lord, who hast form'd me out of mud,
And hast redeem'd me through thy blood,
And sanctifi'd me to do good;

Purge all my sins done heretofore:
For I confess my heavy score,
And I will strive to sin no more.

Enrich my heart, mouth, hands in me,
With faith, with hope, with charity;
That I may run, rise, rest with thee.[15]

Intensity characterizes this verse. In nine lines we have a condensed theology: a God who forms, redeems, sanctifies, purges, and enriches. More is said here than in many theological tomes. Intimacy can be felt as the poet's heart expresses deep affection and longing for spiritual depth. And, yes, intimidating, for we as readers must examine our personal lives to review how we relate to this triune God who purges so as to enrich us.

The diocesan priest straddles the prosaic and poetic worlds. Much of his life is routine, ordinary, somewhat undramatic. By contrast, much of his life is intense in searching for the right words to console the parents of a suicide or to use condensed language to capture the meaning of an anniversary or graduation. Much is intimate: witnessing the exchange of marriage vows, listening and responding to someone lost in sin and seeking forgiveness, sitting with the dying, moments before they encounter the mystery of God. Much is intimidating: meetings at which power plays are employed or board sessions involving accountability and evaluation. A poetic life—intense, intimate, intimidating—indeed!

One of the excellent poets of our century, Denise Levertov, provides a formula that underlies the dynamics of a poetic life.[16] It begins with reverence, a deep respect for all of life. This reverence leads to attention that is focused and concentrated. Then intense seeing or hearing enables the creative person to enter the mystery at hand, be a child's face, a rainbow, the Eucharist. A fourth element now comes into play: the discovery (or revelation) of form. A structure is needed whereby the intense experience of life can be expressed so as to be shared. If the form or structure is appropriate and relevant, then the song is sung, the homily is preached, the bonding of minds and hearts miraculously happens.

All of this involves a price, of course (no free lunches—no free homilies). Energy and discipline are requirements if the creative circle is to be run and enjoyed in any consistent manner. But the cost, however high, is worth the effort since it leads to a qualitative ministerial life. Parishioners will sense a degree of presence that touches their lives in a significant way. A "spirit" (*the* Spirit) will be experienced, guiding one to transformation at many different levels. Such poetic (creative) living nurtures the goal of the spiritual life: union with God, unity among ourselves.

Each of the five elements in this dynamic process deserves consideration. Reverence is that disposition that acknowledges the presence of the sacred. Moses, realizing that he was on holy ground, removed his sandals. The diocesan priest, whether at a wake service, teaching confirmation class, meeting with various councils, kneeling before the Blessed Sacrament, treads upon holy ground, and removes the inner sandals of his soul. God is present; reverence assists us in recognizing and responding to the mystery of Grace. Then St. Paul's strong advice that we pray always and everywhere becomes an actuality.

Attention or attentiveness, the second ingredient to living a creative-poetic-spiritual life, faces a number of immense obstacles.

Hurriedness begins the litany. Racing from one experience to another without reflection or brief pauses stunts our spiritual development and diminishes the quality of life. Would that the great evangelist John Wesley had told us the secret of his "though I am always in haste, I am never in a hurry." Parish work embraces a multitude of activities. Unless time is taken or a methodology is found to process the more significant moments of the day, one's whole existence can easily take on the metaphors of a rat-race, a merry-go-round.

Hurriedness is followed by a second obstacle infringing upon quality of life, *sic.*, an undeveloped hermeneutics. Each event in life demands some degree of interpretation, some discernment as being of God or not of God. Without a mature faith life, we interpret our lives in a secular fashion, failing to see the work of Providence. Wisdom is the gift needed whereby we trace the happenings of our days to their proper source. Third, narcissism prohibits attention because of excessive self-preoccupation that cuts us off from reality. No surprise that alienation and loneliness criss-cross our hearts. The diocesan priest, not immune from the rampant individualism of our age, is vulnerable to this narcissistic life-style that precludes a focusing on the common good and a passionate commitment to the Kingdom.

A diocesan priest hears and sees a lot. Many voices cry out and many needs become manifest to him, plunged as he is into the many-layered life of the parish. What spirituality brings to this situation is an intense seeing and hearing, at the level of the soul that enables the priest to "put first things first." To observe a branch severed from the vine calls for an immediate and radical response. A less intense hearing and seeing misidentifies the problem and the proposed cure can even worsen, rather than abate, the illness. Again, a price must be paid. Self-forgetfulness is part of the bill, a profound charity and concern for the other. There is, however, a payoff, a bonding between the priest and his people, a union that overflows into peace and joy. And, of course, to experience this intimacy arising out of intense hearing and seeing falls under the category of happiness.

The poetic life of the diocesan priest, a life that is creative and generative, enters a fourth phase: discovery or revelation of form. Christian spirituality is incarnational; it demands enfleshment. This belief comes out of an anthropology that links the sensory and spiritual spheres of human life. Amphibious by nature, we humans need a process of translation whereby the compassion and intense love planted in the heart by God now finds expression in word-deed-symbol consequent upon reverent attention to life. At times the expression (discovery of form) is sheer gift, a revelation from God as how to manifest one's inner experience. *The Confessions of St. Augustine* is an example of this grace. More often, perhaps, a diligent struggle and considerable amount of sweat is necessary in writing a homily, constructing a new religious education program, implementing decisions of the parish council.

Finally, the song must be sung, the vine must produce the grape, ministry must meet the need that results in peace. Apostolic action is an essential ingredient in the spirituality of the diocesan priest. This is a natural (supernatural) consequence of reverence, attention, intense seeing and hearing, discovery of form. What good is faith that fails in expression? It is dead, according to St. James. But when life given is shared, all is made new and the kingdom is enhanced. The mission of Jesus, fullness of life (John 10:10), finds articulation in the daily instrumentality of the diocesan priest.

Joseph Conrad, the great novelist, suggests that the task of the artist (poet, priest perhaps) is to make people pause for a moment to look at reality as if for the first time.[16] Even if the stopping is only for a sigh, a smile, a brief glance, the artist has achieved his/her goal. Spirituality aims at bonding us to Reality, the Reality of a creating, redeeming, sanctifying God. The spirituality of the diocesan priest has this same goal. Through Christ and in the Spirit, the priest points to the mystery of our Triune God and leads the people through the narrow gate of faith in quest of holiness. A poetic path, indeed, containing little that is prosaic.

Conclusion

The road to Emmaus led to a table upon which bread was broken. But before the breaking of the bread, wisdom was shared and hearts were kindled. After the bread was broken, good news was shared and Jesus was proclaimed as alive and risen. The spirituality of the diocesan priest, without being reductionistic, comes down to a lively encounter with the Lord, a sharing of life and food, a being sent forth to give what has been received. It is a spirituality of discernment, stewardship and evangelization. One concluding poem from George Herbert, a poem which confirms the thesis that Don Jean-Baptiste Chautard presented in his classic *The Soul of the Apostolate*: the effectiveness of our ministry is dependent on our interior life. Herbert's poem gives us the invitation; we must make the response:

Love (III)

Love bade me welcome: yet my soul drew back,
  Guilty of dust and sin.

But quick-ey'd Love, observing me grow slack
   From my first entrance in,
Drew nearer to me, sweetly questioning,
   If I lack'd anything.

A guest, I answer'd, worthy to be here:
   Love said, You shall be he.
I the unkind, ungrateful? Ah my dear,
   I cannot look on thee.
Love took my hand, and smiling did reply,
   Who made the eyes but I?

Truth Lord, but I have marr'd them: let my shame
   Go where it doth deserve.
And know you not says, Love, who bore the blame?
   My dear, then I will serve.
You must sit down, says Love, and taste my meat:
   So I did sit and eat.[17]

Notes

[1] *George Herbert: The Country Parson, The Temple,* Edited, with an introduction by John N. Wall, Jr., preface by A. M. Allchin (New York: Paulist Press, 1981) 178.

[2] *The Documents of Vatican II,* ed. by Walter M. Abbott (New York: Herder and Herder, 1966) 565–566.

[3] *George Herbert: The Country Parson, The Temple,* 183.

[4] *The New Oxford Annotated Bible,* ed. by Bruce M. Metzger and Roland E. Murphy (New York: Oxford University Press, 1991) 320.

[5] Fred. B. Craddock, *Preaching* (Nashville: Abingdon Press, 1985) 90.

[6] *George Herbert,* 83.

[7] Hans Urs von Balthasar, *Prayer,* trans. by A. V. Littledale (New York: Sheed & Ward, 1961) 204.

[8] *George Herbert,* 171.

[9] *The Documents of Vatican II,* 15.

[10] Ibid., 408.

[11] George Eliot, *Middlemarch* (London: William Blackwood & Sons, 1871) 427.

[12] William Shakespeare, "The Merchant of Venice," V, i., 89–91.

[13] Ralph Waldo Emerson, "Nature," *The Selected Writing of Ralph Waldo Emerson,* edited, with a biographical introduction by Brooks Atkinson (New York: Random House, 1940) 11.

[14] Ralph Waldo Emerson, "Art," 309.

[15] *George Herbert,* 184.

¹⁶In her essay "Origins of a Poem," Denise Levertov writes: "All the thinking I do about poetry leads me back, always, to Reverence for Life as the ground for poetic activity; because it seems the ground of Attention . . . Without Attention—to the world outside us, to the voices within us—what poems could possibly come into existence? Attention is the exercise of Reverence for the 'other forms of life that want to live.' The progressions seem clear to me: from Reverence for Life to Attention to Life, from Attention to Life to a highly developed Seeing and Hearing, from Seeing and Hearing (faculties almost indistinguishable for the poet) to the Discovery and Revelation of Form, from Form to Song." (essay found in Donald Hall's *Claims of Poetry,* 264)

¹⁷*George Herbert,* 316.

9

Heralds of the Gospel and Experts in Humanity

Sylvester D. Ryan

On May 3, 1957, I was ordained a priest. On May 31, 1990, I was ordained a bishop. So, for thirty-three years I lived and worked as a priest in a variety of ministries. I engaged in the ministries of an associate priest and pastor, as an instructor in religious education and a teacher and principal in Catholic schools. At present my life as a diocesan bishop involves a significant amount of time in administration. Yet I am able to spend large portions of my days in the pastoral ministry of the care of souls.

I find it simpler, therefore, as I write on the spirituality of the diocesan priest to use the language of "we" rather than "you." I believe the same realities apply as equally and as urgently to the spirituality of the diocesan bishop as they do to the spirituality of the diocesan priest. At least, that is my personal conviction and the way I struggle to live my life and carry out my ministry as a bishop.

During the 1990 Synod of Bishops on the topic "The Formation of Priests in Circumstances of the Present Day," Bishop Joseph Abangite Gasi of the Sudan described the prevailing image of the priest held by the people of his diocese:

> The priest is seen as a messenger of God, sent to preach His word. . . his local nickname is "Carrier of God's Word." He teaches the faith as well as secular sciences, builds houses, is a carpenter, dispenses medicines besides administering the sacraments. The priest is seen as a man of God. He is expected to spend part of his time in union with God: talking and listening to him.[1]

Msgr. John J. Egan of Chicago makes the point that the Church ought not to ordain anyone "who doesn't give clear indications of loving people. A priest has got to be vulnerable. He must be willing to let people take little chunks out of him. A priest must always be open to people."[2]

During the Synod of 1990 several attending bishops quoted John Paul II:

> We need heralds of the Gospel, who are experts in humanity, who have shared to the full the joys and sorrows of our day, but who are at the same time, contemplatives in love with God.[3]

As we listen to contemporary reflections on the pastoral ministry of priests, such as those quoted above, we realize that they reflect and echo an understanding of the pastoral and missionary ministry of the Church that Jesus himself initiated:

> Jesus went around to all the towns and villages, teaching in their synagogues, proclaiming the gospel of the kingdom and curing every disease and illness. At the sight of the crowds his heart was moved with pity for them, for they were troubled and abandoned like sheep without a shepherd (Matt 9:35-39).

Yet the reflections and convictions of a Polish pope, an African bishop, and a midwestern American priest show that the mission and ministries Jesus shared with his apostles and disciples continue in the Church today. Jesus, the itinerant preacher, teacher, healer, and compassionate shepherd, finds new places, new people, as well as a dizzying variety of new circumstances in which to become embodied in the pastoral ministry of the Church and her priests.

Jesus wove the spirituality of his apostles and the disciples into the manner in which they shared in his power to preach the kingdom and heal the sick. Likewise, the spirituality of the diocesan priest is rooted in and flows from his pastoral ministry. The same elements of preaching, healing, caring for the neighbor, prayer, hospitality and table fellowship that we find in Jesus' formation of his disciples, remain true today for those engaged in the pastoral ministry.

This spirituality builds upon a sacramental foundation. It has its origins in the sacraments of baptism, confirmation, and eucharist. These sacraments of initiation provide the primary identity of the priest as one who comes from and engages in a pastoral ministry for the people of God. As in the life of Jesus Christ, our baptismal event becomes an initiation experience of the Father's love and the Spirit's power in all our lives. Jesus' baptism and prayer at the Jordan river ushered in the descent of the Holy Spirit, and the Father's outspoken love: "You are my beloved son; with you I am well pleased" (Luke 3:22).

In Acts 1:5, the risen Christ promised the nascent community of disciples that they also would "be baptized with the Holy Spirit." The infusion of the Holy Spirit and the Father's affirmation to each one of us that we are "his beloved," begun in baptism and continued in the ongoing Pentecostal experience of the Church, establishes our faith journey in the truth of God's love for each of us. Whatever the combination of human means or events by which we come to the awareness and acceptance of this good news, we begin and continue our authentic spiritual journey in the personal conviction and experience of the Father's love for us in Christ and the Holy Spirit.

Baptism, confirmation, and eucharist, therefore, constitute each of us as members of the community of faith. In a special sense these sacraments provide the same foundation for the spirituality of the diocesan priest as they do for the spirituality of God's people. The sacrament of baptism plunges us into the mystery of Christ's dying so that we may share with him in his victory over sin and death. Through baptism, the passion, death, and resurrection of Christ stand as the primary symbol of the realities of our journey of faith whatever our specific role within the Church.

The sacrament of orders places the priest (and the bishop) in the midst of the Church as one invested with the role and service of pastoral leadership. This pastoral mission of the diocesan priest empowers us to minister to human and spiritual needs "of the crowds" even as Jesus did in the Gospels. This mission constitutes a spirituality formed from our relationship to God the Father, in Christ, and through the Holy Spirit, and our relationship of love and service to all our sisters and brothers. The people of God whom we serve in our priestly ministry become for us our "religious community." Our spirituality and our mission coincide in Christ's commandment: "I give you a new commandment: love one another. As I have loved you, so you also should love one another. This is how all will know that you are my disciples, if you have love for one another." (John 13:34).

Word and Sacrament

The Gospel of St. Luke, chapter 9, marked a watershed moment in the public ministry of Jesus. He had proclaimed the good news of salvation to the crowds. He called people to discipleship. He established the foundations of the new Israel. Now he must journey toward Jerusalem. It was time for him, therefore, to focus his attention on the formation of his apostles and disciples for their mission of evangelization. He had to prepare them for their responsibility to continue his work of teaching and healing:

> He summoned the Twelve and gave them power and authority over all demons and to cure diseases, and he sent them to proclaim the kingdom of God and to heal the sick (Luke 9:1-2).

As Jesus did then, the risen Christ does now, calling us through the sacrament of holy orders to share in his power and authority to preach the kingdom of God and to heal. To preach the kingdom means to undertake the responsibility of hearing and spreading God's message of love and mercy. In preaching the kingdom we assume the task of becoming the "Carrier of God's word." All of our pastoral ministry, therefore, as priests and bishops involves, in a primary way, the word of God.

We preach the word on Sundays and feast days. The Church urges and expects us to prepare a brief homily even for our daily Masses with people. All the sacramental rites include selections of the Scriptures as special envelopes of the grace of the sacraments. We ground our teaching, catechizing, evangelizing, and liturgical actions as well as our commitment to social justice in the word of God.

In doing so, we nourish a profound appreciation of the sacredness and power of the Scriptures for the life of the Church and our ministry. The decree of Vatican II on the liturgy expressed this appreciation in these words: "Christ is present in his word, since it is himself who speaks when the Holy Scriptures are read in the Church."[4]

The crafting and preaching of the word of God challenges our minds, hearts, and imaginations. It demands time, creativity, and authenticity. Somewhere I remember reading that preaching is the task of breaking through the screens people have in front of them so that the word of God can reach into their hearts. This breakthrough, however, starts with ourselves. The word of God calls to us, speaks to us, searches out the innermost rooms of our heart and affections. We must allow the word its entry into the sanctuary of our own souls.

Jesus gave us the model of authentic preaching. After his baptism at the Jordan and the temptations in the desert, he returned to Nazareth full of the Holy Spirit, and on the Sabbath, he entered the synagogue. He was given the scroll of Scriptures, and having unrolled the scroll, read from Isaiah 61. Then he said to the assembly of his own townspeople: "Today this scripture passage is fulfilled in your hearing" (Luke 4:21).

Jesus returned to his own town imbued thoroughly with the word of God. From childhood his spiritual understanding and sensitivity had been nourished by the Hebrew Scriptures. The desert experience became an immersion experience into the word of God. He spoke from a self steeped in the word.

We do not approach the Scriptures first to find a homily. We go to the Scriptures because we, ourselves, hunger and thirst for the word, the word made flesh in the person of Jesus Christ, and the word inspired by the Holy Spirit. We wrestle to comprehend the word because our souls are at stake, and because we want to open our hearts so that the word may penetrate into the inmost places of our souls. The word calls us to conversion, and conversion enables us authentically to preach the word of God.

St. Paul provides us with this insight when he writes in Hebrews:

> Indeed, the Word of God is living and effective, sharper than any two-edged sword, penetrating even between soul and spirit, joints and marrow, and able to discern reflections and thoughts of the heart (Heb 4:12).

When we preside at a Sunday liturgy, for example, and have proclaimed the Gospel and begin our homily, we are measured not only in terms of what we have crafted for the homily and how we deliver the word, but also how we have (with the grace of God) crafted our life of faith and our personal character. Both are inextricably wrapped together. We are vulnerable when we preach. The ambo does not allow anonymity. It is evident to people when the word we preach flows out of the word implanted in our own hearts.

None of this should intimidate us. Sometimes we find clarity and security in God's word. Sometimes we wrestle with the word and find ambiguity and even a sense of our own unworthiness. We fear we cannot live up to all that God asks of us, and what people expect of us. "Depart from me, for I am a sinful man, O Lord," Simon Peter exclaimed to Jesus after he saw the astonishing draft of fish in his nets. In reply Jesus said to him: "Do not be afraid: from now on you will be catching men" (Luke 5:8, 10).

First, we pray over the Scriptures we preach, searching and studying them, for they are God's word speaking directly to us. We listen to the Holy Spirit, struggling, sometimes, in our attempts to respond generously to the word in faith, and then we move to the tasks of preparing and preaching the homily. Prayer and the work of preaching, then, serve as the anchors of our spirituality.

Since our ministry is the stuff of our spiritual life as diocesan priests, the work of preparing and preaching homilies and celebrating the sacraments constitutes an integral part of the depth of our relationship with Christ. As ministers and presiders of the liturgy and sacraments, we need to enter into the mysteries we celebrate just as wholeheartedly as do those who are the recipients and collaborators of these sacraments with us.

All sacramental liturgies are acts of worship, prayer, and redemption. Therefore, this collective prayer of the community moves us priests, as both believers and ministers, as closely into union with Christ as is possible. Liturgy is not something we do after we pray, but the primary prayer of our lives. The ministry of liturgy is the school of our spirituality.

It does not take much time in our pastoral ministry to appreciate the power of sacramental grace even for ourselves as ministers of the sacraments. Which one of us has not had times when, because of fatigue, discouragement, or for some other reason, we were not looking forward to another scheduled wedding, baptism, hearing of confessions, or the Sunday's final Mass and homily, only to find ourselves energized by the sacramental celebration itself?

The Healing Ministry

"Then they set out and went from village to village proclaiming the good news and curing diseases everywhere" (Luke 9:6).

Most of us diocesan priests do not minister as itinerant preachers, although the growing shortage of priests may demand of some of us a ministry of serving several parishes at the same time, not unlike St. Luke's narrative picture of the apostles. We are, however, called to be the shepherds and healers of the people we serve whatever the manner and place of our diocesan priestly ministry.

Preaching the word of God and healing, moreover, are tied together. Faith in general and preaching in particular requires that we take the truth of the incarnation most seriously: "The Word became flesh and made his dwelling among us" (John 1:13). Jesus Christ was truly Son of God, and Son of Mary. From this fundamental truth of our faith we learn to reverence our own humanity because God himself has taken our humanity so seriously both in creation and the incarnation.

Human experience serves as an important source both for the healing ministry and the effective preaching of the word of God. As shepherds we are drawn into the lives of people. Our availability and compassion serve as the signs of our authenticity as priests. Availability and compassion require empathy, not detachment from the human struggle of the people we serve.

Priests involved in parish ministry or its pastoral counterparts in schools, hospitals, and institutions, deal with the everyday drama of people's lives. The empathetic priest rejoices and celebrates with people the birth and baptism of children, first communions, confirmations, weddings, and the many other occasions of joy and splendor that sanctify the human experience. Such a priest also aches with people in their sorrows, tragedies, and disappointments. He listens to their troubles, counsels them in their decisions, supports them during prolonged difficulties and problems. He may share many a meal with the people he serves, and learns firsthand the interpersonal dynamics of each family life. He becomes aware of their individual and collective struggles to be faithful to themselves, their families, their commitments, indeed to the faith itself.

Such priestly availability and empathy is both joyous and painful. One pays a price for sharing in people's lives so completely. Yet, because of this fact, we preach to people we know perhaps more intimately than anyone outside of the family circle. This kind of knowing gives realism and humanness to our preaching that translates the gospel message into a compelling one as we struggle to articulate the good news with honesty and care.

In fact, the NCCB publication *Fulfilled in Your Hearing* on the preaching of God's word makes a powerful point of the priest-homilist averting to the ongoing connection between God's word and people' struggles of faith:

> If the homily must be faithful to the Scriptures for it to be the living Word of God, it must also be faithful to the congregation to whom this living Word of God is addressed. The homily will be effective in enabling a community to worship God with praise and thanksgiving only if individuals in that community recognize there a word that responds to the implicit or explicit questions of their lives.[5]

Our involvement in the lives of people permits us to take their spiritual pulse and to respond competently and compassionately to their needs. Ministry and spirituality combine in our love and service to the neighbor. Here is where each of us with our own unique set of gifts and limitations, finds a richness of spirituality in carrying out to the best of his ability the compassionate mission Christ and the Church have entrusted to him.

God, as Father, Son, and Spirit, stands as the fundamental revelation of our faith and the Gospel. It is a revelation that God in his inmost being is relational. We, as human beings, made in God's image and likeness, are relational. The sacraments, the ritual inter-actions of the risen Christ and his people, are relational. Priestly ministry, at its highest level, is relational. How we relate to our God, who is for us, and to our neighbor, who is with us, sums up the whole law and the prophets.

A priest's availability and compassion for his people, his readiness to share their lives, ministering to them with empathy, skill and time, all are vital elements in our ministry as diocesan priests. Such tasks are demanding. They can be overwhelming at times. Moreover, although the pastoral ministry requires nurturing skills, it calls for leadership skills as well. Shepherds must be prophets. But anyone who dares to respond to God's call as a priest-prophet will inevitably meet with contradiction and opposition in his care of the flock.

The Cross and Discipleship

> Herod the tetrarch heard about all that was happening, and he was greatly perplexed because some were saying, "John has been raised from the dead." . . . But Herod said, "John, I beheaded. Who then is this about whom I hear such things. And he kept trying to see him" (Luke 9:7, 9).

In the person of Herod, the long shadow of the cross moves across Luke's narrative of the mission of the apostles and the identity of Jesus. Jesus had set his face like flint for Jerusalem, and in the following chapters Jesus makes the point over and over that those whom he has chosen as disciples must associate themselves with him in his passion and death.

We meet aspects of the cross in the reality of ministry itself. We find it in our actual day to day experience of priestly service: in the demands on our time, the complexities of administration, the numbers of people approaching us, and the flood of human needs that surround us. We can be the targets of harsh criticism sometimes coming from the very people we are called upon to serve. We often find ourselves caught in the middle of the conflicting understandings of

Church and priesthood that so often polarize our Catholic people today.

We also wrestle with our own weaknesses, loneliness and isolation. We can be dismayed by the absence of tangible results in our ministries. We may find ourselves discouraged by the recent bitter scandals of brother priests, and the strident harshness of public criticism of the Church and the priesthood. We may have our own difficulties with what appears to be the rigidity or insensitivity of the official Church to the issues and concerns that fall heavily on the shoulders of people in our parishes.

As diocesan priests, especially those responsible for parish life, we seek to master the demands of collaborative leadership. Many priests have discovered undreamed of blessings for their pastoral practice in the collaboration and cooperation of brother priests, deacons, religious, and highly educated and trained lay people as partners and team members for ministry. This developing pattern of ministry and evangelization in our parishes, however, has presented priests with its own set of challenges and difficulties, misunderstandings and friction in the pastoral work of a priest.

Our vision of the Church may present a source of difficulty for us when we see so clearly what needs to be done to accomplish the mission of the Church today: that is to evangelize, to catechize, to instill a sense of stewardship; to empower a truly participatory and worshipping community; to serve the needs of the poor in our community; to form our youth as the mature, committed, active Catholics the Church desperately needs now. Yet, all too often our resources appear inadequate to the task.

We can add to all the above our family responsibilities and ties, special demands of ministry, our personal emotional patterns of response and inter-action with people, as well as our health concerns and just ordinary daily endurance. We need not, then, search outside our own lives and ministry for the asceticism and place of the cross in our spiritual journey. We encounter the cross in the very nature of things involved in priesthood and ministry.

In these circumstances and demands of pastoral life, the Gospel calls for us to strive for patience, understanding, kindness, forgiveness, healing, and the perseverance that leadership demands. All of which embodies Jesus' instructions on the cost and the spirituality of discipleship:

> "If anyone wishes to come after me, he must deny himself and take up his cross daily and follow me" (Luke 9:23).

Apart with the Lord

> When the apostles returned, they explained to him what they had done. He took them and withdrew in private to a town called Bethsaida (Luke 9:11).

As priests we speak constantly, in season and out of season, of God's love for every human person. It is our task, our mission, our "business." Somehow or other, though, we priests find it difficult to internalize the truth that God loves us—loves me! We certainly are aware that there are people who find it hard to believe that anyone really loves them, just for their very own sake. Yet it is the basic conviction of our belief that God loves us so! We need to accept that love, to feel it profoundly, individually, in our being! We, the ministering persons, need our own conversion experience or even several conversion moments in order to own and cherish this truth for ourselves.

The entirety of salvation history, especially the Gospels, contains and proclaims one fundamental truth: God loves us with an everlasting love. This love is personal to each one of us. Jesus Christ is the love of God "made flesh" and shows forth this love as a sharing in his own relationship with his Father.

Jesus makes this "grace," this unconditional and deeply human love, the hallmark of his bonding with his apostles:

> "As the Father loves me, so I also love you. Remain in my love . . . I have called you my friends because I have told you everything I have heard from my Father" (John 15:9, 15).

In our priestly journey faith moves us to appropriate this love of God for us. We yearn for this love. We are made for this love. We hunger for this love of Christ in our lives. We believe deeply in the truth of the words of our own ordination: "With a brother's love, Christ chooses men to share his sacred ministry by the laying on of hands."

When the apostles returned from carrying out the mission Jesus had entrusted to them, he took them and withdrew apart. He withdrew apart with them precisely to reaffirm his love and his Father's love for them. He did not love a generic group of people, the crowds if you will, but THIS group of apostles. He knew them intimately and loved them completely as brothers and friends.

Christ has chosen us to be his friends and his priests. We are called to the same intimacy with Christ as Jesus shared with Peter, James, John, Martha, Mary, and Lazarus. We are his beloved disciples. He shares with us his own Father's love. He entrusts his mission to us in the special charism of the priesthood, a mission he received from his Father, and a mission he has consecrated through his death and resurrection.

We catch glimpses of this love in the many facets of our ministry. We priests, however, need time apart with Christ just as did the apostles. We need a time and a place, our Bethsaida, to focus on the love of Christ in our lives. Prayer is our privileged time when Christ takes us with him and draws us apart from the crowds

John Paul II called for priests who are "contemplatives in love with God." Bishop Gasi's image of the priest maintained that the priest is "expected to spend part of his time in union with God: talking and listening to him." Indeed, all that has been stated so far about the spiritual life of the diocesan priest as a relationship with God flowing from one's ministry in the pastoral care of people depends on the priest's decision to pray. Inevitably without prayer the spirituality of the diocesan priest, a spirituality rooted in ministry, will unravel.

I have always been amazed at the scope of human talent I observe in musicians. They have an incredible gift for music's many aspects: melody, harmony, structure, cohesion, tempo, and contrasts, just to name a few. They detect disharmony instantly, almost unconsciously, and recognize musical talent and competency in others, effortlessly. This musical conaturality emerges from a lifetime investment in studying, practicing, performing, and listening to music.

Personal, persevering prayer serves the same purposes for the priest, because prayer produces in us an affinity with the music of grace as played in the midst of God's creation and mingled within all human experience. Our Christian Catholic identity emerges from our baptism. Yet, as in the baptism of Jesus, the heavens continue to open and the Spirit descends in the rhythms and cadences of our own prayer.

The Holy Spirit interlaces salvation with our daily lives. The Spirit vitalizes our sacramental ministry, both in spite of our human weaknesses and by reason of them. The Spirit guides the Church, the parish, the Church's ministers. We need to be connected to the Holy Spirit, responsive to the Spirit's movements, intent to read and understand what the Spirit of Christ wills for us in our lives and ministry. Prayer is the indispensable instrument for such an openness to the Spirit.

The *Catechism of the Catholic Church* includes in its lengthy treatment of prayer a remarkable paragraph that takes its theme from the episode of Jesus and the woman at the well (John 4:10):

The wonder of prayer is revealed beside the well where we come seeking water: there Christ comes to meet every human being. It is he who first seeks us and asks us for a drink. Jesus thirsts; his asking arises from the depths of God's desire for us. Whether we realize it or not, prayer is the encounter of God's thirst with ours. God thirsts that we thirst for him.[6]

Each day begins as a gift which we acknowledge when we start with morning prayer, and conclude our day's work with evening prayer, especially the morning and evening prayers of the Hours. As important, if not more important than anything else we might do in a given day, is the time we set aside with the Lord. The classical description of Christian prayer is conversation with the Lord Jesus, who, as St. Augustine points out, is closer to our inmost being than we are to ourselves.[7] These moments, therefore, become the place where our hearts abide with the Lord

The *Catechism* adds a further reflection on this truth of the heart in prayer:

The heart is our hidden center, beyond the grasp of our reason and of others; only the Spirit of God can fathom the human heart and know it fully. The heart is the place of decision, deeper than our psychic drives. It is the place of truth, where we choose life or death. It is the place of encounter, because as image of God we live in relation: it is the place of covenant.[8]

Somehow, even with the accumulation of tasks that fall upon all parish priests, the individual priest who plans his day around his prayer time rather than the other way around, finds an encouraging strength and peacefulness transforming his ministry. One reason is that persevering, contemplative prayer attunes us to the myriad and marvelous ways the Holy Spirit moves in and through our pastoral ministry.

Human Friendships and Intimacy

There is another aspect of the love Christ has for us as his friends and disciples and our love for Christ and our love of him in return that impacts significantly on the spiritual life of the Diocesan priest. It is the place and importance of human friendship and intimacy in the life and ministry of the priest.

Cardinal Newman, in a sermon entitled "The Love of Relations and Friends," makes the strong case that the love involved in human friendship is not only invaluable of and by itself but also an essential preparation for our love of Christ. He emphasized the point in this sermon given on the feast of St. John the Evangelist: "Yet we find our Savior had private [friends]; and this shows us, first, how entirely He was a man, as much as any of us in his wants and feelings."[9]

He concludes, therefore, that not only are special friends consistent with the Gospel and the fullness of our own humanity, but that they are critical to our capacity to love Jesus Christ as he has loved us. Unless we know what it is to relish and maintain human friendships, we will not have the fullest capacity to truly love our Lord.

Erasmus characterized St. Thomas More as a man "born and made for human friendship." But we are all born and made for friendships, friendships that are deep and enduring. Human friendships, with their reciprocal bonding, are a grace themselves. They are a sustaining and ennobling resource of our wholesomeness and happiness: the friendship of our families, our brother priests, religious and lay people, male and female friends.

As priests we sacrifice marital intimacy and parenthood. We cannot, however, without severe emotional harm, detach ourselves from healthy and necessary human intimacy and friendship. Human friendships can at times be difficult, even painful, certainly demanding. They require balance, prudence, generosity, and honesty for everyone, including the celibate person.

Human friendships are essential to our humanness, and contribute to our ability to respond with the gift of our heart to the question Christ posed to Peter, (and, therefore, to each of us): "Simon, Son of John, do you love me?" (John 21:16).

Creative Ministry

> The crowds, meanwhile, learned of this and followed him. He received them and spoke to them about the kingdom of God, and he healed those who needed to be cured (Luke 9:11).

What is striking about this scene of Jesus receiving the crowds, speaking with them of the kingdom and healing the sick, is his effortless response to the onrush of the crowd. He easily moves from his retreat with his apostles to his acceptance of people.

This spontaneity indicates an enjoyment of the task and a creativity in responding to the crowds with a warmth of welcome, gathering them to himself in his teaching and healing. Jesus seems incapable of becoming weary in carrying out his mission of preaching the kingdom of God and healing the sick. His mission is his strength, and his strength is his mission. Precious secrets of spirituality for the diocesan priests and those in pastoral ministry lie in this attitude of Jesus.

Creativity in our ministry has much to do with our staying "alive" in our priestly work. The Church moves and acts in an institutional mode, whether we speak of the Church universal, the Church on a national level, a diocesan pastoral agenda, or even the parish structure. Because we are an enormous universal community of peoples, structures are necessary.

These institutional aspects of Church are intended to enhance the order and function of the Church and promote the mission of Christ. Sometimes, however, the opposite seems to occur, when the sheer size and complexity of it all seems to stifle the Spirit and our enthusiasm for spontaneity and creativity in ministry.

While supporting with faith and fidelity the institutional realities of the Church, the priest must retain and nourish creative ambitions for pastoral ministry. The two aspects of the Church, the institutional and the charismatic, complement the mission of Christ. In the Apostolic Period there were several decisive turning points in the growth and development of the Church that came from creative movements of ministry.

For example, we can look to the establishment of the order of deacons as a solution to the problem of the care of the Greek-speaking Jewish Christians, especially widows and the needy. Another example is the dream of Peter in the Acts of the Apostles where he was commanded to eat all the food from the cornucopia, even food otherwise forbidden to the Jews; a dream that provided the motive for Peter to visit the home of the gentile Cornelius and to baptize the first non-Jewish family into the Christian community. Paul's confrontation with Peter, when Peter appears to pull back from his bold initiative to bring the Gentiles into the Church on an even footing with the Jewish converts was another decisive turning point in the ministry and the apostolate of the Church.[10]

These were decisions filled with certain risks, yet decisions made by the inspiration of the Holy Spirit and the courage of pastoral leaders.

Creativity belongs in the personal and pastoral lives of diocesan priests. The gifts of the Spirit showered upon us in ordination are given for the building up of the Body of Christ, the Church. There is, however, no reason why we can't thoroughly enjoy using these gifts, as we search for ways to use them ever more effectively for serving the people of God.

Joy is synonymous with the presence of the Holy Spirit in our lives. The joyful priest who can spontaneously welcome people and minister to them creatively reveals an authentic spirituality at work in his life. Looking for ever more effective ways to minister involves risks, criticism and misunderstanding. Yet it also allows the Holy Spirit to touch people and to shape communities of faith in a new manner.

Loving our priestly ministry as our *opus*, our life's work, allows us to invest ourselves entirely in what we are doing. We can strive to be the best priest we can be, taking pride in a level of our pastoral skills that grow through our various experiences of ministry. This love and commitment to our priestly ministry as diocesan priests, and a continual search for doing our tasks ever more lovingly and competently, inevitably brings us rewarding satisfactions along with a profound sense of trust in God's presence and gracious activity in our ministries.

As diocesan priests we are called to minister to and to affirm one another. When we let our brother priests know how much we care about them and appreciate the effectiveness of their ministry, we can enthuse them to minister even more effectively and with increasing satisfaction in their ministry as priests. Nothing can encourage us more than the approval of our peers.

As we accept affirmation gratefully and graciously from our brother priests, from people, even from ourselves, we hear an echo of God's affirmation of us and our work. It is genuine humility to recognize our own gifts and achievements and to be grateful for them and people's appreciation of them.

Taking time to develop our gifts and talents, and looking for innovative ways to minister enriches our personal lives and our work. As we know the key to priestly growth and a sense of the value of our ministry doesn't come only from what we learned in the seminary but what we learned there about the love of learning. As our curiosity and wonder continue to expand, we as persons and priests grow in wisdom and grace.

Spirituality requires the ongoing development of all of our human gifts: intellect, will, imagination, intuition, emotional maturity and physical skills. So as we cultivate the sources for creative growth, we cultivate our own personal and ministerial richness. The opportunities for study, continuing education, sabbaticals, reading, writing, graduate education, study days, aesthetic pursuits such as music, art, theater, literature and poetry, movies, media, hobbies, travel, and sports feed our lives in indispensable ways.

Time away from ministry, time for leisure and recreation, family and friends, have their own place in our ministry. The weekly day off or overnight, reasonable vacation time, retreats and days of prayer make critical contributions to our emotional and physical health, and indeed our ability to carry out our pastoral ministry in a wholesome and inviting way. Sometimes the best gift we can give to those with whom we collaborate in ministry is to just get away for a while to regain our inner serenity or internal rhythm when we sense we are losing it.

The Spirit seizes us most powerfully through our emotions, imagination, and intuition, and investing time in these dimensions of our lives will ultimately serve to enhance our spiritual growth and our priestly service, and consequently the people of God in substantial and enduring ways.

The Priest and the Eucharistic Banquet

> As the day was drawing to a close, the Twelve approached him and said, "Dismiss the crowd so that they can go to the surrounding villages and farms and find lodging and provisions; for we are in a deserted place here." He said to them, "Give them some food yourselves." They replied, "Five loaves and two fish are all we have, unless we ourselves go and buy food for all these people." Now the men there numbered about five thousand. Then he said to his disciples, "have them sit down in groups of fifty." They did so and made them all sit down. Then taking the five loaves and the two fish, and looking up to heaven, he said the blessing over them, broke them, and gave them to the disciples to set before the crowd. They all ate and were satisfied. And when the leftover fragments were picked up, they filled twelve wicker baskets (Luke 9:12-17).

In biblical history a table of rich food and choice wine became the sign of the Messiah. In St. Luke's narrative the first missionary journey of the apostles was associated with "an experience of abundance mediated by Jesus" in this story of the multiplication of the loaves and fish in the feeding of the five thousand.

Most important, however, is that fact that the story of the feeding of the five thousand, as with the other meal stories in St. Luke's Gospel speaks of the origins of the eucharist in the New Testament.[11] The operative eucharistic formula of "take, bless, break, and give" supplies the eucharistic overtones in this story of the multiplication of the loaves and fish.

The apostles wanted to send away the people who had gathered to hear Jesus. They quickly learned that they cannot send them away; rather, they themselves must feed the crowds. "You give them something to eat." Suddenly the apostles realized their own poverty. They did not possess enough to feed the crowds who had come to Jesus.

They had to rely on nourishment provided by Jesus. Indeed, even when Jesus had prepared the food for the multitude, he gave it to the apostles to distribute.

The apostles became the servants of these hungry people. Apostleship exists for the sake of the Church, and the people of God. All leadership in the Church is of its very nature, servanthood. St. Paul makes the point utterly clear to the Corinthians: "Thus should one regard us: as servants of Christ and stewards of the mysteries of God" (1 Cor 4:12).

In the most memorable fashion possible Jesus tied servanthood and eucharist irrevocably together at the Last Supper. Having washed the feet of the disciples, even the reluctant Peter, he told them,

> "You call me 'teacher' and 'master,' and rightly so, for indeed I am. If I, therefore, the master and teacher, have washed your feet, you ought to wash one another's feet. I have given you a model to follow, so that as I have done for you, you should also do" (John 13:13-15).

The eucharist claims a centrality of place and importance in the Church all its own. We are all aware of the primacy given to the eucharist in Vatican II's document on the liturgy. We priests, and especially those involved in pastoral ministry, contract a profound and abiding relationship to the eucharist. We are ordained to act in the person of Christ, to preside at the eucharistic banquet, leading the assembly to the meal and the memorial of the death and resurrection of Jesus Christ.

When Vatican II in its document on the sacred liturgy spoke of the ways Christ is present in the liturgical celebrations. It began with Christ's presence in the priest as well as the eucharistic species:

> Christ is always present in His church, especially in her liturgical celebrations. He is present in the sacrifice of the Mass, not only in the person of His minister, "the same one now offering through the ministry of priests, who formerly offered himself on the cross," but especially under the Eucharistic species.[12]

Each Sunday, feast day, or daily Mass we celebrate with God's people, we recapitulate not only the Last Supper but the feeding of the multitude. We invite our people into the prayer of Christ to his Father, the renewal of the gift of his love and his life for the salvation of all humankind. We bring our people to the word of God that stirs faith and hope. We feed our people the bread and share the cup that bestows the life, love, and person of Jesus Christ.

As presiders we empower those assembled to participate consciously and fully in the eucharistic mysteries of the passion, death, and resurrection of Christ. In our eucharistic ministry we priests lead our communities of faith to the source and the summit of the Church's power in the most privileged sacramental experience available to us.[13]

As leaders of the worshipping community, we ourselves enter into the same mystery of faith. We are never more a priest than when we, the leaders of the assembly, engage ourselves most deeply with this eucharistic encounter of the risen Christ, and through Christ and the Spirit, with the Father.

Our relationship and devotion to the eucharist, with and for the sake of the assembly, presents the most important and enduring aspect of our spirituality as diocesan priests charged with the pastoral care of God's people. Enabling a parish community or its institutional counterparts in schools, hospitals, and other gatherings of the faithful, to have a full, active, and conscious participation in the liturgy of the eucharist ranks first and foremost with our responsibility as priests. It also comprises the heart of our spiritual life and the primary source of our strength and zeal for the mission entrusted to us.

Each of us understands that when we pray the Eucharistic Prayer of the Mass, with the assembly and proclaim the words of consecration, we are acting in the person of Christ. These are *his* words we say: "Take this, all of you, and eat it; this is my body which will be given up for you." And in the same way: "Take this, all of you, and drink from it; this is the cup of my blood, the blood of the new and everlasting covenant. It will be shed for you and for all so that sins may be forgiven."

Yet as we progress in our understanding and love of Christ and the Church in the eucharist, and our own mission to act in the person of Christ, these words can become more and more personal and priestly: "this is *my* body . . . given up for you . . . This is the cup of *my* blood . . . shed for you." A shepherd must be ready to lay down his life for his sheep. A shepherd must be prepared to nourish the flock, whatever the cost to himself. It's true, at times our personal resources may seem as impoverished as those of the apostles facing the hunger of the five thousand. We, however, do not rely on our own store of goods to help others. Christ takes whatever we have to offer, transforms it, and gives it back to us to share with the community.

A spirituality anchored in the eucharist is a spirituality nourished and vitalized by the liturgical year. The two are inseparable, so that we continually follow Our Lord in the unfolding of his life ritually renewed in the seasons of the liturgy: Advent, Christmas, the Christmas season, Lent, the Triduum, Easter, the Easter season, and Ordinary time. We enter into these seasons each year as familiar ground, yet each liturgical year and season communicates graces anew and insights previously unseen and unsuspected!

The liturgical seasons draw us into the most profound depths of the mystery of the life, sufferings, death and resurrection of Our Lord, and reveal in progressive and sometimes startling ways how Christ and the Holy Spirit move in and through our human history. The Church uses sacramental ritual, symbol, and the liturgical year to discover the riches of God's unfolding truth in the times and cultures of our day.

As diocesan priests we must claim a mastery of the knowledge and skills associated with the celebrations of the liturgical year, the rites of the sacraments, and the Order of the Christian Initiation of Adults. We need to do so both spiritually and pastorally and allow the Holy Spirit to lead us continually into their meaning and applications to our ministry.

It is a solid truth, ever ancient, ever new. The eucharist makes the Church, and the Church makes the eucharist. We as priests are servant leaders of this eucharistic mystery. As priest-disciples the eucharist nourishes our unity with Christ and with the Church in an irreplaceable and transforming way.

Pastoral Charity, the Presbyterate, and Our Humanity

> He summoned the Twelve and gave them power and authority over all demons and to cure diseases, and he sent them to proclaim the kingdom of God and to heal (Luke 9:1).

Jesus summoned the Twelve, a distinct group, and gave them a mission. He appointed them as shepherds to care for his people. Their care as shepherds included preaching the kingdom, healing, and leading them to the Father. There is a distinct link between this mission of the apostles and our mission as diocesan priests ministering to people. Pope John Paul II, in his exhortation entitled *Pastores dabo vobis,* described for us the operative virtue of this mission, for the sake of both our ministry and our spirituality:

> The internal principle, the force which animates and guides the spiritual life of the priest in as much as he is configured to Christ the head and shepherd is pastoral charity.[14]

Pastoral charity directs us to deal with people in a kindly, generous, and thoughtful manner, always ready to minister in such a way as to draw them to Christ and to extend to them a heart full of compassion, especially for those in pain, the alienated, the troubled, and the sick in soul or body.

The Holy Father, in this same exhortation, points out two other realities that shape the mission and the ministry of the diocesan priest. The first is that as diocesan priests we are ordained into the presbyterate of the local church. By our ordination we are conformed to Christ the good shepherd, and placed into a special relationship with our bishop and our brother priests. The Holy Father stresses the importance of this truth in saying: "The ordained ministry has a radical communitarian form and can only be carried out as a collective work."[15]

As we, priests and bishops, wrestle with our contemporary crisis of decreasing numbers of priests and increasing numbers in parish populations, our collaboration as priests, as well as with deacons, religious and lay people takes on growing importance. Yet as the presbyterate of the local church, there is an urgent theological reason for the collaboration of priests in ministry, namely our sharing in a collective identity as the ordained priests of Jesus Christ.

We have, therefore, a bonding not only of affection and friendship with one another and for each other, but we are merged into a special relationship by our ordination, our membership in the presbyterate.

The second reality is akin to the first. We are ordained into the local church, the diocese, and we minister collectively with one another in our own presbyterate under the leadership of the bishop. There is a specificity about the mission and ministry of the diocesan priest. We have a care and responsibility, by reason of our ordination, to the service of a diocese, and always to look toward the good of the whole of our local church, along with our parochial concerns and commitments. The Holy Father emphasizes the importance of this relationship to the local church when he writes:

> The priest needs to be aware that his being in a particular church constitutes by its very nature a significant element in his living a Christian spirituality. In this sense, the priest finds precisely in his belonging to and dedication to the particular church a wealth of meaning, criteria for discernment, and action which shape both his pastoral mission and his spiritual life.[16]

Naturally, we will focus on our ministry, our mission, our parish, and most of our working hours will be devoted to this work. Yet we belong to the local church, and exercising a deep devotion for all that has to do with the mission and the needs of the entire Church along with our own particular work or responsibility enhances our priesthood and enriches our own lives.

Jesus Christ was so thoroughly human he scandalized his neighbors when he told them, upon reading Isaiah 61, that the "Scriptures had been fulfilled in their hearing" (Luke 4:14). We also understand and believe that his humanity was the instrument of our salvation. As the author of Hebrews has shown us, we have access to grace and salvation through the humanity of Jesus Christ (Heb 5:1-10).

In embracing the fully human, Jesus Christ experienced on the cross the two great sufferings of humanity: physical pain and a sense of abandonment. He also laughed, cried, rejoiced, befriended, loved, rested, ate, and worked hard. He went to homes and shared meals with his friends. He confronted evil and endured his own dark night of the soul. He was betrayed by one he loved deeply. He grew in wisdom and age and grace.

Gethsemani and Golgotha were not play acting. Jesus never put aside his humanity. As Son of Man he was in fact transformed and transfigured, not discarded, in the mystery of the resurrection, when he was filled with the abundance of the Holy Spirit.

As priests we need to embrace our own humanity with all of its strengths, weaknesses and vulnerabilities. We must imitate Christ, who, "Son though he was, he learned obedience from what he suffered" (Heb 5:8). Through the challenges, sufferings, and satisfactions connected with our priestly ministry, individually and collectively we become pliable to the movements and the power of the Holy Spirit in our priestly life.

Since we are human we all fail at different times and in different ways. Through our sufferings and failures, however, we learn to be compassionate and companions of our people in our mutual struggle to be faithful. People we serve look to us not to be perfect, but to be kind, gracious, available and Christ-like. That's who we are:

> Therefore, since every priest in his own way, represents the person of Christ himself, he is endowed with a special grace. By this grace the priest, through his service of the people committed to his care, is able the better to pursue the perfection of Christ, whose place he takes.[17]

Notes

1 *L'Osservatore Romano* 43 (October 22, 1990) 8.

2 Tim Unsworth, Ed., *Last Priests in America* (New York: Crossroads Publishing Co., 1991) 229.

[3] *L'Osservatore Romano* 42 (October 15, 1990) 3.

[4] Constitution on the Sacred Liturgy, *Documents on the Liturgy,* Walter M. Abbott, ed. (New York: America Press, 1966) no. 7.

[5] *Fulfilled in Your Hearing,* NCCB, The Liturgy Documents, A Parish Resource (Chicago: Liturgy Training Publications, 1991) 56.

[6] *Catechism of the Catholic Church* (Mahwah, N.J: Paulist Press, 1994) #2560, 614.

[7] St. Augustine, *Confession,* Henry Chadwick, trans. (Cambridge: Oxford University Press, 1991) Book X, #38.

[8] *Catechism* #2563, 614.

[9] Henry Cardinal Newman, *Parochial and Plain Sermons* (San Francisco: Ignatius Press, 1987), Sermon 5, "Love of Relations and Friends," 257–63. See also: "Christian Sympathy," Christmas Sermon, Sermon 9, 1030: "It were well if we understood all this. Perhaps the reason why the standard of holiness among us is so low, why our attainments are so poor, our view of the truth so dim, our belief so unreal, our general notions so artificial and external is this, that we dare not trust each other with the secret of our hearts."

[10] Bernard Haring, *Free and Faithful in Christ,* vol. 1, General Moral Theology (Middlegreen, England: St. Paul Publications, 1978) ch. 2, part II, *Creative Fidelity in the Apostolic Church,* 32.

[11] Eugene LaVerdiere, *Dining in the Kingdom of God* (Chicago: Liturgy Training Publications, 1994).

[12] Constitution on the Sacred Liturgy, no. 7.

[13] Ibid., no. 10.

[14] John Paul II, "Formation of Priests," *Pastores dabo vobis,* no. 22. *Origins* 21, no. 45 (April 16, 1992).

[15] Ibid., no. 17.

[16] Ibid., no. 31.

[17] Ibid., no. 20.

10

A Kindled Heart

Frank McNulty

When I was asked to be part of this venture, I mentioned it to a priest friend. He is a published writer, a serious reader, and an excellent communicator. His reaction was, "I think I would have said no to that request. Good luck with it." His answer came out of a knowledge of the current literature around priesthood. When there are so many questions about identity, how can one write about spirituality? With the diocesan priesthood in crisis and with morale problems galore, what does one say about the inner life? But just because we live in a time of evolving ideas about priesthood, it should not stop us from saying something. Not the final word, of course, but something.

Another thing. There seems to be a reluctance among priests to admit to a pursuit of holiness or to be accused of holiness. Just as I began to think about this chapter, a close priest friend died. I was asked to preach the homily at his funeral Mass. As I thought about Vince and sorted out my memories of him, one theme jumped out at me: holiness. Could I stand up there in a church half full of priests and accuse him of holiness? Those kinds of homilies seldom come right out and say, "Listen up, all of you! This was a holy man." So I said, "I don't mean holiness of the stained glass window kind or halos and miracles, but the holiness that gets worked on in the nitty gritty of life, in joy and sorrow and relationships and success and failure and starting over again. Ordinary living, the stuff of being holy." It surprised me how many of the priests thanked me for talking about holiness. I don't know how many were surprised.

Men Without Illusions

Maybe it goes back to seminary days. The kind of holiness we admired was the quiet, unobtrusive, almost secret kind. What people termed "pious" seemed a little too showy or different and, to be honest, sometimes a bit strange. Looking back after all these years, it's hard to remember at all, no less figure out, the reasons for that mentality. In a novel called *Prince of Peace,* James Carroll offers his own:

> What counted for success in the seminary was mastering that peculiar mode of high toned mediocrity—to be devout but not pious, savvy but not intellectual, athletic but not physical, self-confident but not arrogant, deferential but not insecure, jocular but not sarcastic, friendly but not intimate with anyone. That developed as the dominant personality type of the American Catholic priest.

His statement is too sweeping and a little harsh but he is not too far from the truth.

There was a time in our lives when holiness or even sanctity could be termed a realistic goal. But, as the years went by and life went on, most priests would file that kind of thinking under "first fervor." On priest retreats I often quote a scene from Thornton Wilder's *Our Town:*

> The heroine Emily convinces the stage manager to allow her to go back from the land of the dead to the land of the living to relive her 12th birthday. It doesn't work out and she delivers a touching farewell speech to the world ending with, "Oh Earth, you're too wonderful for anyone to realize you!" Thinking a moment she questions the stage manager, "Do any human beings ever realize life while they live it—every, every minute?" He answers quietly, "No—saints and poets maybe—they do some."

These men who have been in the ring for lots of rounds give me a look that says, "Hold on, Frank. Don't take us up that road again. It might have worked on an ordination retreat but my sights are a lot lower now." Could it be that we confuse holiness with perfection? Clergy representatives from England and Wales met in September 1995. They discussed low morale and low self-esteem among the clergy and found one cause to be the type of spiritual training they received. Because we were expected to be perfect, we feel we are always failing. American priests could identify with that statement. Thomas Merton once mused that, for the saint, there were absolute and heroic answers to temptation like flinging himself or herself into ice water. "Indeed the perfect in this fearsome sense are elevated above the necessity or even the capacity for a fully human dialogue with their fellow men. They are without humor as they are without wonder, without feeling and without interest in the common affairs of mankind."

Wounded Healers

Recent studies of Merton's life have revealed some of his personal struggles; yet, people seem to admire him as much as they ever did. Maybe even more so. No one explicitly taught it but somehow we picked up the false notion that to be holy meant to stop being human.

Fortunately, the thinking is much different now. Pope John Paul II in *Pastores dabo vobis* points out the significance of human development. "Future priests should therefore cultivate a sense of human qualities, not only out of proper and due growth and realization of the self, but also with a view to ministry." Priests who think along the same lines were captivated by the title of Henri Nouwen's book *Wounded Healer.* You cannot be fully human without some wounds and you cannot be fully human without relationships. The U.S. Bishops' *Spiritual Formation in the Catholic Seminary* clearly states: "The real growth in the spirituality of a person occurs in the realm of personal relationships; that is, the relationship of the person with the mystery of God in Jesus, with oneself and with other personas."

The official thinking may be drastically different now but priests trained the old way still carry some of the scars. In the celibate lifestyle, we have no spouse or children of our own so we lack some ordinary, normal experiences so helpful to people learning relationship skills. The lifestyle along with past policies in training and clerical life cause a unique kind of suffering. This, too, becomes part of our spirituality:

> He (the priest) was trained to live a life apart, independent, otherworldly, solitary. Personal warmth often broke through these artificial barriers, but on the whole, priests tended to avoid close friendships and involvements. Even today when the attitudes toward real intimacy in the priest's life have changed to more positive, affirming ones, there are still legitimate personal misgivings because of the hazards involved and built-in difficulties because of the life style of the celibate priest.[1]

Parishes Rather Than Monasteries

Some priests feel that our training was built on a monastic model which did not prepare us for the pastoral ministry that awaited us. As seminarians we came together in the chapel to pray a number of times each day. After ordination we were left to pray alone. In larger parishes, other priests might live with us but schedules and differences in temperament seldom allow for communal prayer. Presiding at Eucharist and celebrating the sacraments fits in well with our lifestyle; praying in common in the rectory does not. Members of religious orders working in parishes seem to manage it but it is not all that appealing to most diocesan priests.

The spirituality of the diocesan priest? In some ways it is the same as for other members of the Church and in some ways different. Vatican II emphasized the universal call to holiness and dispelled forever the idea that holiness was the domain of the ordained and the vowed:

> The Lord Jesus, divine teacher and model of all perfection, preached holiness of life (of which he is the author and maker) to each and every one of his disciples without distinction: "You, therefore, must be perfect, as your heavenly Father is perfect" (Matt 5:48). For he sent the Holy Spirit to *all* to move them interiorly to love God with their whole heart, with their whole soul, with their whole understanding, and with their whole strength (cf. Mark 12:30), and to love one another as Christ loved them (cf. John 13:34; 15:12).[2]

It seems to me that a good starting place is to appreciate, even reverence, the gift of life and live it fully. Inscribed on my chalice are the beautiful words of the psalmist, "What shall I give to the Lord for all that he has given to me." I have come to believe that his basic gift to me was not priesthood but life itself and he wants me to live it fully. Thus, I give him glory by being a person fully alive (Irenaeus). How would you feel if you gave a friend the gift of tickets to a Broadway show and he didn't bother going? How does God react when we become one of those people who die in their forties and wait around a few more decades to be buried.

He made us little less than the angels, put us here in this beautiful world and equipped us well for enjoying it. He is like a waitress in an Italian restaurant who puts a dish of pasta before us and with exuberance almost shouts, "Enjoy!" See: a sunset, smiles, the ocean. Hear: laughter, a compliment, music. Touch: water, hearts, a dying person's hand. Smell: coffee, salt air, Fall. Taste: a hot dog, ice cream, a cold beer. Feel: wind, joy, affirmation. We need to realize life, while we live it every moment because there is saint and poet in each of us.

In 1988 the Committee on Priestly Life and Ministry of the National Conference of Catholic Bishops published a short but significant document called *Reflections on the Morale of Priests*. The document is a well researched, practical one with workable suggestions for improving morale. For me, the saddest observation was

> Among some priests, there are a significant number who have settled for a part-time presence to their priesthood. Many feel they have worked hard and long to implement, or at least adjust to, the practical consequences of Vatican II. They sense that much of that effort is now being blunted or even betrayed and they elect to drop out quietly. This is particularly true of those in the 45 to 60 age group who are willing to go through the necessary minimum of motions but whose hearts and energies are elsewhere. Many more of our priests believed in renewal, were willing to adapt, worked hard and now are just plain tired.[3]

Fortunately, they are in the minority but each of us knows men who are no longer fully present to life, to fellow priests or to ministry.

The love command of Jesus is also common to all of our spiritual journeys. If we say we love God and not other people, John tells us we lie. How often we preach to people that our nearest neighbor lives in the same house we do. If we are assessing our own spiritual growth, a logical question is, "How do we contribute to rectory living? How do we treat our nearest neighbors—priests and other staff members?"

Richard Foster, in *US Catholic*, wrote about the signs of a solid spirituality. "Usually the signs are that a person is easy to live with, more human, unpretentious and exhibits a holy hilarity. In other words you would want to be around that person." Holy hilarity might be too strong for priestly spirituality but Foster makes a good point. If you live in a rectory with other priests or if you work on staff, you know what he means. Too many people have adopted the philosophy of W. C. Fields, "Smile early in the morning and get it over with."

Like all people, we are called to prayer. Much of our prayer is the same but for a priest there are some wrinkles, mostly centered around ministry. Many of us, ordained or not, picked up the erroneous notion that spirituality was something imposed on life, a series of good things I did by leaving real life for awhile. You step out of life into a church to make a visit, celebrate Eucharist, say the rosary and so on. You step out of life into your room to read the Bible or to meditate. That was a result of the duality of the holy and worldly, the sacred and profane. That is why some of us were surprised and enthused even about the title of the Vatican II document, The Church in the Modern World. We are persons in the world and not expected to move into a hermitage or make the rectory into one. Yes, we must be countercultural at times but you cannot do that by hiding or taking flight.

Meaning Through Function

The spiritual life is, above all, life, concerned with ultimate meanings and values but incarnated in human circumstances. It happens through my life, now, interfacing with American culture, living in this rectory with all these human encounters. It happens through the tasks that fall to me precisely because I am a diocesan priest. Daily life is the matter to be transformed: every event, every experience, every relationship, every joy or pain or friction or twist in the road. That is what we say yes to: the rhythm, paradoxes, mysteries, polarities, questions and, if you are a parish priest, even the interruptions. A priest friend, in describing the expectations of people, claims we are bombarded by marshmallows. Those, too.

Spirituality doesn't happen by searching for a God way out there but learning to notice and surface the God right here, under our noses. We live out the paschal mystery we have been caught up in through our Baptism and we do so precisely in our daily life. Through all that happens we struggle to stay aware of the reality and mystery of that which is ultimate. Life is so busy that we don't succeed in doing that as much as we would like.

Fr. Michael Himes, theology professor at Boston College, uses an image to say all of the above and illustrate what grace is: You visit a dentist's office for a root canal and your mind is very much on what is to come. Another patient asks you, "What is that music they are playing?" All of a sudden, you realize you hadn't heard the background music at all. Around Thanksgiving time, I was having breakfast in a diner with a friend and sharing that image. The waitress came over and said, "Can you believe that music?" We both said, "What music?" and, at the very moment heard the Christmas carol that was playing. Maybe part of our task is to keep reminding each other of the music always there: grace. And maybe preaching is saying to others, "Can you believe that music?"

The Diocesan Priest's Spirituality

Most of what I have written so far applies to spirituality in general. What about the spirituality of the diocesan priest? Can we get more explicit? We have much in common; is there anything distinctive?

These questions put us smack in the middle of an ongoing theological discussion on the identity of the priest. Most of us were attracted to diocesan priesthood more by what the priest does, his functions, than by what he is. We did know that priesthood would mark us in a special way, set us apart and commission us to a leader-ship position in the work of salvation. The council spells that out. "Through that Sacrament (Holy Orders) priests by the anointing of the Holy Spirit are signed with a special character and so are config-ured to Christ the Priest in such a way as they are able to act in the Person of Christ, the Head."[4] But the same council also expanded ministries for laity and stressed that all members of the Church have gifts and charisms. The authors of the documents use the mystical body image and remind us that all the members share the mission of the whole body. They spell it out more clearly when they say: "Though they differ essentially and not only in degree, the common priesthood of the faithful and the ministerial or hierarchial priesthood are none the less ordered one to another; each in its own proper way shares in the one priesthood of Christ."[5]

The next question is obvious. How do they differ *essentially?* A few people have helped me through these muddy waters. Robert Schwartz, another contributor to this volume, published his doctoral thesis *Servant Leaders of the People of God—An Ecclesial Spirituality for American Priests.* He analyzes well the expression *in persona Christi,* one used again and again by the Holy Father. He points out that using it only for the ordained was a deliberate choice of the coun-cil Fathers. We serve in the Person of Christ, the Head, so our style of leadership should be the complete opposite of clericalism or an ap-proach from a pedestal. Servant leadership means care, compassion, fi-delity, real service. In a retreat talk to priests gathered in Rome, Pope John Paul II talks of sacramental actions performed *in persona Christi* and adds, "But it must likewise find expression in the fervor of your prayer, the consistency of your lives, and the pastoral charity of your ministry as you reach out tirelessly for the salvation of others. In other words, it demands your personal sanctification.

The Redemptorist priest poet, Andrew Costello, has written a poem priests find appealing. He calls it "Two Hands":

"I am a fist,
   a sign of fear,
   a sign of anger,
   a sign of greed,
   a sign of tension.

I can pound a desk,
I can hoard money,
I can try to scare you,
I can punch you
   in the mouth.

I am a fist.

What do you think of me?

I am an open hand,
   a sign of calm,
   a sign of ease,
   a sign of peace,
   a sign of relaxation.

I can dial a phone,
I can shake a hand,
I can change the diapers,
I can play cards,
I can break the bread,
I can pass the wine,
I can heal the hurt,
I can write the poem.

I am an open hand.

What do you think of me?[6]

Thus, should not a style of servant leadership include the cross, asceticism, reconciliation, availability? On ordination day, we opened those hands and a bishop poured oil on them and begged God to give us strength. Then he predicted suffering would play a role by making a Sign of the Cross with the oil.

Bearer of the Mystery of God

At a 1995 meeting of the National Federation of Priest Councils, Joseph Cardinal Bernardin reminded us that we are more than "functionaires" in the Church. He noted that the two essential dimensions of priestly life are these: bearer of the Mystery of God and doctor of the soul.[7] People are hungering, the cardinal said for those words, insights, visions and dreams that speak of the "deep things of God." We bring people into this powerful force: the passionate, unconditional, unreasonable and excessive love of God. We tell them of this mystery and draw them into it especially by our preaching and our preaching is, in turn, formed by our prayer life. But we must be convinced to deliver the message.

In the *Mystery of Commitment,* Fr. Edward O'Toole puts it this way. "I accepted what I was told that religion could be taught. I should have known, fool that I am, that Christ said *preach* the Gospel.

The House of God is not a classroom, it is a hillside. The word of God is not a text. It is a message."[8] As messengers, we must sound like we mean it and act like we mean it. And prayer is at the heart of it. That is why we usually preach more effectively after a retreat. Faith can allow for doubt but our faith must be evident. I was a visitor standing outside a church after Mass one Sunday. Over the years, the priest presiding had settled into a style that seemed bored, hurried, matter of fact and routine. A young man said to me on his way out, more in sadness than anger, "Does that guy really believe?" No doubt the priest did, but it had stopped showing.

John Sheehan wrote an article for *America*[9] called "Recollections From a Distant Planet" in which he tried to find words to express the extreme pleasure he has found in priesthood. He regularly celebrated Mass in a jail and one of the convicts commented, "When you picked up the cup, I saw the tears in your eyes and I thought—Christ, he really believes it." Tears are not there often but faith should be and conviction and enthusiasm. It is for Sheehan and caused him to say about priesthood—"It is all I ever wanted."

For Cardinal Bernardin, the priest is also "Doctor of the Soul," He is the instrument through whom God heals broken hearts and minds. He brings to bear the healer and nothing of humanity is untouched by that power. Could the Eucharist and the sacrament of reconciliation be the most evident places? I think so.

If there is something distinctive about our spirituality, it must have something to do with our identity—who we are as priests. The last word has not been spoken in that theological discussion and mystery is part of it. But spirituality must also have something to do with our ministry, what we do as priests, the spelling out of those "Doctor of the Soul" activities. The studies on priesthood all affirm the fact that happy and effective priests enjoy ministry. They love their people and that love is mutual. They are invited into the deepest place in people's hearts and lives and enter therein with awe. They are present for all the key moments, from womb to tomb.

A life of prayer has a necessary place in all this. When I was a seminarian the classic by Dom Chautard *Soul of the Apostolate* was required reading. His thesis was convincing and powerful. He warns that our deeds could become "the heresy of good works" unless informed by the soul: a prayer life. Of course, but to me, it has always been a challenge to balance time in prayer with ministerial activity. Most priests work hard but my guess is that they fight to make time for prayer. When I began giving retreats to priests, I visited with a veteran and respected Jesuit who specialized in priest retreats. I asked what his goals were for his retreatants and he said, "I just want to get them praying again."

A helpful insight for me comes from John Shea and several other theologians. They tell us that faith is not so much a belief in what we cannot see but an interpretation of what cannot be escaped. We surface the God who is everywhere rather than search for him up there somewhere.

> A Prayer to the God Who Fell from Heaven
>
> If you had stayed
> tightfisted in the sky
> and watched us thrash
> with all the patience of a pipe smoker,
> I would pray
> like a golden bullet
> aimed at your heart.
> But the story says
> you cried
> and so heavy was the tear
> you fell with it to earth
> where like a baritone in a bar
> it is never time to go home.
> So you move among us
> twisting every straight line
> into Picasso,
> stealing kisses from pinched lips,
> holding our hand in the dark.
> So now when I pray
> I sit and turn my mind
> like a television knob
> till you are there
> with your large, open hands
> spreading my life before me
> like a Sunday tablecloth
> and pulling up a chair yourself
> for by now
> The Secret is out.
> You are home.[10]

"You are home." In the beauty of nature, if we are aware; in the word, if we are attentive. In sacraments, in liturgy, in a homily, an event, a coincidence, a conversation. So many ways but especially in ministry, what we do to advance the mission of the Lord. It is to this mission that the priest commits his very life. It is worked out more often through persons than projects and programs.

People bring to us so much and, if I am praying, I can catch the anguish beneath the words. My Mom has cancer . . . the baby is a Down Syndrome . . . I am lonely and afraid . . . our son has AIDS . . . my daughter never goes to Mass . . . it looks like I'm pregnant . . . we fought over the will . . . he is back in intensive care. We stand with people in the mystery of life to give them hope and help them search for meaning. An older priest once said to me after several hours of Christmas confessions, "Mac, we ought to be able to cry with them". Yes, and we ought to laugh with them, too, as they invite us into the joyful moments of life. Through it all, we meet God and all that happens becomes part of our prayer. Malcolm Muggeridge said it well. "Every happening, great and small, is a parable whereby God speaks to us and the art of life is to get the message." Yes, but how come we so often miss the message? A story out of my own life might help here.

Catching the Signals

"So, this is what third base feels like," the grammar school baseball player said to himself. He was, at best, a singles hitter but this day had gotten to third on a rare occurrence double plus a helpful error. "So this is what third base feels like," he said to himself as he adjusted his cap, relocated his chewing gum, straightened his socks, cleaned his spikes, hitched up his pants, and surveyed the crowd. Surveying the crowd was the best part. Who is that cute little blond? I wonder what she thought of the double? Is Dad still clapping or cleaning off his hands? What in the world has gotten into the coach? Why is he making all those faces? Has he picked up a nervous twitch of some kind? I wonder why he has me bat ninth all the time? My average . . . let's see . . . 0 for 3 today . . . 0 for 3 last week . . . 0 for 3 the week before . . . 0 for 3 the first game . . . that makes . . . suddenly he was distracted from his mathematical musings. The batter squared his stance, put the bat in front of his chest and pushed a perfect bunt to the pitcher. The pitcher fielded the bunt and glared over to him; he glared back and just then it struck like a bolt of lightning. The reason for the bunt—a squeeze play; the reason for the nervous twitch—the squeeze play. That marvelous strategy to surprise the enemy: a bunt and a head start by the runner and a score. The squeeze play—we practiced it just this week.

The stay at third base is now full of concentration but very short as the next batter struck out. The grammar school baseball player headed in for his glove . . . face flushed . . . eyes on the ground. For a second he thought about mentioning the nervous twitch but then thought better of it. Being a good Catholic boy he decided on a complete confession. His speech came out in a faint whisper. "I missed the signal, coach." "Missed the signal! Missed the signal! Missed the signal! I gave it to you ten times. Everyone saw the signal: the other pitcher, all the fielders, your father, the little blond—everybody saw it."

As priests, it is our mission to catch the signals, those moments of communion that reveal God's spirit in the most ordinary or most dramatic of human events. Only if we are men of prayer can we catch the signals. Of course, celebrating Eucharist and praying the breviary make us prayerful people. But here I mean the personal, private kind of prayer. What we used to call meditation. When we engage in it on a fairly consistent basis, we develop an alertness, an ability to notice. When we are not praying much, we easily become insensitive to the privileged moments, the subtle and profound ways of the Lord. There is prayer on the knees and prayer on location. You pray and it helps you notice; you notice and it helps you pray. Ignatius called it "contemplation in action." We enter into ministerial moments just as in Ignatian contemplation we enter into the scene described in the Scriptures. We are really there!

When I stood there admiring the view from third base, it would have helped me if we had a third base coach. This is what a spiritual director can do for us. He can gently suggest that we may be missing some important signals. Even in baseball, signals are not always easy to read. In life they can be even more difficult.

Priests have found lots of other effective ways to pray. I've just shared one helpful to me and am not citing it as the best method. It is for me. But whatever method has proven helpful to you, it has to be related to your ministry, it has to become the soul of your apostolate.

Jessica Powers, a member of the Discalced Carmelite Order, has left behind a legacy of inspiring poetry. Her poem "The House at Rest" speaks well to the busy diocesan priest:

> How does one hush one's house,
> each proud prossessive wall, each sighing rafter,
> the rooms made restless with remembered laughter
> or wounding echoes, the permissive doors,
> the stairs that vacillate from up to down,
> windows that bring in color and event
> from countryside or town,
> oppressive ceilings and complaining floors?

The house must first of all accept the night.
Let it erase the walls and their display,
impoverish the rooms till they are filled
with humble silences; let clocks be stilled
and all the selfish urgencies of day

Midnight is not the time to greet a guest.
Caution the doors against both foes and friends,
and try to make the windows understand
their unimportance when the daylight ends. . .
Persuade the stairs to patience, and deny
the passages their aimless to and fro
Virtue it is that puts a house at rest.
How well repaid that tenant is, how blest
who, when the call is heard,
is free to take his kindled heart and go.[11]

We take our kindled heart and go and, because it is kindled, we love more profoundly, we heal hearts and minds more often, hear the background music called grace and speak of it to others more eloquently. And we find the God who called us.

Notes

[1] *Spiritual Renewal of the American Priesthood* (Washington, D.C.: United States Catholic Conference, 1972) 28

[2] Pastoral Constitution on the Church in the Modern World, ch. 5, par. 40

[3] "Reflections on the Morale of Priests," *Origins* 18, no. 31 (January 12, 1989).

[4] Decree on the Ministry and Life of Priests, ch 1, par. 2.

[5] Pastoral Constitution on the Church in the Modern World, ch. II, par. 10.

[6] Andrew Costello, "The Two Hands," *Listenings* (Chicago: Thomas More, 1980) 107

[7] Joseph Cardinal Bernardin, "Bearers of the Mystery of God," NFPC Newsletter *Touchstone* X, no. 4 (summer 1995).

[8] Edward O'Toole, *The Mystery of Commitment* (Staten Island: Alba House, 1968).

[9] John Sheehan, "Recollections from a Distant Planet," *America* (November 12, 1994).

[10] John Shea, "The God Who Fell from Heaven" from *The God Who Fell from Heaven* (Allen, Texas: Argus, 1979) 90.

[11] Jessica Powers, "The House at Rest" from *The House at Rest*.

11

The Conciliar Documents and the 1983 Code

Edward G. Pfnausch

Memories of life in the seminary during the 1960s occasion no sentimental nostalgia. Rather, they evoke quaint and curious images of a silent, regimented world focused on study and prayer. The model for spirituality, taken from a number of wise spiritual writers from a variety of backgrounds, was reflected in the schedule. Early morning meditation and Mass, visits to the chapel after meals, late afternoon spiritual reading, and the end of the day's evening prayer in chapel were practices ordered to the seminarian's growth in holiness. This model, rooted in the teaching of the Council of Trent, succinctly incorporated in the 1917 Code of Canon Law and developed by papal teaching in this century, was meant to be a formation in values and practices that would last a lifetime.

Many of us realized that the model was changing. Alongside the institutional formation we were being formed by the excitement of the "innovations" generated by Vatican II, despite the lack of enthusiasm that we observed in our professors. That, too, was a part of the seminary in the 1960s. By reason of a number of factors—experience, virtue, and personality—we became traditionalists or innovators, supporters of Hans Küng or Cardinal Ottaviani. We followed the literature to the extent we were able and within the limits of our knowledge and we relished the gossip of council day by day. Our spiritual formation was influenced, particularly by liturgical change, as well.

Ordination and immersion into ministry brought new adjustments and changes. The model for institutional formation that was meant to shape the spirituality of the diocesan priest was gone. For many it never worked. We found ourselves in uncharted waters, left to develop a new model on our own—integrating those methods of the past with the new demands of ministry. Many of us found pastors and other experienced presbyters unaware of or unenthusiastic about conciliar change, a laity polarized by liturgical change and Paul VI's encyclical *Humanae vitae* and a demanding round of activities and new experiences that left little time for the Liturgy of the Hours let alone the other practices so encouraged in the years of formation.

Thirty years later we know that all that has changed. The world has changed and the Church has changed. Some changes in the Church were obvious to all whereas other new practices, such as the institution of consultative bodies on the diocesan and parochial levels, had a more limited impact on the people of God but touched the lives of diocesan presbyters in an immediate way. Some presbyters responded to the challenge with generosity and new energy. Many, however, found that the changes touched so many aspects of their lives that the very nature of the priesthood had changed. All these changes, however, were not just changes in practice but reflected a deeper change in theology occasioned by Vatican II. As memories of the council fade and enthusiasm is dimmed, the diocesan priest finds new challenges in more demands on his talents and energies with the declining number of presbyters, merging and closing of parishes and a perception of being abandoned by the episcopal order. The quaint and curious practices meant to form us in the spiritual life are now clearly inadequate to nourish the busy pastor.

The world has changed, the Church has changed and the law has changed. The revised code of 1983 institutionalized both the theology and practices taught at Vatican II. Although its ultimate goal is the "salvation of souls" (c.1752), the Code of Canon Law, of course, is not a handbook of spiritual theology. One does not find, and should not expect to find, anything but a skeleton, or blueprint, for the minimal expectations demanded of disciples. Both codes oblige members of the clergy to pursue holiness, but the codes are quite different. This study is an examination of the differences and the reasons for the change—the change in the basis, principles, and goals of the law—old and new. These reflections are rooted in the conviction that the revised code provides a suggestion for new models for the spirituality of diocesan priests who are engaged in parochial ministry. Such a study provides a starting point, a common ground, for further discovery of the implications in prayer and study. Before examining the present code, it is necessary to see how far we have come.

Before Vatican II

The succinct legal formulation of the cleric's obligation was found in canon 124 of the 1917 Code of Canon Law:

> Clerics must live interiorly and exteriorly a holier life than lay persons and must be superior to them in giving an example of virtue and good deeds.

The canon is directly and principally related to the teaching of the Council of Trent, which was normative for four hundred years. The teaching that underlies the canon was well expressed by Pius X who was responsible for the codification of 1917. In his exhortation *Haerent animo* of August 8, 1908, he wrote:

> . . . there should be as much difference between the priest and the good layman, as there is between heaven and earth, and therefore the priest's life should be free not only of the graver defects, but even of the least.[1]

The basis for the difference was grounded in the dignity of the ordained priest's special identification with Christ.

The pre-conciliar view held that holiness of life was a necessary prerequisite for good example and for ministry. A corollary of this teaching was that ministry endangered holiness of life:

> It would be a grave error fraught with many dangers should a priest, carried away by false zeal, neglect his own sanctification and become overly immersed in the external works, however holy, of the priestly ministry. Thereby he would run a double risk. In the first place he endangers his own eternal salvation. . . . In the second place he might lose, if not divine grace, certainly that unction of the Holy Spirit which gives such a marvelous force and efficacy to his external apostolate.[2]

As a consequence of the need for the priest to be holier than the laity and the necessity of holiness for effective ministry, the 1917 code established daily and frequent practices to assist the diocesan priest in striving for holiness. Each day, he was to spend time in mental prayer, visit the Blessed Sacrament, pray the divine office and the rosary, and examine his conscience. He was to confess his sins frequently and make a retreat every third year. Papal teaching and commentators on the code suggested other means that could be useful to clerics in that pursuit, e.g., days of recollection, spiritual conferences, use of spiritual directors. Training in these valuable practices was the purpose of the daily routine of the seminary.

The beginnings of change were evident before Vatican II in an intense debate in Europe and later in the United States about the dignity, ministry, and spirituality of the *diocesan* priest.[3] An important part of that discussion was on the importance and propriety of the ministry of the diocesan priest in collaboration with his bishop:

> These considerations lead us to conceive of the priestly state as being capable by itself of furnishing its members with means of perfection through and in the exercise of the duties which it imposes upon them, for these duties are acts of charity, and therefore acts of perfection. A diocesan priest who has a true understanding of his state, that is, of its relations with the state of life of his bishop, and who acts accordingly, is perpetually training himself in charity, and therefore training himself in holiness.[4]

Gustave Thils, in a work that appeared in English in 1964, provided a particularly influential contribution to this discussion in his attempt to develop a spirituality of the diocesan priest.[5] Based on the premise that the diocesan priest is consecrated *for action*, Thils argued that his spirituality should be determined by his actions and that his ministry is central.

When John XXIII announced the convocation of Vatican II on January 25, 1959, the issues involved in the discussion of priestly holiness had not been settled by theologians and would provide the occasion for lively debate when the council Fathers began their discussions on holiness in general and on priestly life and ministry in particular.

Presbyteral Spirituality and Vatican II

The relationship between ministry and holiness and the means to achieve holiness was developed in the council schemata, the public discussion, and the written observations of the bishops which led to the Constitution on the Church and its practical application in the Decree on the Ministry and Life of Priests.

Developing the teaching on the universal call to holiness, the dogmatic Constitution on the Church established the fundamental framework for understanding the diocesan priest's pursuit of perfection by emphasizing the nature of the presbyterate and the call of presbyters to holiness. In the constitution the diocesan presbyter's life is based on three key principles. First, by ordination he is consecrated to Christ and shares, with the bishop, in the one priesthood of Christ. Presbyters are not just "helpers" for the episcopal order, but "cooperators." The unity of the episcopal and presbyteral orders with Christ by ordination is the basis for any juridical relationships between them. Second, the priest is consecrated to Christ not merely in view of the celebration of the Eucharist; rather he participates with the bishop in the threefold mission of Christ to teach, sanctify, and govern the people of God. It is that mission which shapes the presbyter's life. Third, like all Christians, the presbyter is called to holiness. The Constitution on the Church describes the specific nature of presbyteral spirituality in terms of conditions, duties, and circumstances of his ministry in cooperation with the divine will.[6]

The relationship between a priest's spiritual life and his ministry received considerable attention during the complex development of the Decree on the Ministry and Life of Priests, which was promulgated in December 1965. The discussion focused on two questions. First, was holiness a prerequisite for ministry and, second, does ministry contribute to or detract from holiness? It is well known that the council fathers, led by some of the bishops of France, put ministry in the first place:

> It is through the daily sacred actions, and through the whole of their ministry, which they carry out in communion with the bishop and his priests, that they [priests] are led to perfection of life. . . . Priests will achieve this holiness proper to their state by sincere and untiring fulfillment of their duties in the Spirit of Christ.[7]

It was in the discussion of the aids to the development of the spiritual life that the special needs and way of life of the diocesan priest received attention. The council fathers recognized a harmonious relationship between ministry and the priest's life of prayer. Two extremes were observed—some diocesan priests were totally immersed in pastoral action and neglected their spiritual lives; others dedicated so much time to the spiritual life that they neglect their duties. Still others were torn between pastoral ministry and the spiritual life. The primary aid for the development of a harmony in the priest's life, the council taught, was the nourishment provided by the twofold table of holy Scripture and the Eucharist. In addition, the council did not endorse any specific form of the spiritual life but rather encouraged presbyters to use any means at their disposal, especially those that had been found to have been helpful in the past, to develop unity and harmony between ministry and their interior lives. Such an emphasis is strikingly different from the emphasis on personal holiness as a prerequisite for ministry found in papal teaching before the council and in the 1917 Code of Canon Law.

The Decree on the Ministry and Life of Priests was not entirely successful in dealing with three issues that played an important role in the conciliar debates, the formation of the revised code, magisterial teaching, and ultimately the lives of diocesan presbyters.

Is there a distinctive presbyteral spiritual? It was clearly the hope and intention of the fathers to identify the presbyteral consecration and ministry as the cornerstone of the presbyter's spirituality as well as the means he is to use to pursue perfection. In the light of the universal call to holiness in the Constitution on the Church, however, and the baptismal consecration of all believers, the Decree on the Ministry and Life of Priests does not completely or adequately separate presbyteral spirituality from the spirituality of all believers. That may very well be due to the uncertain role of the evangelical counsels in the lives of presbyters and the desire not to introduce distinctions in the one priesthood of Christ shared by all presbyters whether diocesan or religious. As a consequence, the fathers were not able to develop a distinctive spirituality for either diocesan or religious presbyters.

Second, the identification of priesthood with both consecration to Christ and mission is not without difficulties. Such a twofold formulation provides the basis for further discussion about priority of emphasis and the relationship of the presbyter to the mission dimension of the entire Church. If, for example, the emphasis is placed on sacramental consecration, there is a tendency to emphasize the unique cultic functions of the presbyter's mission that distinguishes him from other members of Christ's faithful and a consequent tendency to diminish his mission to be a teacher and pastor. On the other hand, an emphasis on the presbyter's participation in the common mission of all believers can lead to a loss of appreciation for the distinctive ministry of the presbyter or lead to the danger of activism.

Finally, a more practical difficulty arises in the desire to harmonize the external ministry of the presbyter, especially the diocesan presbyter, with his interior life. The Decree on the Ministry and Life of Priests proposes Christ's desire to do the will of his father as a model for achieving that harmony. The practical relationship between presbyteral consecration, his intention to do the will of Christ in hierarchical communion, his pastoral ministry, and the aids to his pursuit of perfection is not adequately integrated in the third chapter of the decree. In addition to the ministry of the word and sacraments, the ministry of governing or shepherding God's people demands special virtue and sacrifice and includes a wide range of activities that include taking "new pastoral initiatives" when necessary.[8] Although the harmony between external ministry of the presbyter and his interior life might be effectively achieved in some aspects of the presbyter's life such as preparation and preaching the word, prayer, and the celebration of the sacraments, such a harmony is more elusive in his attempt to harmonize his spiritual life with the responsibilities, for example, as the administrator of temporal goods, the demands that arise from the need to be present to the people committed to his care, the needs for continuing education and formation and the changes that are a part of the fabric of the modern pastor's care for the people of God.

The insights and directions, as well as the ongoing difficulties, in the teaching of Vatican II were much discussed in the post conciliar Church and are echoed in the 1983 code.

The 1983 Code of Canon Law

It is not surprising that the teaching of the council was incorporated in the revised code. At the very beginning of the process of revision of the code, Pope Paul VI said, "Canon law must be accommodated to the new manner of thinking, in accord with Vatican II, which stresses very much the pastoral ministry. Canon law must, therefore, consider the new needs of the people of God."[9] Pope John Paul II has expressed the same intimate connection between the code and the council and the newness of conciliar teaching, most pointedly in *Sacrae disciplinae leges* as he promulgated the code:

> The instrument which the code is fully corresponds to the nature of the Church, especially as it is proposed by the teaching of the Second Vatican Council in general and in a particular way by its ecclesiological teaching. Indeed in a certain sense this new Code could be understood as a great effort to translate this same conciliar doctrine and ecclesiology into *canonical* language. . . .

> Hence it follows that what constitutes the substantial "newness" of the Second Vatican Council, in line with the legislative tradition of the Church, especially in regard to ecclesiology, constitutes likewise the "newness" of the Code.[10]

The obligation of the cleric to pursue holiness of life has been formulated in the light of the new way of thinking and the "newness" of Vatican II. That is evident in the changes incorporated in the revision.

The New Canon

The new juridical formulation can be found in the 1983 Code of Canon Law among the obligations and rights of clerics in Book II, Part I, Title III, chapter III:

Canon 276 - §1. In leading their lives clerics are especially bound to pursue holiness because they are consecrated to God by a new title in the reception of orders as dispensers of God's mysteries in the service of His people.

§ 2. In order for them to pursue this perfection:
1° first of all they are faithfully and untiringly to fulfill the duties of pastoral ministry;
2° they are to nourish their spiritual life from the two-fold table of Sacred Scripture and the Eucharist; priests are therefore earnestly invited to offer the sacrifice of the Eucharist daily and deacons are earnestly invited to participate daily in offering it;
3° priests as well as deacons aspiring to the priesthood are obliged to fulfill the liturgy of the hours daily in accordance with the proper and approved liturgical books; permanent deacons, however, are to do the same to the extent it is determined by the conference of bishops;
4° they are also bound to make a retreat according to the prescriptions of particular law;
5° they are to be conscientious in devoting time regularly to mental prayer, in approaching the sacrament of penance frequently, in cultivating special devotion to the Virgin Mother of God, and in using other common and particular means for their sanctification

Who is bound?

For diocesan presbyters and deacons, canon 276 constitutes a fundamental obligation that is to be the focus of their pursuit of perfection. The obligation to pursue holiness in canon 276 binds all clerics, that is, bishops, presbyters both diocesan and religious and deacons both transitional and permanent. Diocesan bishops, however, are also bound to set "a personal example of holiness, in charity, humility and simplicity of life" and the bishop "is to make every effort to promote the holiness of the Christian faithful according to each one's own vocation."[11] Religious presbyters and deacons, in addition, are bound not only by other canons but also by the distinctive obligations of their institutes.[12]

The nature of the obligation

As norms for action, it ought to be clear whether an individual is bound by the action called for in such canons. The mind of those drafting the canon was that clerics be canonically bound to the daily recitation of the liturgy of the hours and an annual retreat, according to the prescriptions of particular law is not only clear from the language *(obligatione tenentur),* but by their own report:

> Not all the means are juridically imposed. Clerics are juridically or canonically bound only by the daily recitation of the canonical hours according the proper and approved liturgical books and to a retreat, according the prescriptions of particular law. The other means of sanctification, of which the most important are enumerated, are only recommended.[13]

Dedication to ministry and the nourishment found in Sacred Scripture, however, are more than simple exhortations.[14] The language could have been more precise.

A comparison of the two codes

In the light of the universal call to holiness, the obligation of the clergy to be *holier* than the laity was omitted. There were also a number of additions to the obligation to pursue holiness. The first addition, in canon 276, §1, is that the basis for the pursuit of holiness is the consecration of orders by which the cleric becomes a dispenser of the mysteries of God in service to his people. In the previous code the cleric was to be holier than the laity and superior to them in both virtue and example. It was the importance of setting good example which was emphasized by the Council of Trent, papal teaching and commentators on the 1917 code that formed the basis for the need for the cleric to pursue perfection. The identification of the consecration of ordination as the basis for the pursuit of perfection is a welcome addition to the new code since it not only gives the diocesan presbyter a sacramental foundation for his pursuit of holiness but also indicates the basis for the distinctive nature of that pursuit. Just as religious are to pursue perfection within the context of the evangelical councils and the distinctive nature of their own religious institutes[15] and married couples are to pursue perfection within the context of their own sacramental consecration and responsibilities as spouses and parents,[16] clerics are now asked to develop their pursuit of holiness in the light of their own distinctive sacramental consecration. It is within that context that the other addition to the canon, dedication to ministry as the *first* means to pursue holiness, provides a clear focus for clerics, especially diocesan clerics, in their pursuit of holiness.

Although there is a certain logic in including ministry among the means of pursuing holiness in the second paragraph of the canon, the decision to separate ministry from the consecration of orders is somewhat unfortunate. Rather than emphasizing the importance of ministry described in the conciliar documents, the final formulation is misleading because it separates ministry from its base which is consecration. The council was clear. Ministry in the life of a priest, especially the diocesan priest, is not one of the traditional *subsidia* (aids) for the pursuit of holiness, but rather is essentially connected with the distinctive consecration of the sacrament of orders. Without that essential connection, ministry seems to stand on its own. Such a separation, which was at the core of the struggles to develop the spirituality of the diocesan priest immediately before and during Vatican II, can lead to that "activism" which had been identified by popes in this century as a danger. Those popes were concerned about the priest becoming so absorbed in and dependent upon external activities that he would lose sight of the nature of the priesthood and his need to develop his spiriual life. That fear suggested that even legitimate and obligatory ministry can be seen as unrelated to the consecration and holiness and thus could become an obstacle to holiness.

A second unfortunate result of the final formulation of the canon, as a consequence of having to place ministry "in the first place," is the fact that the nourishment found in the twofold table of holy Scripture and the Eucharist takes the second place. In the Decree on the Ministry and Life of Priests that twofold table is the primary aid *(subsidia)* by which the priest is to nourish his spiritual life.

A third unfortunate consequence of the promulgated formulation is the suggestion of a separation of ministry from the other means available to the priest. An important part of the discussion during the council focused on the need to identify means by which the priest could deepen his sacramental relationship with Christ in the context of ministry. The separation of ministry from prayer, especially mental prayer, and those other aids to holiness that have been found helpful not only fails to keep them in proper perspective but also does not identify them as means to maintain a unity and harmony in the priest's life between his consecration and mission.

Despite the difficulties with the formulation of the canon, however, the fact that the key concepts of the new way of thinking of Vatican II have been incorporated into the code is an exceptional achievement. The difference between the two codes and additions to the 1983 code suggest that the only similarity between them is that both deal with the spiritual lives of clerics and some of the same means are included in both! The differences and the additions are so substantial that the canon can only be interpreted in the light of the teaching of Vatican II. The consequence for the diocesan priest is clear: the consecration of his ordination and the ministry that flows from it determines how he is to pursue holiness.

A Commentary on the Canon: *Pastores dabo vobis*[17]

The apostolic exhortation *Pastores dabo vobis* is the papal reflection on the 1990 Synod of Bishops on priestly formation. Although it is surprising that the pope makes no reference to canon 276 of the 1983 Code of Canon Law, he relies heavily on those sections of the Constitution on the Church and the Decree on the Ministry and Life of Priests that are the foundation of the canon. Consequently, the apostolic exhortation provides a valuable commentary on the canon.

Within the context of the universal call to holiness and the presbyter's specific vocation to holiness because of his configuration to Christ by the sacrament of orders, John Paul II succinctly presents the essential elements of the priest's pursuit of holiness. Because of his configuration to Christ, the presbyter's spirituality should be marked by total, humble, loving dedication and service to the people of God.[18] That service, which is a characteristic of the spirituality of all presbyters, is a specific and principal mark of the diocesan presbyter's ministry. To specify that service, John Paul II recaptures the terminology that was associated with the search for the distinctive spirituality of the diocesan presbyter before and during Vatican II that was incorporated into the Decree on the Ministry and Life of Priests.

> The internal principle, the force which animates and guides the spiritual life of the priest inasmuch as he is configured to Christ the head and shepherd, is pastoral charity, as a participation in Jesus Christ's own pastoral charity, a gift freely bestowed by the Holy Spirit and likewise a task and a call which demand a free and committed response on the part of the priest. The essential content of this pastoral charity is the gift of self, the total gift of self to the church, following the example of Christ.[19]

It is the gift of self which is the source and synthesis of pastoral charity and the concrete way by which the presbyter can love the universal Church and that part of it entrusted to him. It is pastoral charity that impels and demands in a particular and specific way of developing his personal relationship with the presbyterate, united in and with the bishop.[20] Pastoral charity is both nourished by the Eucharist and "is the dynamic inner principle capable of unifying the many different activities of the priest."[21]

That activity of the presbyter which is ministry is directly related to the consecration of the sacrament of orders:

> The priest's mission is not extraneous to his consecration or juxtaposed to it, but represents its intrinsic and vital purpose: consecration is for

mission. In this sense, not only consecration but mission as well is under the seal of the Spirit and the influence of his sanctifying power.[22]

Just as consecration determines presbyteral spirituality so too dedication to ministry characterized by pastoral charity is intimately connected with his pursuit of perfection:

> The relationship between a priest's spiritual life and the exercise of his ministry can also be explained on the basis of pastoral charity bestowed by the sacrament of holy orders. The ministry of the priest, precisely because of its participation in the saving ministry of Jesus Christ the head and shepherd, cannot fail to express and live out his pastoral charity which is both the source and spirit of his service and gift of self.[23]

In order for ministry to contribute to the growth of the spiritual life, the pope wrote, the presbyter must continually renew and deepen his awareness of being a minister of Jesus Christ by consecration so that he is a living instrument of Christ who has chosen him not as an object but personally:

> In this way the exercise of his ministry deeply involves the priest himself as a conscious, free and responsible person. The bond with Jesus Christ assured by consecration and configuration to him in the sacrament of orders gives rise to and requires in the priest the further bond which comes from his "intention," that is, from a conscious and free choice to do in his ministerial activities what the church intends to do. This new bond tends by its very nature to become as extensive and profound as possible, affecting one's way of thinking, feeling and life itself: in other words, creating a series of moral and spiritual "dispositions" which correspond to the ministerial actions performed by the priest.[24]

John Paul II then applies the consecration and mission of the presbyter united by pastoral charity to the ministry of the word and sacraments and those virtues which must be a part of the life of the presbyter[25] and ends the chapter with the reminder that it is "the Spirit of the Lord which is the principal agent of our spiritual life. The Spirit creates our 'new heart,' inspires it and guides it with the 'new law' of love, of pastoral charity."[26]

Within that context, the pope specifically discusses the spirituality of the diocesan priest and teaches that it is intimately connected with the unique historical and contextual conditions associated with the diocesan priest's membership in and dedication to a particular church:

> The priest needs to be aware that his "being in a particular church" constitutes by its very nature a significant element in his living a

Christian spirituality. In this sense, the priest finds precisely in his belonging to and dedication to the particular church a wealth of meaning, criteria for discernment and action which shape both his pastoral mission and his spiritual life.[27]

In *Pastores dabo vobis* Pope John Paul II has reaffirmed the essential connection, developed during the council, between priesthood and ministry and between ministry and holiness which is the basis for canon 276. They are united in faithful and untiring pastoral charity, that is, the presbyter giving of himself to Christ and to collaboration with his bishop and other presbyters, in service to the people of God. To develop that unity, in addition to the traditional means identified in canon law, the pope has indicated the need for the presbyter to pay special attention to the unique situation and circumstances of his particular church.

Like other Christians, the diocesan priest finds holiness, an awareness of God in his life with resulting patterns of activity, in the conditions, duties, and circumstances of his life.[28] Unlike other Christians the central condition and circumstance of the diocesan priest's life is his consecration to Christ by the sacrament of orders that identifies his ministry. A starting point for the spirituality of the diocesan priest, then, is to begin to identify those elements of ministry that contribute to his growth of awareness of God's presence in his life. "A new way of thinking" suggests a number of questions for further reflection.

There are two fundamental characteristics of the ministry of *each* diocesan priest that influence his spirituality. The first is the fact that he belongs to a particular church and thus needs to reflect upon the distinctive elements of his particular church that shape his ministry, his use of time, and his priorities. Is his particular church, for example, an older church with unique traditions and deeply rooted practices or a new church that is developing its own identity? What is the ethnic composition of that church? Does the Catholic population predominate or form a substantial majority or are Catholics in the minority and the church more missionary of necessity? Do priests have easy access to one another and to their bishop, or are they more isolated because of great distances? Such characteristics might be further specified by whether the particular priest's formation took place in his diocese of origin or somewhere else. Each suggests possibilities for the predominance of particular characteristics not only of ministry but of spirituality. A priest, for example, in an older diocese on the East Coast with its own seminary might find that his ministry's focus is on the maintenance of the familiar, the celebration of local feasts and the struggle to reorganize and re-educate the Christian faithful in the face of changing demography. On the other hand, a priest formed outside of his native diocese and returning to a diocese in the Southwest might need to focus on developing an appreciation of different cultures and the rediscovery of the richness of his own local church. Another priest, returning to a diocese with few Catholics might need to focus on the missionary aspects of his ministry and encourage and develop lay ministry. Each personal experience of the joys, the challenges, and the stresses of ministry needs to be harmoniously integrated into his awareness of God in developing a spirituality which is both personal and unique to the diocesan priest.

The second relationship which is fundamental for all diocesan priests is their relationship with the diocesan bishop and other members of the presbyterate. Those relationships, rooted in the sharing of the one priesthood of Christ by the consecration of orders, form the primary communitarian dimension of the priest's ministry and spirituality. The priest's ministry, as well as his morale, is shaped by the personality, style of governance, age, theological preferences, concerns and priorities of the diocesan bishop. Ideally by his own respect for and generous cooperation with the bishop as the pastor of the particular church the priest finds support and encouragement for his own ministry. Strengthened by this bond, he can celebrate the presence of God not only in more effective ministry and participation in the consultative bodies of the diocese, especially the presbyteral council, but also in public and private prayer and a deeper appreciation of the universal Church. Unfortunately, that is not always the case. An unfortunate overemphasis on personality and particular preferences can lead to a lack of communication and misunderstanding. Although greatly influenced by geography and available personnel, much the same can be said of the relationship of the diocesan priest with other members of the presbyterate.

Just as the relationship of the priest to a particular church and his relationship with his diocesan bishop and other presbyters are fundamental to developing a spirituality which grows out of ministry, those same relationships also suggest a certain danger. Exclusive focus on the particular church can result in a loss of the union of the priest with the universal Church and cause a provincialism that limits personal growth, a passionate concern for others in different places and circumstances, and a deepening of missionary zeal. An immature relationship with the diocesan bishop and other presbyters can cause excessive dependency which can lead to a loss of self worth, over emphasis on personality, and loss of focus for ministry in a particular community.

What most diocesan priests do, however, is more specific. They are dedicated to parochial ministry. Within a particular church and in collaboration with the bishop, the diocesan priest is identified with a particular community often with unique characteristics and challenges. A general "job description" of the priest's ministry of the word and of sacraments and of service in the parish can be found in the Code of Canon Law (cc. 528-29). That ministry of the word and sacraments provides the parish priest with clear opportunities to discover God's presence and make that presence known to his own parish family. Unlike other members of the clergy, the parish priest has a frequent, special, and demanding opportunity to experience first hand the beauty and value of all life in the celebration of baptism, the weakness of the human condition, and the destructive power of sinfulness in the celebration of reconciliation, the transforming power of love in the celebration of marriage and the inevitable goal of all human life in anointing those who are sick and dying. Such ministerial experiences should contribute to an ever deeper appreciation of God's power and love and the need for God's supporting and empowering grace in his own weakness as he pursues eternal life. Those experiences, common to all parish priests, can be made more specific by the individual priest as he reflects on his own care for a particular community and develops the virtues that his ministry demands. It may be, for example, that the virtues that characterize the life of the priest in an aging community might be understanding and patience, whereas a priest in an impoverished or crime ridden community might need to develop the virtue of justice appropriate to a prophet. The priest's consecration for ministry, however, is more than just a "job." His living in the midst of the community and acting in cooperation with all the members of the Christian faithful suggests that his ministry, and his spirituality, is influenced and developed by his interaction with the people he serves.[29]

In the end, the world has changed, the Church has changed, and the law has changed. Developing a "new way of thinking" about the spirituality of the diocesan priest is not an easy task. Most diocesan priests have been formed in other "spiritualities" which have been tried and true in the past but might not be appropriate in the face of the expectations, demands, and challenges presented to a priest today. Following the teaching of Vatican II, the 1983 code suggests that there is no one model, but rather many, for the spirituality of the diocesan priest. All need to be developed in the light of consecration and ministry, in the local church in union with the bishop and other presbyters. In addition to the obligations and suggestions for the development of clerical spirituality in the 1983 code, clerics are reminded to use "other common and particular means for their sanctification." Among those means, in addition to the twofold table of Scripture and the Eucharist, both conciliar and papal teaching have emphasized daily mental prayer as the primary aid for a new way of thinking. Aware of God's presence, a starting point for that prayer might be the simple question "What do I do and how do I do it?"

We live in new times, times of change and challenge, but the noble mission of the presbyter, especially diocesan presbyters, is timeless:

> People need to come out of their anonymity and fear. They need to be known and called by name, to walk in safety, along the paths of life, to be found again if they become lost, to be loved, to receive salvation as the supreme gift of God's love. All this is done by Jesus, the good shepherd—by himself and by his priests with him.[30]

Notes

[1]*ASS* 41 (1908) 560. The translation is taken from *The Popes and the Priesthood* (St. Meinrad, Ind.: Grail Publications, 1953) 14.

[2]Pius XI, encyclical *Ad catholici sacerdotii*, December 20, 1935: *AAS* 28 (1936), 23. The translation is taken from Claudia Carlen, ed., *The Papal Encyclicals 1903–1939* (Raleigh, N.C.: McGrath, 1981) 504. See also Pius XII, exhortation *Menti nostrae*, *AAS* 42 (1950) 677; John XXIII, (who emphasized obedience as the basis for holiness and effective ministry), encyclical *Sacredotii nostri primordia*: *AAS* 51 (1959) 375.

[3]There were several important theological works that contributed to this discussion. For a helpful review of European debate and the nature of the debate see Joseph C. Fenton, "The Spirituality of the Diocesan Priesthood," *The American Ecclesiastical Review* 116 (1947) 126–140.

[4]Eugene Masure, *The Parish Priest* (Chicago: Fides, 1955) 106.

[5]*The Diocesan Priest*, Albert J. LaMothe, trans. (Notre Dame: Fides, 1964).

[6]See *LG* 41. The obligation of all Christians to pursue holiness is included in canon 210: "All the Christian Faithful must make the effort, in accord with their own condition, to live a holy life and to promote the growth of the Church and its continual sanctification." All translations of the 1983 code are taken from *The Code of Canon Law. Latin-English Edition* (Washington, D.C.: Canon Law Society of America, 1983).

[7]*PO* 12, 13.

[8]See *PO* 13–14.

[9]Allocution to the cardinals and consultors of the pontifical commission for the reform of the Code of Canon Law, November 20, 1965: *AAS* 57 (1965) 988.

[10]Apostolic constitution *Sacra disciplinae leges*, January 25, 1983: *AAS* 75 (1983) xi–xii. The translation is taken from *The Code of Canon Law, Latin-English Edition* (Washington, D.C.: Canon Law Society of America, 1983) xiv–xv.

[11]See canon 387.

[12]See cc. 573–78; 662–72.

[13]*Communicationes* 3 (1971) 193.

[14]See *LG* 41; *PO* 18.

[15]See cc. 573–78.

[16]C. 835, 4.

[17]The Latin text appeared in *AAS* 84 (1992) 657–804. The translation here is taken from *Origins* 21:45 (April 16, 1992) 717–59.

[18]*Origins*, 728.

[19]Ibid.

[20]See also *PO* 14.

[21]*Origins*, 729.

[22]Ibid.

[23]Ibid.

[24]Ibid.

[25]Like the documents of Vatican II, the pope discusses the virtues of obedience, virginity, or celibacy, poverty, membership and dedication to a particular church and missionary zeal. See, ibid., 729–33.

[26]Ibid., 733.

[27]Ibid., 733.

[28]See *LG* 41.

[29]See c. 529, especially c. 529, §2.

[30]*Pastores dabo vobis* in *Origins* 757.

12

Confessions of a Pilgrim Pastor

William D. Hammer

When I was invited to participate in a discussion on diocesan priestly spirituality, it was helpful to know that I was not to bring together a complete synthesis on diocesan spirituality. What I offer, therefore, is a confession, a personal witness to the marvelous mystery of grace unfolding in my life as a priest.

Two limits that I recognize at the outset—I do not have the experience necessary to reflect on such important aspects of the diocesan priest as artist, prophet, or missionary, and I have no explicit reflections on contemplation as a part of diocesan spirituality. Also, I have never served, as many diocesan priests do, as a full-time teacher, chaplain, or chancery staffer. My witness is shaped by my pilgrim journey as a pastoral leader. Struggling to put into words my understanding of diocesan priestly spirituality reminds me that I am a pilgrim, that the journey itself is holy, even though I may be far from the journey's end.

The context in which I write is that of a pastor of seven years, ordained fifteen years, trained in Sulpician seminaries, raised in the suburbs of a mid-sized city. In the seminary I felt a special resonance with existentialist and phenomenological philosophies rather than with the more classical philosophies. This background prepared me to be open to the process of critical reflection on my lived experience as the starting point in my prayer. I bring to prayer a love of Jesus that is deep and personal and grounded in both Scripture and sacraments. My reading of church history has shown me that the Church at its best has always changed and grown and adapted, incorporating what is good, critiquing what is evil. Thus, I have tried to use this historical consciousness to guide my spiritual life and ministerial journey.

This diocesan priest's spirituality is first and foremost Eucharist centered. There is nothing I do that is more important than sharing in the Eucharist with the faith community to which I belong. I feel I do many things that are very important. I have come to recognize from feedback given to me that I do well in such ministry as helping people prepare for death, proclaiming and teaching the Gospel, administering the sacraments, and counseling people in time of crisis or tragedy. I enjoy celebrating life and working with children. All these activities of ministry and many more are important and naturally affect my prayer life. The heart and soul of my spirituality, however, remains the Eucharist.

These past years have revealed to me that the Eucharist is the summit and font for my day, my week, my priestly life. The Eucharist is the means by which I stay connected with the faith community I am serving and with whom I am working. We believe that we become what we receive. The time after Communion, the few prolonged moments of silence, is a way that I join with God, the faith community, the needy, those who mourn, the people of Guatemala or Bosnia or . . . , my family, my friends, my neighbor. This post-Communion quiet time becomes a moment to be savored. In this quiet communion I am freed to be present in a way more real and more sustaining than if I were actually physically present, addressing those needs or standing beside those people I call to mind. This time of life-sustaining connection and unity enables me to draw strength from those I love and to be present in a way of loving care for those in need. Before ordination, some of my classmates and I committed ourselves to pray for each other, but we also committed ourselves to *unite* with each other in communion. In the silence I call to mind those intentions and those friends who are in different parts of the world, the country, the state, the city, the parish. I invite God to fill me and to fill them with that divine life, light, and love. I ask God to help us, hold us, keep us, sustain us; and to never let us be parted from such an abiding care that has been promised to us. There is no time of prayer that is more important to me spiritually and that sustains my priestly ministry more than these moments of quiet contemplation. My life is disconnected without them. The rest of the day, week, or lifetime is a prolongation of living the implications of Eucharist as an ordained priest.

By sheer repetition, the prayers of Mass become an indelible imprint upon the ordained priest's spiritual life and ministerial life. Over and over again we sign ourselves with the cross, we wish people the grace and peace of Jesus Christ, the love of God, and the fellowship of the Holy Spirit. These gestures and greetings (or others like "The Lord be with you") become such a part of a priest's vocabulary as to permeate his life. The meaning of these words of greeting and this gesture of signing with the cross—owing to their repetition—is often overlooked. However, at the unconscious level they sustain their power and influence. When the meaning of the gesture and prayer takes hold the ritual allows the assembly to experience the transforming power of the Lord's supper. Being signed with the cross and inviting others to share this gesture calls the believer to embrace the cross in loving trust. In embracing the cross we actually embrace the entire paschal mystery of Jesus' birth, ministry, suffering, death, resurrection, and ascension into heaven. This mystery of Jesus' life is ultimately the mystery of the priest's life as he seeks to make Christ present through his priestly life and ministry.

To praise God, to thank God, to seek mercy, to consecrate to God, to petition God on behalf of others and oneself, to preside at prayer especially the Eucharist; these are the imprints of priestly spirituality. Additionally there is the action of entrusting people's needs along with our own to our gracious God, both at Mass and when the priest as leader of the community is called upon to lead prayer. This role of prayer leader happens quite naturally on behalf of the sick, at the wedding rehearsal dinner, before a meeting, and around a family's dinner table on a night out. The priest is both host and servant of the prayer life of the community. These types of daily experiences also set the tone of his private prayer. And it is in prayer that the priest deepens his own faith, a faith shaped by his role reaffirms all those deep held beliefs that he has found for himself of leading others in their prayer. I find myself consistently beginning prayer with a litany of thanksgiving for all the wonders of God in my life, my day, my ministry. Each moment in prayer is an occasion to thank God for the gift of the day, my life, my faith, my friends, the communion we have shared, the sun or the rain.

Another sacramental moment that has a profound impact on a diocesan priest's spirituality is mediating God's healing forgiveness to a penitent in the sacrament of reconciliation. Some of the most powerful moments of my priestly ministry have been in the context of confession. To acknowledge another's conversion of heart, to wipe away the tears of sorrow that come with the act of contrition or the tears of joy that come with the prayer of absolution, these and similar moments are strongly etched upon my psyche. If others can change with God's grace, then I can also do better in my life. When I examine my own conscience before receiving the sacrament, I find myself having to confront my own selfishness, self-centeredness, jealousies, and possessiveness. But then, I also remember my words of consolation to others: You have already punished yourself more than God will, just as Jesus did not yell or strike the adulterous woman nor will I yell at you. However, Jesus also offers a "tough love" challenge to go and to sin no more, to be as generous with mercy for others as God has shown to us.

Core to Jesus' ministry was reconciling sinners; equally core to the spirituality of the ordained priest is praying the words of absolution ". . . through the ministry of the Church may God grant you pardon and peace and I absolve you. . . ." Sometimes the change in a penitent's life is so radical that they truly have become a new person, leaving old ways behind. I rejoice with the penitent as I also rejoice in my own steps in ongoing conversion. As one who mediates God's endless wealth of forgiveness over and over again I am called to let go and forgive those who may take advantage of my trust, those who are mean spirited, and those who unjustly criticize me. To help myself and to offer to others who are overwhelmed in their pain, I find myself on occasions falling back on the words "Father, forgive them; for they know not what they do" (Luke 23:34). As a priest I strive to maintain the same calm and tranquillity in my life as Jesus manifested in his life. I find when my life is out of balance that I need to return to the healing balm of forgiveness for my sins, or else to forgive those who have wronged me.

Poverty

The diocesan priest, while not vowed to poverty, must embrace the gospel call to a lifestyle that is neither ostentatious nor given to the pursuit of wealth. As a priest, he is called to sacrifice for the good of the Church and its people. There are countless times he challenges others in their times of need to trust in God's care and divine providence: when illness or tragedy strike, when a job layoff occurs, when a spouse dies, when carefully laid plans are frustrated. In these and in countless other situations, the ordained priest must reaffirm the belief that all he is and all that he has are first God's gracious gift. All that is accomplished is ultimately the work of God. We are blessed with the gifts of our time, talents, and treasure. Each day serves as an invitation to serve, to be better stewards, to model a profound trust in God's abiding providence.

Obedience

The seminaries I've attended, the parishes to which I have been assigned . . . never were these my choices. I had another plan or proposal in mind. In retrospect I have come to see that God's plan was actually at work, but only after getting over the initial disappointment of *my* plan not working out as I had hoped. So now, I still plan, but I remain open to the "surprise" options that suddenly appear.

My present assignment as pastor was totally unexpected. I understood that I would likely be named a pastor later in the year to a certain type of parish that would naturally complement the other archdiocesan work I was doing. Quite unexpectedly a call came asking me to consider an immediate opening. I was given a very few days to consider accepting the call to be pastor, very little time to "research" the parish. In fact, I did no checking up on the parish except to attend Mass there that weekend. Later that Sunday evening I was attending a meeting about a few hours from the city. On the way home, knowing I needed to have an answer by the morning, I remembered that all my plans had never really worked out for me, but had always worked out much better than ever I could have planned. Since this was a pattern in my life, I saw that this invitation was likely another occasion of God's hand at work. And so, I decided that because it was not my plan, I should accept. I called my contact person on the personnel board that night, rather than wait until the morning. I can understand clearly now that this parish is the right place for me, and that it has been a good match for the community

At the time of ordination a priest promises obedience not only to a bishop and all those who come as successors but also an obedience to God's plan for that priest. Early in the ordination rite, as a sign of complete, defenseless vulnerability, the candidate lies face down on the sanctuary floor. During the chanting of the Litany of Saints, the priest submits to the mystery of God's call and God's plan in his life. The priest, then, in prayer and in life, is continually in discernment of God's will and plan. By a willingness, like Abraham and Sarah, to forsake stability and instead to move as the needs of the diocese call, the promise of obedience inevitably shapes the diocesan priest's spirituality.

Celibacy

Both the promise of obedience and the promise of celibacy shape the spirituality of the diocesan priest. However, unlike obedience, celibacy is not a requirement for all diocesan priests, as witnessed by our embrace of married Protestant clergy who have joined the Roman Catholic Church and now serve as priests. At this time, however, in the Latin Rite the promise of celibacy is the norm; married diocesan clergy the exception. When I was ordained, I accepted the promise of celibacy. Understood positively, celibacy is a charism of empowerment and freedom. The celibate priest's spirituality is further shaped by this additional recognition of dependence upon God's love, not mediated through a spouse, but rather through a faith community, a circle of friends and family. To remain faithful over the long haul, the celibate priest is greatly aided by a spiritual companion or director and a few close friends with whom he can be himself. These friends and guides help the priest to experience God's unconditional love. Through them, God's love for the priest takes on flesh.

Being Present

As a man marked for service, I find a natural desire to be present with the faith community I am called to serve and lead. I feel an abiding ache when I am unable to be present with my community before and after Mass. This desire to meet and greet people is more than hospitality. I will hear about what has happened the past week or what is anticipated for the upcoming week—this will often supply the matter for my prayer life. It is a ministry of presence that submerges me in the life of the people, in the joys and crises of their lives. And the ministry of presence leads to awareness which in turn calls me to service, to the ministry of being priest. This decision to be present, to listen with reverence, touches my soul and shapes my prayer and preaching. Without holy listening, without the ministry of presence, my spiritual life is diminished and my prayer becomes shallow.

Preaching the Word

At the time of his ordination to the diaconate, he was handed the gospels and instructed, "Believe what you read, teach what you believe, and practice what you teach." At his ordination to the presbyterate, the priest is publicly examined, "Are you resolved to exercise the ministry of the word worthily and wisely, preaching the Gospel and explaining the Catholic faith?" While there are different views on homiletics, different schools of preaching, all insist that the effective preacher first prays over the Scripture passages. The passages need to speak to the soul and mind of the preacher. After grappling with its meaning in the homilist's own life, the next movement is to explore the possible meanings for the assembled community. When one is part of a faith community, especially in the role of pastor or associate, then quite naturally the homily will be grounded in God's Word and the community's experience.

I have noticed that most often when I receive considerable feedback on a particular homily, I have been challenging myself or preaching to myself. I have been able through my prayer to experience that passage's call to live the Gospel and to bring that experience to words. My struggle, my insight, my life has somehow been able to touch a cord within the assembly. The reading and praying the daily Scripture readings calls the priest to an ever greater integration of his words with the Word.

Liturgy of the Hours

Praying the Liturgy of the Hours allows the Scriptures to permeate the day of the priest. Morning Prayer and Evening Prayer become the hinges of the day. Often the psalms capture the varied life experiences of the believer: hymns of thanksgiving, lament, praise, trust, hope, cries for justice and remembrance of deliverance. First, at the start of each day as it is anticipated, then throughout the tasks of that day, and finally upon reflective examination at day's end, the emotions and experiences of the priest echo the emotions and experiences of the psalmist. As the psalms remember the action of God in the life of the chosen people, God's fidelity and vindication, so the priest is to remember God's same action for the sake of God's children today.

The Canticle of Zechariah (Luke 1:68-79) and the Canticle of Mary (Luke 1:46-55) have become anchors for my spiritual life. When praying Zechariah's Canticle, I recall that my ministry is one of preparation for the coming of Christ again in glory—working to further the establishment of the reign of God and pointing to its continued unfolding in the midst of the faithful. "In the tender compassion of our God the dawn from on high shall break upon us . . . ." (Luke 1:78). Each morning Zachariah's canticle motivates me to announce the dawn of a new day of compassion and hope.

Come evening, Mary's prayer reminds me that I have been called to serve the poor and the lowly. In many different ways, God's mercy has sustained me through my day: "The Almighty has done great things for me, and holy is his Name" (Luke 1:49). As I say my daily "Yes, let it be done to me according to your will," I hope to grow each day a little closer to Mary's confident proclamation of God's greatness.

Each night I try to make Simeon's Canticle (Luke 2:29-32) the last thought I have as I pull back the covers and climb into bed. "Lord, now let your servant go in peace; your word has been fulfilled: my own eyes have seen the salvation you have prepared in the sight of every people: a light to reveal you to the nations and the glory of your people Israel." Each night I am ready to be dismissed should I not awake, each night I know I have seen God's salvation at work during that day, a light revealing itself to the world and to me. This prayer certainly took on a new meaning for me after my experience of a malignancy, subsequent surgery and radiation treatments, and the knowledge that my type of cancer had an above average chance of reoccurrence. I hope each night that I, too, have fulfilled God's plan for me so that I can be dismissed if that is God's will. All too often, however, I recognize that I am not quite ready to be dismissed. I hesitate in my prayer as I recall that I have left some loose ends during the day. Thus, Simeon's prayer becomes for me more like my hope that my life's ministry thus far has been enough for God. I reaffirm my faith that my desire to be ready for dismissal will suffice for God.

Regularly I share this prayer of Simeon with others who are struggling with approaching death due to a terminal illness. They know that death is coming; many are longing for death and the freedom from pain that it will bring. They struggle with the way their own family and friends must wait with them for the inevitable end. As I pray with them, I encourage them to say Simeon's prayer or their own prayer of readiness as they feel themselves drifting off into sleep. I share with them that one time when they do go to sleep, their prayer will come true and they will be dismissed in peace.

The frequent experience of preparing others for death, of burying the dead, of comforting those who mourn have had a great impact on my priestly spirituality. Using Scripture readings chosen by the family, the homilist is led to share the good news of the promise of eternal life: that death has been conquered and that in dying we pass over to God. Death is the door to the fullness of life. Often I am struck by the difference in the kinds of responses to death that are shown by those who have a strong faith in God and share in the life of the Church; greatly differing from the responses manifested by those who have no sense of God and for whom Church is not a part of their lives.

In celebrating a Mass of the Resurrection with the deceased and family, the priest not only looks back but also looks forward in time. The family and friends and priest are invited to affirm their belief in a place where there is no more tears or pain or crying out. The words of the creed professed on Sunday take on a much more personal meaning when we say we are awaiting the resurrection of the dead. Death is never easy when we love someone, no matter how long we have to prepare. I have never found myself with an "easy" funeral, but certainly some are more of a "celebration" than are others. Regardless, death is not my great enemy nor is it for any Christian. The homilist knows it is in the letting go of life in this world that we can come to embrace the fullness of life while awaiting the body's final healing at the resurrection of the dead.

The other sights and sounds of the funeral liturgy continue to shape my prayer life. Each time I pour the waters of baptism over a child or catechumen, I know that in their death I will once again sprinkle their casket with holy water, as I will be sprinkled one day. Each time I watch a child or adult clothed in their baptismal gown, I know they will wear it again as the pall is placed upon their coffin and my coffin. Each time a baptismal candle is lit from the Pascal Candle, I know the Pascal Candle will again be there burning for them and for me on the day of our funeral. As the Book of the Gospels is placed upon the casket I reflect upon how, "In life N. cherished the Gospel of Christ. May Christ now greet him/her with these words of eternal life: Come, blessed child of God." As I hope the deceased has sought to live the Gospel of Christ, so I hope it will be able to be said of me. Every funeral, if I am honest, stokes the embers of my own, often unnoticed, grieving. I grieve not having a family of my own, a home of my own. Even as I recount the ways my soul is nurtured in my ministry as celibate priest, and give thanks, I feel the quiet ache that reminds me of my own passover journey.

A further influence on my priestly spirituality is the patron of the parish where I am a member and serve. With the annual celebrations around the patronal feast day, the saint has a continuing intercessory place in the life of the priest and parish, as well as serving as a role model for how God's life was revealed through his or her life. And if the parish is named after an aspect of divine mystery, then its meaning for our understanding of God and the divine plan of salvation becomes the focus of the annual celebration.

I serve now as pastor of St. Gabriel's Church (God's strong one). The traditional Gabriel reading from Scripture is that of the annunciation of Mary. However, Gabriel does serve as a bridge figure in the Bible. The angel has a role in the New Testament as God's messenger to both Zechariah and Mary, but also serves God in the Book of Daniel. Gabriel comes as God's messenger to explain Daniel's visions (8:15-27; 9:20-27). For a parish to do more than survive, the community needs to be a people of vision and certainly its leaders must also be visionaries. It takes vision to start with a piece of vacant land and to begin to build up a faith community; it takes vision to build upon someone else's foundation; it takes vision to strategically plan for the future. Each succeeding generation is called to be keepers of the vision and to discern the signs of the times in each new age. We share a common vision with our forebears, but we must continually refocus the lenses of faith through which we see. Here I'm not referring only to a parish's vision for itself but also the vision of our faith in Christ Jesus. Jesus was a visionary who saw the blessedness of the sorrowful, the blessedness of those who hunger and thirst for justice, those who are merciful and peacemakers, those who in their poverty recognize their dependence upon God. Jesus' vision was of a time when we would all be one, when mercy and forgiveness would reign, and we would welcome everyone as our brother and sister. The vision is also a promise that offers hope in times of struggle and suffering. The diocesan priest can be no less a visionary. Having received the vision from our parents, pastors, and teachers, he takes responsibility for passing it on to the next generation.

There is one last dimension to my spirituality as a diocesan priest—that of the clown. For all the world's lunacy and chaos, silliness and foolishness, the clown is able to invoke a sense of sanity to it all. When the priest becomes a clown-like figure, he gives to the people he serves the gift of grace through laughter. The clown, as an archetype of priestly ministry, goes through the process of dying in the putting on the "ghostly" white grease paint, and experiences new life as the colors are applied to the face. As the clown goes silent with the completion of applying make-up, the words cease so that the Word may more clearly be spoken in gesture, smile or mimed story. As a clown I seek to die to myself, so that Christ may more clearly shine through. Clowns stand up for their beliefs no matter how that belief or view may be different from the world. In the clown as a universal person, people see their own battles, triumphs, struggles, and failures. The clown is a "wonderer." The fool reminds us that all the pride, pomp, and circumstances mean nothing ultimately. In admitting their own vulnerability, clowns remind us not take ourselves too seriously. In effect, clowns become useless for a while, hoping to create a time and space "outside of time and space" where God's grace takes hold. It is in the act of making believe, that the chance for belief is created.

Jesus established his "kingdom" in a backwater section of an empire and then told his followers to create a new world. He promised that we would be at peace and filled with joy, but that we would be thought of as crazy. Jesus warned that we were going to get into trouble with the world. Jesus also promised that we would be most powerful when we would give all our power away. The great enemy of the clown is not death—the clown can never die—he or she pops back up after every fall. Rather, the enemy of the clown is the living dead. In his death, Jesus was costumed by his enemies, mocked and lampooned. As a clown-like figure, the diocesan priest takes on the simple, direct, compassionate vulnerability of Christ. The priest is to let pain hurt and joy show forth. If I preach love of one's enemy, then I am treated as a fool. However, as a clown or a pastor, I can strive to love everybody, and invite everyone to get up and join the dance.

My experience is that the longer I clown, the better I am able to offer authentic and spontaneous pastoral ministry. I am better able to offer sympathetic and concerned eye contact, to give frequent, startling hugs, to reflect a playful delight in God's gift of humanity and creation. The clown celebrates a holy humanness in which there is neither male nor female, rich nor poor, Gentile nor Jew—no race, nationality, or age—there is only the clown. As a clown I give up my voice, give up my old self and identity, even the right to die. In the giving up of all these things, I become more like Christ in certain aspects of my priesthood. Like the true clown, the ordained priest is not a performer; but rather one who creates an atmosphere of excitement, laughter, and delight. This type of atmosphere is a welcome addition to most pastoral settings as the priest strives to be ever more in touch with the activity of God in the world. Through it all, I struggle to strive to be an ever more authentic symbol of joy, symbol of hope, a symbol of vulnerable lover, a symbol of the Suffering Servant.

I remember once hearing about the reflections of a survivor of a plane crash. The survivor observed that people reacted to disaster in much the same way as they related to minor inconveniences in everyday life. If their reaction during the flight to an inconvenience or a spilled drink had been to get upset or curse, then in the confusion and panic of trying to get out of the burning plane, their reaction was to curse and scream. On the other hand, the survivor noted that the people who had displayed patience and courtesy during the first part of the flight were the ones who reacted with quiet resolve and cooperation during the struggle for survival.

This anecdote keeps me focused on the ordinary events, the tedious tasks of everyday life. As a pilgrim pastor, I seek each day through prayer, service, and reflection, ever greater conformity to the life of Christ, so that in the end I may take the next and final step boldly but naturally into Christ.

Afterword

Something happens to the human soul when it is subjected to trial upon trial, to sustained criticism, and to the anxiety that follows the apparent loss of place and identity. Either it surrenders to despair or chooses to stand in the fire until purified and transformed into a stronger, more compassionate human being. Both the life and the graceful dying of Chicago's Cardinal Joseph Bernardin illustrate the depth of soul and tranquillity of spirit that may be brought about in the crucible of ordeal and suffering. The quiet dignity he displayed in bearing cross after cross won the respect and admiration of believers and nonbelievers alike.

The priest's winter of discontent—his loss of trust in the eyes of many, his crisis of confidence and identity—shows signs of a similar depth of soul and renewal of spirit. One can observe small triumphs of grace coalescing into fresh configurations of spiritual depth and vigor in the lives of diocesan priests. With humility and new found confidence, priests are lifting their heads and opening their eyes to the mystery of God's presence in the midst of their present painful crisis. In spite of the serious personal failures of some priests involving sexual misconduct with minors, in spite of the energy-absorbing polarization between traditionalist and progressive Catholics, in spite of drastic declines in the number of candidates preparing for priesthood and the stretching of clergy personnel to meet expanding pastoral needs, rumors of spring persist. Leaning into the chilling winds, priests are weathering their winter of discontent with a maturation of spirit and soul that deserves reflection and analysis.

This reading of the soul of the priest is drawn from my experience as vicar for clergy in a large midwestern diocese and is supported, I believe, by the essays in this volume. It carries with it, nonetheless, all the limitations of projection and wishful thinking that accompany reflective examinations and analyses of this kind. Yet, what I have seen

184

and heard and what I have read in these pages convince me that God's spirit is not only sustaining priests during this winter of discontent but deepening their lives of faith and service.

The Ordeal of Suspicion

Before turning to the signs of spring that support the present reading of the priest's renewal of spirit, a word about the winter's discontent.

Clearly, the sharpest pain, the cruelest suffering is the result of clergy sexual misconduct with minors. I have seen it in the eyes of those making a report of clergy sexual misconduct—the fear that they will not be believed nor understood, the pain of years of abuse congealed into a hard lump high in their stomachs. Most of the people making reports of this kind of misconduct during my years as vicar came forth only after drawing upon all the reserves of courage at their disposal.

And how does one tell a brother priest an allegation has been brought against him? My message, no matter how carefully framed, brought his world to a sudden halt—the fear in his eyes suggesting the panic in his soul. I remember the chilling silence as the accused priest read a brief description of the allegation. We both understood that this was the beginning of an ordeal. It was little comfort to be reminded of the good he had done as a priest. All was eclipsed now by the report of betrayal and seduction.

While the pain of clergy misconduct is felt most keenly by the victims of clergy misconduct, their families and friends, it overflows into the daily lives of the vast majority of priests who are innocent of abuse. The suspicion they read in the faces of parents is confirmed when parish secretaries receive calls inquiring if other chaperones will accompany Father on the teen retreat. A certain self-consciousness hangs over their conversations with the youth and young adults of their parish. They search for ways to signal parents that their children are safe with them. The confidence of previous generations dissolves into awkward encounters with both young and old.

A recent conversation with a seminary colleague illustrated not only parental suspicion but hostility. Driving home after celebrating Mass at an upscale suburban parish, he was preoccupied with perhaps the saddest words he had ever heard, "No son of mine is going to be a damn priest." At the door of the church, a teenage boy stopped to talk and expressing interest in the possibility of studying for the priesthood, accepted a brochure on seminary life. Suddenly the young man's mother abruptly stepped between them, took the brochure out of his hand and said with a steely voice, "No son of mine is going to be a damn priest." When he asked for an explanation my colleague was told that it had nothing to do with him personally. The mother's animus toward the priesthood in general, however, was deep and powerful—no son of hers was going to be a priest! Incidents like this certainly sadden priests, but they appear not to dampen the emerging confidence and quiet resolve of the presbyter's will to carry on.

The Ordeal of Evolving Identity

The metal of priests continued to be tested on other fronts as well. Conciliar developments, in particular *Lumen gentium's* first two chapters ("The Mystery of the Church" and "The People of God") and *Presbyterorum ordinis* re-framed the issue of the priest's identity. With all the baptized, priests were to enter on the common paschal path to holiness, no longer taking for granted that priestly spirituality was inherently superior to the laity's spirituality. They were to preach the Word as men who listened to the Word proclaimed by voices other than their own, by parishioners and other believers more at home in the market places of city and suburb. Leaders still, but more than ever, servant leaders pursuing holiness *with* their parishioners. As presbyters they were to minister in collaboration with religious and lay ministers whose gifts were manifest and whose numbers were growing. At the same time, priests were to be elders to the community as representatives of the diocesan bishop and brothers to their parishioners. While the essence of the priesthood remained consonant with the tradition of the Church, the new context and consciousness of priestly ministry shook the foundations of the priest's sense of identity.

It was not always so. Since the time of Trent, the priest's identity was clearly defined, safely moored in Trent's theological harbor. Few winds of change threatened the safe mooring. It was a time when the status of the priest went unquestioned and his authority unchallenged. So it followed right up to the eve of the Second Vatican Council. The housekeeper, altar boy, and the parish's lay leaders regularly responded to the pastor's directives with "Whatever you say, Father." That era, of course, has passed and for many the perceived loss of a central and special place in the life of the parish challenged their very identity as priests and stoked the coals of their anxiety and fear.

It would be trying enough to be caught between parishioners' affirmation and suspicion, between pre- and post-conciliar theologies of priesthood, between traditionalists and progressives, but priests are further burdened with the drastic decline in the number of seminarians, with the graying and thinning of their ranks. In the midst of this winter of discontent, a surprising turn has been taken that should not go unnoticed.

A New Priestly Culture

A new, if uncertain priestly culture is taking shape. Stripped of the status and privilege that allowed priests to ignore the personal signs of anxiety and loneliness that often touched their lives, priests have been forced to address their human condition without the defenses and rationalizations of previous clerical cultures. Now as men without illusions, they are free to own their humanity with a humility and freedom that, not surprisingly, has renewed their hope and confidence.

For the most part, priest gatherings no longer have the same ring of bravado as in the past. They meet now as men chastened by the ordeals of suspicion and criticism. And the common trial has deepened their regard and respect for one another. Real and serious issues still divide them—issues relating to identity and to variant theologies of priesthood—but the signs point to a sustaining fundamental unity which transcends the current tensions. They have survived a common threat, weathered the same ordeal, and they know they are the stronger for it, individually and collectively.

In general, relationships with authority are improving. While many remain frustrated by the deafness of some bishops to issues arising from their experience of priesthood, for the most part, priests demonstrate a growing sympathy for the relentless challenges and pressures facing their bishops. Their deference to the diocesan bishop remains appropriate, but recognizing that bishops have been tested by many of the same ordeals they themselves have undergone, the bishop-priest relationship seems stronger, more fraternal. In his presidential address at the November (1996) meeting of the National Conference of Catholic Bishops, Bishop Anthony Pilla of Cleveland spoke to the need for a stronger bond between bishops and priests. "We bishops," he said, "should ask ourselves about the extent to which we truly empower our priests in their ministry, especially our pastors who so directly participate in our role as shepherds of the flock. Priests, in turn, should ask themselves about the extent to which they truly empower us Bishops as their leaders through support and assistance . . . this can and should be a source of unity and understanding among us." On October 7th, just weeks before his death, the priests of Chicago assembled in Holy Name Cathedral for a prayer service for their dying archbishop. In his remarks, Cardinal Bernardin returned to his installation homily fourteen years earlier. Acknowledging his approaching death, Bernardin pointed to the path leading to honest fraternity between bishop and priest:

> As our lives and ministries are mingled together through the breaking of the Bread and the blessing of the Cup, I hope that long before my name falls from the eucharistic prayer in the silence of death you will know well who I am. You will know because we will work and play together, fast and pray together, mourn and rejoice together, despair and hope together, dispute and be reconciled together. You will know me as a friend, fellow priest, and bishop. You will know also that I love you. For I am Joseph, your brother!

A Turn to Holiness

Dismissed by secularists, disdained by fundamentalists, discredited by a few of their own, priests are falling back on their primal relationship with Jesus Christ. Not only do they remain men of prayer, their preaching and interactions with parishioners suggest that their prayer is more mature and contemplative. And this in turn has both renewed their ministry and strengthened their confidence. While their preaching may still be wanting, it is more and more grounded in a faith tried by the fires of ordeal. No strangers to pain and poverty, they more easily connect with parishioners as pilgrim partners.

The present crisis has gone a long way to dismantle the "lone ranger" motif that characterized previous generations of priests. Tried in the crucible of suspicion and anxiety, priests are acknowledging their need for a deeper and more mature spirituality. What is of particular interest here is that the turn is collective rather than individual. While priests are more ready to schedule and honor individual time for prayer and reflection, they are, at the same time, turning to each other. Priests are far more ready than in past generations to share their spiritual journey with brother priests. The *Jesus Caritas* and *Emmaus* programs for priests, along with a number of other community based renewal movements have provided critical support during difficult and painful years.

The reason the present turn to a richer life in the spirit is significant, a priest friend reminded me, is that it is a turn to holiness *with*—holiness *with* the people they serve and lead, holiness *with* their brother priests, holiness *with* their bishop, holiness *with* the poor and marginalized. This communal and fraternal dimension to priestly spirituality signals a maturing of soul and promises a greater pastoral sensitivity. More conscious than ever both of their wounds and strengths, they sense that their wounds have not been wasted.

Through the ordeals and struggles of recent decades, priests have experienced again the pain and the privilege of priesthood. There are signs that they are now entering a new spring after the rigors of a long and hard winter. Tested by the same fires, they regard each other with deepened affection and with a new sense of the bond uniting them in the ministerial priesthood. As one survivor to another, they whisper the enduring words of Dag Hammarskjold, "Cry. Cry if you must. But do not complain. The path chose you. And in the end you will say, thank you."

Donald B. Cozzens

Contributors

DONALD B. COZZENS is president-rector of St. Mary Seminary and Graduate School of Theology in Wickliffe, Ohio, where he is professor of pastoral theology. A former vicar for clergy and religious of the Diocese of Cleveland, he has ministered to priests and religious as spiritual director, counselor, and retreat master. He is an associate editor of *Emmanuel Magazine*.

DENIS EDWARDS, a priest of the Archdiocese of Adelaide, South Australia, is lecturer in theology at St. Francis Xavier Seminary. He is author of *Human Experience of God, Jesus and the Cosmos*, and *Jesus the Wisdom of God: an Ecological Theology*.

WILLIAM D. HAMMER, a priest of the Archdiocese of Louisville, Kentucky, is pastor of St. Gabriel the Archangel Church in Louisville. He has served as director of continuing education for the clergy of the Louisville Archdiocese and presently is president of the priests' council.

FRANK McNULTY, a priest of the Archdiocese of Newark, is pastor of Our Lady of the Blessed Sacrament in Roseland. A popular priests' retreat master, he served two terms on the National Conference of Catholic Bishops' *Priestly Life and Ministry Committee*, was vicar for priests in the Newark Archdiocese and addressed Pope John Paul II on behalf of American priests during his 1987 visit to the United States.

ROBERT F. MORNEAU, D.D., a well-known author and retreat master, is auxiliary bishop and vicar general of the Diocese of Green Bay. He is chairman of the *Priestly Life and Ministry Committee* for the National Conference of Catholic Bishops and an associate editor of *Emmanuel Magazine*.

204 The Spirituality of the Diocesan Priest
192   *The Spirituality of the Diocesan Priest*

EDWARD G. PFNAUSCH, a priest of the Archdiocese of Hartford, is presently assistant professor of canon law at The Catholic University of America. He is a past president of the Canon Law Society of America and served as its executive coordinator from 1986–1992. His articles have appeared in *The Jurist, Living Light,* and *The Priest.*

JAMES H. PROVOST is professor of canon law and chairperson of the department of canon law at The Catholic University of America. A former president of the Canon Law Society of America, he is a highly respected and frequently consulted jurist. He currently serves as managing editor of *The Jurist.*

SYLVESTER D. RYAN, D.D., is bishop of the Diocese of Monterey, California. Well known for his retreat work with priests, he has given numerous workshops on theology and catechesis.

ROBERT M. SCHWARTZ is pastor of St. John Neumann Church in Eagan, Minnesota. He previously served as spiritual director of St. Paul Seminary School of Divinity, University of St. Thomas, in St. Paul, Minnesota, and as president of the National Organization for the Continuing Education of Roman Catholic Clergy. He is the author of *Servant Leaders of the People of God: an Ecclesial Spirituality for American Priests.*

WILLIAM H. SHANNON, a priest of the Diocese of Rochester, New York, is professor emeritus of religious studies at Nazareth College. He is the founding president of the International Thomas Merton Society and the general editor of the five-volume collection of Merton's letters. His most recent book is *Seeds of Peace.*

RICHARD J. SKLBA, D.D., is auxiliary bishop of the Archdiocese of Milwaukee. A well-known biblical scholar, he previously served as rector of St. Francis Seminary School of Pastoral Ministry. In 1988 he received the prestigious John Courtney Murray Medal from the Catholic Theological Society of America.

KENNETH E. UNTENER, D.D., is bishop of the Diocese of Saginaw, Michigan. Ordained for the Archdiocese of Detroit, he was president of St. John's Seminary there before his appointment to the Diocese of Saginaw. An outstanding speaker and retreat master, he has addressed important ecclesial and pastoral issues in various journals.